Why I Am A Baptist

Tom J. Nettles
and Russell Moore
Editors

Why I Am a Baptist

WITH CONTRIBUTIONS BY
Wayne Grudem, Carl F. H. Henry,
R. Albert Mohler, Roger Nicole,
Paige Patterson, and others

Broadman & Holman Publishers

Printed in the United States of America

0–8054–2426–1

Published by Broadman & Holman Publishers, Nashville, Tennessee

Dewey Decimal Classification: 286
Subject Heading: BAPTISTS

Library of Congress Cataloging-in-Publication Data

Why I am a Baptist / Tom J. Nettles and Russell Moore, editors.
p. cm.
Includes bibliographical references.
ISBN 0–8054–2426–1 (pb.)
1. Baptists—Doctrines. 2. Southern Baptist Convention—Doctrines. 3. Baptists—Biography. 4. Southern Baptist Convention—Biography. I. Nettles, Tom J. II. Moore, Russell, 1971–
BX6331.3 .W48 2001
286—dc21

2001025070

1 2 3 4 5 6 7 8 9 10 05 04 03 02 01

DEDICATION

To faithful grandparents
Agnes Yancey Moore and the late Rev. Herman R. Moore,
and to the late
T. B. Nettles, Eliza Robertson Nettles, and Betty Webb East,
whom the Lord used to make us Christians, as well as Baptists

CONTENTS

PART SIX: THOUGHTS FROM THE FAMILY ROOM

PART SEVEN: THOUGHTS FROM THE PROFESSOR'S LECTERN

PART EIGHT: THOUGHTS FROM EVANGELICAL LEADERS

PART NINE: CONCLUDING THOUGHTS

FOREWORD

Morris H. Chapman

Baptist is not just my denominational preference. I am Baptist—blood and bone.

Born into a Christian, Southern Baptist family, I trusted Christ at the age of seven, was baptized, and, without knowing everything it meant, became a Baptist. But as I matured, what had been an effortless connection to my Baptist identity was transformed into a matter of deeply held conviction.

Sitting at the feet of faithful Sunday school teachers in my Baptist church in Mississippi, I learned to know and love Jesus better. I was challenged and inspired by the pastor who graced its pulpit. I was trained and shaped in a Baptist university in my home state. In a Southern Baptist seminary I was prepared for a lifetime of service, leadership, and ministry. I learned to love the Word of God from great Baptists and was inspired to evangelistic passion by godly Baptist laymen, evangelists, and pastors with a heart for souls. Baptist saints developed in me a thirst for God-sent revival for our world.

How would we describe what it means to be a Baptist? I submit there are three irreducible minimums for defining Baptists. When these are weak, the Baptist name fades; when they are absent, it has been completely emptied of real meaning.

Devotion to Jesus identifies Baptists. A host of our forebears in the faith "counted not their lives to be precious" and gave them up rather than renounce the Lord. Many had trials of cruel mockings and scourgings, bonds and imprisonment. They were stoned. They were sawn asunder, drowned, tortured to death. What is the source of this persistence in the face of opposition, this willingness to be counted the offscouring of the world? Simple human stubbornness? No, Baptists know that Jesus is Lord, and he alone deserves our ultimate loyalty. Our heritage rebukes those caught up in the spirit of religious relativism and easy convenience. Undivided allegiance to Christ remains our challenge and our calling!

Biblical fidelity identifies Baptists. In the first church, "they continued steadfastly in the apostles' doctrine" (Acts 2:42 NKJV). Baptists have never supported creeds imposed on us from the outside. But Baptists have always embraced strong doctrinal confessions. Baptists have been marked by adherence to the precious, powerful truths of the Word of God. We believe in the great God of the Bible who created us in his image, and, having loved us, gave his own Son for the remission of our sins, reconciling us unto himself. Southern Baptists believe in the autonomy of the local church, the priesthood of believers, soul competency, the preexistence of Christ, his virgin birth, his sinless life, his atoning death, his bodily resurrection, and his glorious return. Southern Baptists believe in the inspired, infallible Word of God, inerrant in the original manuscripts. We have been nurtured and nourished in faith and in faithfulness by stout hearts who hold those convictions—Baptist convictions! We have a charge to keep—to stay the course blazed in days past by our fathers in the faith.

Missionary fervor identifies Baptists. The first Baptist church planted in the South was actually a transplanted church from Kittery, Maine, whose congregation was led to South Carolina by a Maine shipbuilder named William Screven, a man with a great missionary heart. And missions flows through Baptist veins as blood flows through our bodies. Our Baptist heritage induces us to look outside the church body at the people of our land and our world. The needs are so much greater than most could imagine, and the opportunities around the world will not wait. People in both the developed and developing nations are obsessed with newness and novelty, with technology and progress. However, Baptists know that our world is dying not for the modern but for the timeless.

Baptists, we are on a journey. God's two great ambassadors are hard on our heels. They are goodness and mercy. Let us make this journey together, to the glory of God and his Christ. We must not turn back!

The editors of this volume are your fellow Southern Baptists. The writers they have selected to contribute to this book represent Baptists on a multinational scale. All of them are biblically convictional, boldly confessional, and bravely courageous. It is presented as an encouragement to a renewed commitment to our Baptist identity. It is offered with the prayer that the Southern Baptists of our generation may be Baptist—not as an uninformed child would, by effortless connection—but by deeply held conviction.

PREFACE

C. S. Lewis was once asked what propelled him to write his beloved Narnia books. No one would write the books he wanted to read, he replied, so he had to do it himself. While not pretending to be as majestic or as captivating as *The Lion, the Witch and the Wardrobe* and its sequels, the book you are holding right now was born from a fairly similar frustration.

One brisk Kentucky morning, the two of us were walking across the campus of The Southern Baptist Theological Seminary on our way to chapel services. We were flipping energetically through the pages of a book, hot off the presses from Smyth and Helwys publishers. We were especially interested in this new release because of its title, *Why I Am a Baptist.*[1] After all, this title has a grand old tradition in Southern Baptist life. We immediately recalled long out-of-print works by the same name edited by Louie Newton and our fellow Mississippian, the revered Joe T. Odle.[2]

But this book was different. Written by a virtual "Who's Who" of the Baptist left, this volume made a concerted effort to attempt Baptist identity without Baptist theology. "Baptist is not so much about theology," one contributor assured the reader. Rejecting confessional boundaries as creedal straitjackets, these moderate writers presented the alternative: a Baptist identity built upon sociological commonality, shared memories, and not much else. The eclipse of theology in Baptist life was celebrated by some of the contributors because it brings with it a freedom to pursue a "faith journey" without arguing so much about what the faith is.

One contributor began his article by recounting an experience he had preaching in a Methodist church. After the service, a Methodist congregant said to him: "Why are you a Baptist anyway? You sound just like one of our pastors."[3] By the end of the book, the question remained unanswered. The query, "Why are you a Baptist?" seemed to be answered in unison with a simple answer: "I grew up Baptist, and it gave me the freedom to do and believe what I choose, so I remain one." The writers failed to demonstrate why someone who lacks their memories of Training Union socials should become a Baptist. Could a person who rejects the resurrection of Christ (but who is amenable to being dunked in the water) be considered an authentic Baptist? Sadly, the contributors to the Smyth and Helwys book offered no reason why such should not be the case.

This kind of revisionism grieved us. "I wish there could be a book like this written by conservatives," one of us interjected, "making the case that being Baptist is about theological conviction." After a moment of silence, the other responded, "Let's do it." Hence this book is more than just a collection of testimonies. Since we are convinced that Baptist identity is at its heart a matter of theological conviction, we decided to invite some of the most theologically engaged Baptists we knew to make the case for Baptist identity from a conservative, confessional perspective.

Since there is always a danger that Baptist distinctives might be bartered away in favor of lowest common denominator parachurch activism, we chose some committed Baptists who are ministering in the context of the larger world of American evangelicalism. Because there have been all too many Baptists who have found it easy to carry their babies with them into the waters of Reformation confessionalism, we have chosen some committed Baptists in the Reformed tradition, including two who are former Presbyterians and one who has taught for many years in a largely Presbyterian seminary. Because some Baptists in the dispensational tradition have admitted a temptation to cherish the regional prophecy conference over the local church, we chose some faithful Baptist dispensationalists. Because Baptist moderates have long said that a person cannot be a "real" Baptist and a biblical inerrantist at the same time, we chose some of the most stalwart theologians of our denomination's inerrancy controversy. Because there is always a danger of parochialism, we chose some confessional Baptists from as far away as Wales and Zambia.

Readers might notice that there is much reflection here on the community heritage and background experiences that made us Baptists. We are not saying that being Baptist is anything *less* than a sociological phenomenon, but, unlike some, we insist that it is much *more* than that. Hence, many of our contributors write with honesty about their painful journeys in discovering whether their Baptist identity was rooted simply in cultural heritage or in biblical conviction.

On this book project, as in all of life, the Lord also provided us with much-needed iron-sharpeners as we thought about what it means to be convictional, confessional Baptists. Our wives, Margaret and Maria, were, as always, joyful reminders of at least one important truth from an inerrant Bible: "It is not good for the man to be alone" (Gen. 2:18). We were also granted welcome advice and encouragement from some friends who labor every day to pass on a robust Baptist identity to the next generation. These include Juan Sanchez, pastor of Ryker's Ridge Baptist Church in Madison, Indiana; David Prince, pastor of Raleigh Avenue Baptist Church in Birmingham; Gregory A. Thornbury, who teaches Christian studies at Union University; Peter R. Schemm, who teaches theology at Southeastern Baptist Theological Seminary; Tim Harrelson, academic book buyer for LifeWay Christian Resources; and Tony Rose, our pastor. We are especially thankful to Sean M. Lucas, archivist at The Southern Baptist Theological Seminary and a valued member of our Sunday school class, for proofreading this volume and giving much-needed counsel.

Of course, we could not fail to mention the faithful example of R. Albert Mohler, Jr. For one of us, he is a colleague and president, the one who brought me to the faculty of Southern Baptists' mother seminary. For the other, he is a treasured mentor—the one who, in my years of working with him, has taught me more than a thousand divinity schools—usually at three or four in the morning in his basement library or driving down a stretch of highway on the way to the next speaking engagement or walking through the aisles of a Borders bookstore in some faraway city. For both of the editors, he is undoubtedly the towering Baptist theological presence of the twenty-first century, placed by providence at this strategic moment.

We cannot adequately express our gratitude to our Sunday school class at DeHaven Memorial Baptist Church, whom we have the joyful responsibility of teaching together. They love the Word of our God. In their love for us and for one another, they model the kind of kingdom righteousness that comes only from the activity of the Spirit. Every Lord's Day, they remind us how blessed we are to be Baptists.

From the very beginning, Baptists have been accused of being "watery bigots." Sometimes we have deserved it. We offer this book with the full knowledge that we are greatly dependent upon mighty servants of the Lord, many of whom have never been baptized. We long for the day when our Lord Jesus Christ will call from their graves our brothers in Christ—Augustine, Martin Luther, Jonathan Edwards, John Wesley, George Whitefield, J. Gresham Machen, D. L. Moody, and the rest of the great cloud of witnesses. We believe that we will all be Baptists then.

And finally, we praise our triune God for two Mississippi Baptist churches who loved us enough to tell us the old, old story. In fact, they pointed us to the same truth to which a great "small b" baptist once pointed so many years ago: "Behold the Lamb of God who takes away the sin of the world!" (John 1:29 NASB). Through faithful preaching and teaching, they spoke as if speaking the oracles of God "so that in all things God may be glorified through Jesus Christ, to whom belongs the glory and dominion forever and ever. Amen" (1 Pet. 4:11 NASB).

Tom J. Nettles
Russell D. Moore

CONTRIBUTORS

Donna Ascol is a mother of six children and the wife of a Baptist pastor. She has given more than a little time and thought to the duty of teaching truth to the next generation. A Texas native, Donna now resides in Cape Coral, Florida, where her husband has served as pastor of Grace Baptist Church since 1986. She has been active in home-schooling, teaching Sunday school, and helping her church stay deeply sensitive to the obligations of Baptists to be zealous in evangelism and international missions. A native Texan, Donna earned a bachelor's degree in nursing from the University of Texas at Arlington and worked as a pediatric registered nurse before becoming a mother.

Isaac Backus (1724–1806) was a Baptist minister and evangelist in colonial America. His advocacy for religious liberty, including his 1773 treatise entitled *An Appeal to the Public for Religious Liberty Against the Oppression of the Present Day,* was a precursor to the United States of America codifying religious freedom in the First Amendment to the Constitution.

Douglas K. Blount is one of American evangelicalism's premier philosophers. He serves as assistant professor of philosophy of religion and chair of the department at Southwestern Baptist Theological Seminary in Fort Worth. Doug is an active writer, a regular contributor to scholarly publications, an energetic participant in professional meetings such as the Evangelical Philosophical Society and the Evangelical Theological Society, and an insightful reviewer of books. He holds degrees from Baylor

University and the University of Notre Dame. Doug and his wife Andrea have two children. They are members of the First Baptist Church of Burleson, Texas.

Morris Chapman has served as president of the Executive Committee of the Southern Baptist Convention since 1992. He previously served as pastor of the historic First Baptist Church of Wichita Falls, Texas, for thirteen years. He was elected president of the Southern Baptist Convention in 1990 and reelected in 1991. A native of Kosciusko, Mississippi, Dr. Chapman earned his doctor of ministry and master of divinity degrees from Southwestern Baptist Theological Seminary and his bachelor's degree from Mississippi College. Two of his books, *Faith: Taking God at His Word* and *The Wedding Collection,* have been published by Broadman Press. Dr. Chapman and his wife Jodi have two grown children.

Andrew Davis is senior pastor of the First Baptist Church of Durham, North Carolina. Prior to this, he served as a church-planting apprentice with the Southern Baptist International Mission Board in Japan and as pastor of New Meadows Baptist Church in Topsfield, Massachusetts. He received his doctor of philosophy degree in church history from The Southern Baptist Theological Seminary; his master of divinity from Gordon-Conwell Theological Seminary; and his bachelor's degree from the Massachusetts Institute of Technology. A Boston native, Andy and his wife, Christine, have three children: Nathaniel, Jennifer, and Carolyn. The Davises have been active in the pro-life movement and in various cooperative endeavors with other home-schooling families. Having memorized numerous books of the New Testament, Andy consistently encourages his friends to memorize the Scriptures.

Mark Dever is the pastor of Capitol Hill Baptist Church in Washington, D.C. Prior to coming to the nation's capital, Mark served as pastoral assistant at Eden Chapel, a Baptist congregation in Cambridge, England. Mark earned the bachelor of arts at Duke University, the master of divinity from Gordon-Conwell Theological Seminary, the master of theology from The Southern Baptist Theological Seminary, and the doctor of philosophy from Cambridge University. Much sought after by several schools as a professor, Mark sees his ministry as firmly planted in the local church. He has written several books, including *Nine Marks of a Healthy Church* (Crossway). Mark and his wife Connie have two children, Anne and Nathan.

James T. Draper, Jr., serves as president of LifeWay Christian Resources of the Southern Baptist Convention. Prior to his election in 1991 to head the agency then known as the Baptist Sunday School Board, Dr. Draper served as pastor of the First Baptist Church of Euless, Texas. In 1982 and 1983, he was elected president of the Southern Baptist Convention. Dr. Draper is the author of several books, including *Authority: The Critical Issue for Southern Baptists,* a highly influential argument for the inerrancy of the Bible. He and his wife Carol Ann married in 1956. They have three grown children.

Tom Elliff has served as pastor of First Southern Baptist Church of Del City, Oklahoma, since 1985. From 1996 to 1998 he served as president of the Southern Baptist Convention. His tenure as SBC president was marked by an emphasis on the need for repentance and prayer for revival, a message he took to all six SBC seminary campuses. From 1981 to 1983, he served as a missionary to Zimbabwe with the SBC Foreign Mission Board. A third-generation Baptist pastor, he is a graduate of Southwestern Baptist Theological Seminary and Ouachita Baptist University. With a worldwide evangelistic and discipleship ministry, Dr. Elliff has also authored numerous articles and several books, including *The Pathway to God's Presence* (Broadman) and *America on the Edge* (NCM Press). He and his wife, Jeannie, have been married since 1966. The Elliffs have four grown children and are proud grandparents.

Denise George is the author of sixteen books, including *God's Heart, God's Hands: Kids Can Talk to God* and *An Unexpected Christmas: The Story of Johnny Cornflakes.* She is also the co-editor of Broadman & Holman Publishers' multivolume Baptist Classics series. A frequent speaker at church, seminary, and women's conference groups, she is married to Timothy George, dean of the Beeson Divinity School at Samford University in Birmingham, Alabama. They are the parents of two teenagers: Christian and Alyce. The Georges are members of Shades Mountain Baptist Church in Birmingham.

Wayne Grudem serves as professor and chairman of the department of biblical and systematic theology at Trinity Evangelical Divinity School in Deerfield, Illinois, where he has taught since 1981. He received his bachelor of arts from Harvard University, his master of divinity from Westminster Theological Seminary, and his doctor of philosophy from Cambridge University. In addition to his magnum opus, *Systematic Theology: An Introduction to Biblical Doctrine,* Dr. Grudem has authored numerous works, including *The Gift of Prophecy in the New Testament and Today* (Crossway); *The Gender-Neutral Bible Controversy,* with Vern Poythress (Broadman & Holman); and *The First Epistle of Peter* in the Tyndale New Testament Commentary series (Eerdmans). He has edited *Are Miraculous Gifts for Today? Four Views* (Zondervan) and *Recovering Biblical Manhood and Womanhood,* with John Piper (Crossway). He is cofounder and current vice-president of the Council on Biblical Manhood and Womanhood; a past president of the Evangelical Theological Society; and currently a member of the translation committee for the English Standard Version of the Bible, an evangelical revision of the Revised Standard Version. He and his wife Margaret have been married since 1969 and have three adult sons. The Grudems are members of Crossroads Church, a Southern Baptist congregation in Libertyville, Illinois.

Carl F. H. Henry is the dean of evangelical theologians. He has served as the founding editor of *Christianity Today;* as a member of the founding faculty of Fuller Theological Seminary; as president of the Evangelical Theological Society; and as chairman of the 1966 World Congress on Evangelism. In addition to his monumental work, *God, Revelation and Authority* (now republished by Crossway Books), Dr. Henry has authored numerous books of vital importance to the global evangelical movement. This very long list includes *The Uneasy Conscience of Modern Fundamentalism* (Eerdmans), *Christian Personal Ethics* (Eerdmans), and *Toward a Recovery of Christian Belief* (Crossway). Dr. Henry earned the doctor of philosophy from Boston University; the doctor of theology and the bachelor of divinity from Northern Baptist Theological Seminary; and the master of arts and bachelor of arts from Wheaton College.

Erroll Hulse serves as associate pastor of Leeds Reformed Baptist Church in Leeds, England. Prior to this, he served other ministries at Cuckfield and Liverpool. For more than thirty years he has edited and written extensively for the Baptist magazine *Reformation Today.* He has also written several books on topics such as revival, the life of Adoniram Judson, evangelism, and baptism. He is the author of the widely acclaimed volume *Who Are the Puritans?,* published by Evangelical Press. Erroll is a gifted encourager with an irrepressible confidence in the power of the gospel and in the hope for worldwide revival. He maintains an international ministry of preaching and teaching, particularly in areas where Baptists are repressed by government and religious establishments. He and his wife Lyn have four adult children.

Ann Judson (1789–1826) served as a Baptist missionary to Burma. She and her husband Adoniram were appointed to the mission field by Congregationalists, but were baptized on the field after they adopted Baptist views on believer's baptism by immersion.

F. H. Kerfoot (1847–1901) was a Baptist minister and theologian. He served as successor to James P. Boyce as professor of theology at The Southern Baptist Theological Seminary, occupying the Joseph Emerson Brown Chair of Systematic Theology. Kerfoot then served as corresponding secretary for the Home Mission Board of the Southern Baptist Convention until his death.

Michael Lawrence is currently a research doctoral student at Cambridge University. He received his bachelor of arts at Duke University and his master of divinity from Gordon-Conwell Theological Seminary. After shucking the genetic Baptist pedigree, an honest and often agitated search for truth led him into a conscientious and informed commitment to a Baptist understanding of the church. His research gives him a deep respect for this theological struggle as he works through Thomas Goodwin's contribution to the "Puritan Project" of 1600–1704. Michael and his wife Adrienne serve actively in a local Baptist church in Cambridge, where she is involved in women's ministry. They have two children: Michael Jr. and Christian.

Fred A. Malone is pastor of the First Baptist Church of Clinton, Louisiana. He received the master of divinity from Reformed Theological Seminary in Jackson, Mississippi, and the doctor of philosophy from Southwestern Baptist Theological Seminary in Fort Worth, Texas. He is the author of *A String of Pearls Unstrung,* a booklet explaining his journey from Baptist to Presbyterian to Baptist again. Having served churches in Florida and Texas, Fred is active in his local association and in the Louisiana Baptist Convention. Fred and his wife Debbie have three grown children.

Conrad Mbewe has served since 1987 has served as pastor of the Kabwata Baptist Church in Lusaka, Zambia. He received the bachelor of science in mining engineering in 1984 from the University there. Since 1992, Conrad has written as a columnist with the *National Mirror* (a national weekly newspaper) and has functioned as an associate editor of *Reformation South Africa.* Conrad is known throughout his native region as "the Spurgeon of Africa" because of his powerful pulpit ministry. Felistas, Conrad's wife, is a midwifery tutor at the University Teaching Hospital.

Together they have three children, sons Mwindula and Mwansa and daughter Mwape plus a foster daughter Bwalya.

Al Meredith has served as pastor of Wedgwood Baptist Church in Fort Worth, Texas, since 1987. In September 1999, Pastor Meredith became a national spokesman for the truth of Christianity after a deranged gunman opened fire during a youth service at Wedgwood. In nationwide media appearances, Pastor Meredith emphasized the goodness of God and the salvation that can be found in Christ. He received the doctor of philosophy and master of arts from Michigan State University, where he wrote his dissertation on the social and political activism of Charles Haddon Spurgeon. He received the bachelor of religious education degree from Grand Rapids Baptist College. Pastor Meredith has been married to his wife Kay since 1970. They have a daughter, Becky, and a son, Josh.

C. Ben Mitchell is assistant professor of bioethics and contemporary culture at Trinity Evangelical Divinity School, where he has served since 1999. He also serves as consultant on biomedical and life issues with the Ethics and Religious Liberty Commission of the Southern Baptist Convention and as senior fellow with the Center for Bioethics and Human Dignity in Bannockburn, Illinois. Before coming to Trinity, he taught Christian ethics at The Southern Baptist Theological Seminary. He received his doctor of philosophy in medical ethics from the University of Tennessee in Knoxville and his master of divinity from Southwestern Baptist Theological Seminary. Published widely in bioethics, he is presently editing a volume on the ethics of human cloning and is general editor of the forthcoming *New International Dictionary of Bioethics.* In addition to his academic work, he has given testimony on various public policy matters before the United States Congress. He has pastored churches in Mississippi, Texas, Kentucky, and Tennessee. Ben and his wife Nancy are members of Crossroads Church, a Southern Baptist congregation in Libertyville, Illinois.

R. Albert Mohler, Jr., serves as the ninth president of The Southern Baptist Theological Seminary in Louisville, Kentucky. One of the leading conservative evangelical figures of our day, his role as a strategic leader among Southern Baptists and the wider evangelical world has been recognized by such publications as *Time* and *Christianity Today.* He is a widely published author and noted speaker. Dr. Mohler has distinguished himself as a denominational statesman by his leading role in the massive restructuring of the Southern Baptist Convention and on the committee that drafted the 2000 *Baptist Faith and Message.* A frequent guest on nationally televised news programs such as CNN's "Larry King Live," Dr. Mohler is quoted frequently in the *New York Times, Washington Post,* and other major newspapers. His commentaries, "Fidelitas" and "Thoughts and Adventures," appear regularly in Religion News Service, *World* magazine, and other publications. He and his wife Mary have two children, Katie and Christopher. They are members of Highview Baptist Church in Louisville.

Russell D. Moore is a doctoral candidate in systematic theology at The Southern Baptist Theological Seminary. Since 1998, he has served as research assistant to President R. Albert Mohler, Jr., In 2001 he was appointed to teach systematic theology at Southern and to serve as the executive director of the Carl F. H. Henry Institute for Evangelical Engagement. He received his master of divinity from New Orleans Baptist Theological Seminary in 1997. A third-generation Baptist minister, he served as associate pastor of Bay Vista Baptist Church in Biloxi, Mississippi. Prior to entering the ministry, he served as an aide to U. S. Congressman Gene Taylor (D-Miss.). He has written numerous articles and commentaries for publications such as *SBC Life,* the *Southern Baptist Journal of Theology,* the *Council on Biblical Manhood and Womanhood Update,* and various state Baptist newspapers. He and his wife, Maria, are members of DeHaven Memorial Baptist Church in LaGrange, Kentucky.

Tom J. Nettles serves as professor of historical theology at The Southern Baptist Theological Seminary. He has also taught at Trinity Evangelical Divinity School, Mid-America Baptist Theological Seminary, and Southwestern Baptist Theological Seminary. He received the bachelor of arts from Mississippi College and the master of divinity and doctor of philosophy degrees from Southwestern Seminary. He is the author of numerous books, including *By His Grace and for His Glory* (Baker); *Baptists and the Bible,* with L. Russ Bush (Broadman & Holman); and *Teaching Truths, Training Hearts* (Calvary Press). Tom and his wife Margaret have three adult children. The Nettles are members of DeHaven Memorial Baptist Church in LaGrange, Kentucky.

Roger Nicole recently retired as visiting professor of theology at Reformed Theological Seminary in Orlando, Florida, where he has served since 1989. From 1969 until 1986, he served as professor of theology at Gordon-Conwell Theological Seminary in South Hamilton, Massachusetts. Ordained in 1943, he pastored French Baptist churches in Worcester and Marchang, Massachusetts. Dr. Nicole is a world-renowned theologian and is a tireless defender of the inerrancy of Scripture and of the substitutionary atonement of the Lord Jesus Christ. In 1980 he edited and contributed to *Inerrancy and Common Sense* (Baker). In 1985 the book *Reformed Theology in America* (Eerdmans), edited by David Wells, was dedicated to Dr. Nicole on the occasion of his seventieth birthday. Dr. Nicole has been married to Annette Cyr since June 18, 1946. They are members of First Baptist Church of Sweetwater in Longwood, Florida.

Stan Norman serves as assistant professor of theology at New Orleans Baptist Theological Seminary, where he occupies the McFarland Chair of Theology. Stan is the author of *More Than Just a Name,* a book on Baptist distinctives published by Broadman & Holman. He received the doctor of philosophy and master of divinity degrees from Southwestern Baptist Theological Seminary and the bachelor of arts from Criswell College. He and his wife, Joy, a homemaker and schoolteacher, have been married since 1984. They are the parents of three children, Andrew, Daniel, and Stephen.

L. Paige Patterson has served as president of Southeastern Baptist Theological Seminary in Wake Forest, North Carolina, since 1992. He served as president of the Southern Baptist Convention from 1998 to 2000. Prior to his coming to Southeastern, Dr. Patterson served as president of Criswell College in Dallas, Texas, and as associate pastor of First Baptist Church of Dallas. He received the doctor of theology and master of theology degrees from New Orleans Baptist Theological Seminary and the bachelor of arts degree from Hardin-Simmons University. Known by many as the "Martin Luther of Southern Baptists," Dr. Patterson led the way from the 1970s onward for biblical inerrancy and doctrinal renewal in the Southern Baptist Convention. He is the author of numerous articles and books, including commentaries on 1 Peter, 1 Corinthians, and the Song of Solomon. His wife, Dorothy, is also a renowned author and speaker. They are the parents of two grown children and the grandparents of two grandchildren.

Geoffrey Thomas is pastor of Alfred Place Baptist Church in Aberystwyth, Wales, where he has served since 1965. He also serves as associate editor of the *Banner of Truth* magazine. He studied biblical studies at the University College of Wales, Cardiff, and at Westminster Theological Seminary in Philadelphia. He and his wife, Iola, have three grown daughters.

Donald S. Whitney has served as associate professor of spiritual formation at Midwestern Baptist Theological Seminary in Kansas City, Missouri, since 1995. Prior to assuming this position (the first of its kind in any of the SBC seminaries), Don served as pastor of Glenfield Baptist Church in Glen Ellyn, Illinois, a suburb of Chicago. A native of Arkansas, Don received the doctor of ministry degree from Trinity Evangelical Divinity School; the master of divinity from Southwestern Baptist Theological Seminary; and a bachelor's degree from Arkansas State University. He is the author of *Spiritual Disciplines for the Christian Life* (NavPress); *Spiritual Disciplines Within the Church* (Moody); *How Can I Be Sure I'm a Christian* (NavPress); and *Ten Questions to Diagnose Your Spiritual Health* (NavPress). Don's wife Caffy ministers from their home in Kansas City as a women's Bible study teacher, an artist, and a freelance illustrator. The Whitneys are parents of a daughter, Larelen Christiana. They are members of North Pointe Baptist Church, a congregation Don helped to plant and where he serves on the pastoral ministry team.

PART ONE

OPENING THOUGHTS

1

BEING BAPTIST: WE MUST NOT SELL IT CHEAP

Tom J. Nettles

THE CHALLENGE OF DEFINITION

I was Baptist born.
I was Baptist bred.
And when I die,
I will be a Baptist dead.

So stated the great Southern Baptist preacher R. G. Lee, of "Pay Day, Someday" fame. In addition to being brought up as a Baptist, he gave two other reasons for his stance as a Baptist. He compared the beliefs of other denominations, such as the Presbyterians and Methodists, and found them wanting, and he believed the defining doctrinal beliefs of Baptists. In this list of "Baptist Beliefs" he included eighteen statements, some of them in the form of affirmations and denials, in short, simple, pithy epigrams: for example, "In free grace, not sacramental grace . . . In the believer's baptism, not infant baptism . . . That in religion we have no priest but Christ . . . That in sin there is no sacrifice but Calvary . . . That in all things we have no authority but the Bible."[1]

Lee of course would agree that no one is "Baptist-born;" with greater biblical accuracy, he would say "I was born dead in trespasses and sins to Baptist parents." That caveat is necessary in light of his belief in believer's baptism. In fact, Baptists confess a church doctrine in which it is impossible to say, "I was Baptist born." One might be Roman Catholic born, or Anglican born, or Methodist born, or Presbyterian born, but none can be Baptist born. One cannot be Baptist until after personal conversion to faith in Christ alone and His saving work, he or she professes this faith before a Baptist [or baptist] congregation in baptism, that is, immersion in water as a symbol of death, burial, and resurrection. This difference begs for definition.

What makes a Baptist? Not all attempts to answer that question have the simplicity, confidence, and clarity of R. G. Lee's discussion. Some sociologists sort out Baptists as a "sect type" religion because of the voluntary nature of their membership, the congregational nature of church government, and their nonritualistic worship. Some historians give historical origin and continuing historical context the lion's share in developing a definition. Large numbers of denominational insiders perceive Baptist life in terms of their home church, their pastor, various persons that love (or dislike) them, organizations that influenced them, and hymns that they sang in worship.

All of these efforts at definition have validity in helping gain overall perspective. Greater accuracy, however, begs for the doctrinal/biblical component. Through the last four centuries, Baptists generally identified themselves through a discussion of doctrinal commitments, built upon exposition and synthesis of Scripture, espoused by the churches. Typical of scores of such attempts would be *The Doctrines of Our Faith,* written by E. C. Dargan and published by the Sunday School Board of the Southern Baptist Convention in 1905, or *Manual of Church Order* by John L. Dagg. In his preface to the book *Baptist Doctrines,* published in 1882, C. A. Jenkens indicated the certainty with which Baptists affirmed their denominational commitment. Jenkens lamented the tendency to "ignore doctrinal teaching." His hope for the book, however, centered on his desire for "thousands of Baptists" to be brought to "rejoice in the faith once delivered to the saints, and to realize fully that their creed is from heaven."[2]

J. M. Frost, in *Baptist Why and Why Not,* emphasized Baptist identity from three standpoints. First, he emphasized internal Baptist unity. In 1900, Frost was not so enamored of diversity as many seemed to be a century later. "Baptists are one in contending for the faith," in his judgment as well as one in their history and the "heritage of their fathers," one in their "purpose to preach the gospel of the grace of God among all nations." Baptist cohesiveness and doctrinal singularity comes from their Bible centeredness. They receive it as "an all-sufficient and infallible rule of faith and practice" because of the "absolute inerrancy and sole authority of the Word of God." Frost left no room on this point "for division, either of practice or belief, or even sentiment." Unity founded in this conviction is the only kind worth having—"None other is worth the naming."[3] Second, Frost highlighted doctrines held in common with other groups; and third, he pointed to Baptist distinctiveness. "Baptists have a distinctive faith," he wrote, "and yet hold much in common with people of other names."[4] Baptists, it seems, held all that was biblical in other denominations, but, in their distinctives, held more tenaciously to the plain teaching of Scripture than others.

In his book of 1913 published by the Sunday School Board of the Southern Baptist Convention, *What Baptists Believe,* O. C. S. Wallace undertook an exposition of the New Hampshire Confession. He dedicated the book to James P. Boyce and B. H. Carroll as "mighty men in the Kingdom of Christian Teaching." Wallace stated the "creedal statements . . . notwithstanding their essential agreement and conspicuous use" would not be quoted as "exercising authority over the belief of anyone." They are not considered authoritative because they are humanly composed attempts at enunciating distilled truth synthesized for the whole of the Bible. None would claim, therefore, that everything the Bible teaches is in the confession, or that every emphasis is just what it should be, or that on occasion more clear vocabulary could not have been chosen, or more pungently and courageously stated expositions could not have been made. Admitting all this, however, "in an eminent and almost commanding way," Wallace insisted, "they represent the things which are most surely believed among a great people, who recognize the Scriptures alone as the one supreme standard of religious belief and practice."[5]

PUSHING OUT THE BORDERS

In his warm and congenial book by the same title as this one, *Why I Am a Baptist* (1957), Louie Newton includes a chapter entitled "Because of

Books." He mentions books of Baptist history, books of Baptist doctrine, books by E. Y. Mullins, B. H. Carroll, Armitage, Vedder, sermons by George W. Truett and many others. These books convinced him that Baptist doctrine was right. Particularly interesting is the prominence given to E. Y. Mullins as the keenest expositor of Baptist identity. It seems that the generation of Newton considered Mullins's *Axioms of Religion* as the purest distillation of the Baptist genius yet presented to the world.[6]

Unlike earlier books on the subject, however, Newton's book witnessed to greater latitude in doctrinal issues. Mullins had prepared him for this acceptance, maybe glorification, of diversity. In his own testimony, he mentions contacts with myriad sorts of Baptists. Included were Walter Rauschenbusch and Harry Emerson Fosdick. Fosdick's sermon, "Shall the Fundamentalists Win?" preached in 1922 in New York, intensified strife in two denominations, the northern Presbyterians and the Northern Baptists. Newton gave several pages to Rauschenbusch's paper *Why I Am a Baptist,* published in 1905 in *The Rochester Baptist Monthly.* Rauschenbusch emphasized the noncreedal experiential nature of Christianity and, after the style of the German liberal historian Adolf von Harnack, linked orthodoxy with "Greek intellectualism after Christianity had amalgamated with the Greek civilization of the heathen world." This was an old liberal refrain hardly characteristic of Baptists a generation earlier. Newton indicated great admiration for Rauschenbusch and his writings on the Social Gospel and did not feel necessary any warning about its liberal foundation.[7]

After discussing his own pilgrimage, Louie Newton included testimonies of fifty people from different walks of Baptist life. These reflected a wide range of convictions on the issue. James L. Sullivan, then the Executive Secretary of the Sunday School Board of the Southern Baptist Convention, emphasized that Baptists "point to a perfect Christ, have complete faith in the inerrant revelation of God through the Bible, and seek to exalt Him everywhere to the best of their ability." In further highlighting the centrality of Scripture, Sullivan wrote, "God's Word is the infallible guide for life's highway and the most important book on the bookshelf of humanity. It is eternal in duration, complete in revelation, unparalleled in inspiration. Baptists exalt the Bible and delve into its pages constantly to discover truths about the ways of God in earthly life."[8] R. Alton Reed, the Executive Secretary of the Relief and Annuity Board of the Southern Baptist Convention, tells of the advice he received from John R. Sampey for a program of study to answer the question of being Baptist. Reed writes: "At the end of many months of research, study, and prayer, I had come to the conclusion I was a Baptist because I believed the people called Baptists follow out more nearly the principles and doctrinal truths of the New Testament church than any other denominational group."[9]

Another, however, does not share this same certainty but gives his testimony with the greatest brevity and the least conviction.[10]

> In the first place, my family were Baptists. My father was head of the deacons at the Dudley Street Baptist Church.
>
> Secondly, I have seen no particular reason to adopt any other faith or any other church, and
>
> Thirdly, I feel quite certain that the particular church or religious faith one belongs to has no important relationship to his usefulness in life.
>
> *Paul Dudley White, Heart Specialist, Boston, Massachusetts*

Other testimonies among these fifty indicate the breadth of theological diversity that slowly insinuated itself into Southern Baptist life throughout the twentieth century. Theological latitude gained favor by emphasizing the great virtues of diversity and the Baptist love of toleration. This spirit of toleration increased apace in the fifties and was a matter of pride with some. G. B. Connell, president of Mercer University and son of a Baptist minister, noted his early acquaintance with intense discussion on a broad range of doctrinal issues. His Baptist loyalty found root, however, not in the truthfulness of any doctrinal commitment but in a resistance to "authoritarianism in religion and government." He gloried in the four freedoms "in our Baptist faith" and showed that he had drunk deeply from the well of Protestant Liberalism by severing the voice of Christ from the written Word of the Bible.

> Freedom from coercion of creed, freedom from the coercion of ritual, freedom from the coercion of ecclesiastical authority, and above all the freedom to break through a thousand professional interpreters to see the Master Himself, to look upon His gracious and compassionate ministry and to hear Him speak His living word.[11]

Another, J. C. Wilkinson, Pastor Emeritus of First Baptist Church in Athens, Georgia, writes that the "unity of Baptists is also voluntary but very real. The fellowship includes a wide difference on thinking and varied interpretations. To me one of the glories of Baptists is that there is room for the liberal and for the most conservative in preachers and lay people."[12]

Joe Odle compiled testimonies and sermons in 1972 on this subject and called the book by the increasingly familiar title, *Why I Am a Baptist.* Twelve testimonies and six sermons set the stage for Odle's own presentation of "Baptist Distinctives," followed by a sermon by J. D. Grey entitled "Baptist Devotion to Doctrine and Truth." Odle, with the sincere desire to present a compelling case for a conservative view of Baptist identity, personified the ambivalence of a conservative Baptist caught in the middle of the controversy over the Broadman Commentary. While he rejoiced in reports of revival among Baptist youth, he lamented that "far too many of our members do not know what we believe or why we are Baptists. . . . This disturbed me and gave me deep concern."[13] Odle clearly agreed with W. O. Vaught's affirmation of "the infallibility of the Scriptures" and that "the very words of the Scripture [bear] the authority of divine authorship"; also he agreed with M. E. Ramay who said that the "Bible is the Holy Spirit inspired, infallible, unchanging, and unchangeable word of God."[14]

With somewhat less conviction he admitted the position of Grady Cothen who said, "To the degree we try to write and enforce creedal statements, we compromise our Baptist distinctive." Another contributor, at that time the young, sought-after pastor of First Baptist Church, Jackson, Mississippi, Larry Rohrman, seemingly with no sense of ambivalence takes a strong stance on opposing sides of the issue of confessional unity. He writes on one page, "The person wishing to join a Baptist church must wish to do so badly enough to submit to the doctrinal beliefs of the church." This conviction he reinforces in stronger language, "If you wish to be a member of our church, you must submit totally to our theology." Two paragraphs later the same writer with entire candor informs the reader that "no creed will ever be handed an individual Baptist for the purpose of dictating his theological position." The result of this happy condition is that "there are Baptists who disagree doctrinally with other Baptists." Different doctrine, however, in Rohrman's opinion, does not reflect immaturity or instability but is "one of the strongest points for the Baptist faith."[15]

Odle recognized that doctrinal differences not only prevailed but also were admired by many in Baptist life. "Some declare there is no such thing as a Baptist position," he pined, "since Baptists are not a creedal people, and do not require of their members that they accept certain doctrinal positions." But this doesn't quite make sense, given that Baptists are distinguished by their beliefs. Odle's intuitive response is, "Yet something does make men Baptists, and does distinguish them from members of other denominations." What could this possibly be? "There is only one reason, and that is that their doctrines are different. They are separated from others by what they believe."[16] Even then the don't-force-me-to-believe-anything ethos had so permeated Southern Baptist consciousness that Odle would issue a caveat after quoting the 1963 *Baptist Faith and Message* statement on Scripture. "It is not a creedal statement," he demurred, "and therefore is not binding upon any Baptist." An affirmation of the truthfulness of Scripture not binding upon any Baptist! How quaint. How debilitating the slide into latitudinarianism had become, that even Joe Odle would despair of thinking that it was necessary for a Baptist to believe the Bible. Though he would not give such an affirmation the status of a creed, he must at least grasp this much: "Yet it is an enunciation of what Baptists believe about the Bible."[17]

A CONFLICT OF VISIONS

Not only the diversity, but also the definition of toleration that promoted such diversity appeared only in isolated places by the late nineteenth century, spread subtly in the early decades of the twentieth under the guise of Christian experience, and developed more deliberately and completely in the mid-twentieth century. Baptist mammoths such as J. B. Gambrell and B. H. Carroll never interpreted the principle of toleration in such a context. They were only too happy for all sorts of religions and infidels to have freedom in the country. Their freedom in the civil context meant that Baptists could work with fervent conviction for pure congregations and denominational organizations. J. B. Gambrell, in an article entitled "Baptist Rights," noted, "Men who do not preach the accepted doctrines of the Baptists, have no right in Baptist pulpits, and it is not abridgment of their rights nor any persecution to keep them out." Likewise, in the schools a man sometimes thinks that the doctrines of the denomination are wrong or outworn. "No one should seek in the least to abridge his thinking, or his defense of his thinking," Gambrell contended. The world is open to him. But when he uses the money, prestige, and opportunities afforded him by a Baptist institution to oppose its doctrines, "he passes the bounds of liberty and enters the realm of arrogant license."[18]

B. H. Carroll, noting a tendency to doctrinal minimalism in some sectors of Baptist life due to the rise of liberalism in the first decade of the twentieth century, warned against "any teaching that decries doctrines." He considered the mentality of magnifying liberty at the expense of doctrine "a positive and very hurtful sin." The stress on individual liberty meant a sacrifice of the power of united forces and the "trend toward cutting off every article of faith to which some individual crank may object, will, if tamely unresisted, leave the church without a creed and without a moral life."[19]

Baptists had no inclination to increase membership at the expense of conviction. In 1887 the *Alabama Baptist* wrote, "Baptist churches have no use for those who do not believe their doctrines." They wanted no spouse-followers as members but only those who came from "a conviction of duty, and because they believe Baptists hold the truth as it is in Christ." *The Christian Index* responded, "Sound to the core." If they are not of us then they should not be among us was the sentiment. The editor told an anecdote of a woman he persuaded to join the Presbyterians because she wanted to join the Baptists only out of preference. Church membership, however, at least in a Baptist church, "is not a matter of preference, but a matter of conscience. We want no members except those who cannot conscientiously go anywhere else."[20]

A WIDENESS IN BAPTIST EXCLUSIVITY

While taking seriously the necessity of cordial adherence to doctrinal truth as a matter of conscience in the task of defining Baptist, we note that catholicity of spirit is part of the Baptist heritage also. The decade from 1850 to 1860 saw a movement among Southern Baptists that repressed this spirit. The Landmark movement in its most intense days of agitation could ask the question, with the intention of receiving a serious answer, "Can we consistently recognize the ministers of such irregular and unscriptural bodies [non-baptist churches], as gospel ministers in their official capacity?" Their reply was, "Of course not!" This in turn led to the next question, "Can we consistently address as brethren" those who do not adopt our Baptist understanding of the church?[21]

Though sharing the hearty approval of such zeal for the biblical ordinances in their proper relationship, the narrow scope of fellowship implied hardly satisfied the generous spirit of Baptists in other generations. Hercules Collins, a seventeenth-century Particular Baptist, argued strongly for the rightness of believer's baptism and the necessity of restoring it to its rightful place in establishing the "true form of God's House." Lest any misinterpret his zeal in this matter, however, Collins enthusiastically stated his desire for openness of fellowship with all evangelical Christians. Even though "there are some differences between many godly Divines and us in Church-Constitution, yet inasmuch as those things are not the Essence of Christianity, but that we do agree in the fundamental Doctrine thereof, there is sufficient ground to lay aside all bitterness and prejudice, and labour to maintain a spirit of Love each to other, knowing we shall never see all alike here."[22]

Oliver Hart, for thirty years (1750–80) pastor of First Baptist Church, Charleston, South Carolina, embodied historic Baptist purist ecclesiology and evangelical catholicity. His friendship with William Tennent, a Presbyterian minister in South Carolina and son of one of the famous First Great Awakening Tennents, evoked expressions of the highest confidence in the Christian usefulness of other evangelicals. At the death of Tennent, Hart preached a memorial sermon in which his brotherliness with Tennent, his affection toward him, and his high evaluation of his usefulness in the church saturates his words. Tennent came from the "most reputable and pious ancestors." These men Hart described as "great, pious and orthodox ministers of the gospel." He had often heard them preach "with great pleasure, and I hope, some profit." Hart mentions the grandfather, the father, and three uncles—all Christian ministers who were "happy instruments of converting thousands of souls."[23] Hart did not at all reject the Tennents as Christian ministers.

Abraham Booth, one of the most articulate advocates of the exclusivity of Baptist ecclesiology as scriptural, nevertheless maintains a sense of cordiality and respect for evangelical, but ecclesiologically incorrect, brethren. He expressed these parallel commitments in *An Apology for the Baptists in which they are Vindicated from the Imputation of laying unwarrantable Stress on the Ordinance of Baptism; and Against the Charge of Bigotry in Refusing Communion at the Lord's Table to Paedobaptists.* In a most judicious, consistent, clear, candid, and uncompromising way, he contends that none but believers should be baptized and received into church membership and none but baptized believers should be received to the communion of the Lord's Supper. He strongly opposes those churches that have open membership as well as those that have open communion. Portrayed as a "watery bigot," saturated with unbrotherliness, lovelessness, and narrow strictness, Booth maintains his argument with unwavering precision while displaying an amazing breadth of scholarship and intimate knowledge of the writings of Christians of every denomination. At a peculiarly high point of his argument, he proposes the following query and response:

> "Will you, then dare to reject those whom Christ accepts?" Reject, from what? My esteem and affection? Far be it! Under a persuasion that Christ has received you, I love and honour you as a Christian brother. His image appearing in your temper and conduct commands my regard.—"With what consistency, then can you refuse me communion? If Christ has accepted me, if Christ himself has communion with me, why may not you?" Communion with you in the knowledge and comfort of the truth I have; and this would be both my honour and happiness, were you a converted Jew. Communion with you I also have in affection; but fellowship at the Lord's Table is a distinct act, a very different thing; and is to be regulated entirely by the revealed will of Him that appointed it.[24]

As his questioner continues to urge Booth to relent on his position, he suggests that Booth considers him an unbaptized heathen. On the contrary. Booth would say to him, "Quite a mistake. I consider you as a real convert, and love you as a Christian brother."[25] Booth also provides a lengthy defense against an accusation of "notorious inconsistency" in that he would "occasionally admit, with pleasure, Paedobaptist ministers into our pulpits, to whom we should refuse communion at the Lord's Table." The Landmark principle of no pulpit affiliation with non-Baptists had no place in the views of even so well-defined a Baptist as Abraham Booth.

We thus give testimony to being Baptist out of conviction and a desire to embrace joyfully all that our Lord has asked us to do. No desire to exclude from affection or appreciation those whose consciences dictate otherwise motivates these testimonies. We join with Hercules Collins in declaring that the essence of Christianity exists outside the parameters of denominational distinctives. Sharing with other orthodox evangelicals a belief in the inerrancy of Scripture, the Trinity, the deity and humanity of Christ in one person, substitutionary atonement, justification by faith, the necessity of regeneration, God's invincible purpose of holiness for his people, the certainty of Christ's physical return, and the eternal destinies of heaven and hell constitutes a more central Christian commitment than the denominational peculiarities of any group that confesses these same truths. In fact, before distinctives may be discussed meaningfully, friendly disputants must share these certainties of the faith. Before one may be a Baptist, he must first be a Christian. Submission to immersion as a form of adult baptism has no power to make a person a

Baptist if he does not believe the gospel of Christ's saving righteousness and that Jesus is indeed the Christ come in the flesh, God with us.

That believer's baptism and other distinctives have no status as elements of saving faith does not render such elements as optional or nonessential in any sense. They still exist as part of God's positive commands for the formation and order of the church. They constitute aspects of the fulfillment of Christ's missionary imperative and the universal practice of the New Testament church. Errors here create awkward and possibly destructive modifications in one's view of the church and her mission of evangelism, worship, and purity as the Bride of Christ. Though fellowship with all believers in the experience of God's saving grace and the great truths of redemption, the attributes of God, and the person of Christ has an intrinsically surpassing excellence, we may never justify inattentiveness to any positive command. We omit the faithful discharge of these commands of Jesus at the cost of rebellion against our Master and Redeemer.

BAPTISTS ARE PEOPLE

Being Baptist includes more than just subscription to the truth of certain propositions. The curious and energizing interplay between truth and personality that produces unforgettable characters and mountains of memorabilia gives depth and texture to the word *Baptist*. The marvelous natural gifts, spiritual insight, doctrinal astuteness, close attention to experimental Christianity, and personal tragedy that fill the movements and chronicles of Baptist history endow the appellation Baptist with an inexhaustible richness and continue to shape it for good or ill. One must take care how he or she builds thereon.

One can think of scores, hundreds, of personal traits and accomplishments and acts of courage the absence of which would diminish the luster of what it means to be Baptist. Without John Smyth's self-baptism and Thomas Helwys's to-the-death defense of it, our history would be poorer. Without the courage of Benjamin Keach to go to the stocks for his books and without his work on types and metaphors in Scripture and catechism for children and conscientious contention for singing in worship, what shape would Baptist history have taken? How would the whole world be different had John Bunyan not dreamed in prison for cause of conscience and become the chronicler of *The Pilgrim's Progress*? We must have John Gill's unflagging commitment to the cause of God and truth, not just for

Calvinism but for orthodox Christianity, or Baptists could have crumbled into infidelity.

Robert Hall must produce his *Help to Zion's Travelers.* Andrew Fuller must write *The Gospel Worthy of All Acceptation* and the variety of defenses necessitated by its publication. William Carey must produce his *An Enquiry in the Obligations of Christians, to use Means for the Conversion of the Heathens.* Abraham Booth must write *The Reign of Grace,* and Roger Willams must bleed out *The Bloudy Tenent of Persecution.* Can any conceive of what being Baptist would mean apart from these?

Would Baptists be at all what they presently are without the moral courage of Adoniram Judson and his capable wife Ann, who were willing to be left in a foreign land without support rather than perjure themselves before God concerning the issue of baptism? Having received instructions from his Congregational Mission Society to baptize credible believers "and their households," and having subsequently come to the biblical position that only believers should be baptized and that the household baptisms in the New Testament included only such as could be instructed to believe and rejoice in the truth, the Judsons gracefully resigned their positions (while in a foreign land) and began a series of events that would culminate in the inextricable union between Baptist churches and foreign missions. They enfleshed the eloquent conviction of Roger Williams: "Having bought truth dear, we must not sell it cheap, not the least graine of it for the whole world, no, not for the saving of soules though our owne most precious."[26] If being Baptist does not embrace that kind of conviction, we are a sorry lot.

J. B. Cranfill said during George Truett's long pastorate at First Baptist Church in Dallas, Texas, that "George W. Truett is the greatest Baptist in the world, both officially and actually. I regard him as the greatest preacher in the world." That was written in 1937. In 1914 he had noted on November 11 at the death of B. H. Carroll, "The greatest Baptist in the world is dead. On Wednesday morning, November 11, on Seminary Hill at Fort Worth, the spirit of the most majestic man the Baptists of the world have known in this generation swept into the gates eternal."[27] Since their time, one cannot conceive of what it means to be Baptist apart from the names of Carroll and Truett. Perhaps Cranfill may be forgiven for his superlatives; for, in the estimation of any observer, he was not far wrong on both accounts.

Many observers would have said the same thing about Spurgeon. He was enveloped in praise and critical analysis from the earliest days of his ministry and often the subject of scrutiny in Baptist newspapers in America. Some thought his Baptist credentials a bit shaky because of his acceptance of non-Baptists to communion. Others were not willing to ride him out so quickly. He caused a stir on slavery in the southern United States in 1860, created a controversy over baptismal regeneration among evangelical Anglicans, appalled the Arminians with his vivid and energetic Calvinist convictions and preaching, upset the hyper-Calvinists because of the freeness with which he displayed Christ as Savior of sinners, and, at the end of his life, inspired resistance in some quarters due to the stance he had taken in the Downgrade Controversy. Given this he still was universally regarded as the Prince of Preachers and, during the Downgrade Controversy, his name inspired massive admiration in virtually all of Baptist life in America. Helmut Thielicke said of Charles Haddon Spurgeon, "The fire he thus kindled, and turned into a beacon that shone across the seas and down through the generations, was no mere brush fire of sensationalism, but an inexhaustible blaze that glowed and burned on solid hearths and was fed by the wells of the eternal Word. Here was the miracle of a bush that burned with fire and yet was not consumed."[28] Because Spurgeon's well overflowed with inexhaustible resources (to alter Thielicke's metaphor a bit), Thielicke advised, "Sell all that you have . . . and buy Spurgeon."[29] Spurgeon was a Baptist and "Baptist" will evoke a sense of debt from others because of the contribution of Spurgeon.

A CASE OF CLARITY AND CONFIDENCE

The authors have not adopted an attitude of despair in the task of defining what it means to be Baptist. The doctrinal, the charitable, and the personal still play important roles in this task. The assumption of liberalism that refuses doctrinal definition eventually collapses in its effort at denominational definition. Bill Leonard illustrates this perfectly in his advice that Baptists forget the myth that a Baptist identity may be reestablished in our generation.[30] His observation, astute and probably correct, that many young Baptists "have no frame of reference for Baptist beliefs and practices" should not constitute a new paradigm, but only serves to emphasize that Baptists face a challenge. We have faced the same challenge on more than one occasion. Leonard assures the disenchanted among the moderate Baptists that modern people don't care about denominations, especially those that have to look to the past for an outworn creed.

Gary Parker, under the same intellectual assumptions, indicates that protection of the doctrinal aspect of identity somehow works at cross-purposes with evangelism. "Given time, the neo-Baptists [read, Baptists who think that our historic doctrines are important] in our midst can build a wall of doctrine high enough and thick enough that no one will want to come inside and play in our yard." Too much time with doctrine and soon, "Instead of inviting lost peasants into our Baptist home," we will find ourselves "constructing walls of orthodoxy and conformity and creedalism which blocks them out."[31]

Strange that the very ideas that made Baptists strong and gave sharp and recognizable angles to the Baptist profile should be deemed unbaptistic and destructively exclusivistic. Such happened in 1888 to Spurgeon when the Baptist Union refused to adopt a clear and precise evangelical confessional statement. In 1873 the Union had reduced its theological base to the simple assertion, "The immersion of believers is the only Christian baptism." Spurgeon, convinced that "the doctrine of baptism is not sufficient for a groundwork," offered an evaluation of such doctrinal vapidity directly contradictory to the fears quoted above.

> To say that "a creed comes between a man and his God" is to suppose that it is untrue; for truth, however, definitely stated, does not divide the believer from his Lord. So far as I am concerned, that which I believe I am not ashamed to state in the plainest possible language; and the truth I hold I embrace because I believe it to be the mind of God revealed in his infallible Word. How can it divide me from God who revealed it? It is one means of my communion with my Lord, that I receive his words as well as himself, and submit my understanding to what I see to be taught by him. Say what he may, I accept it because he says it, and therein pay him the humble worship of my inmost soul.[32]

In 1888, subsequent to Spurgeon's withdrawal and to a series of strong, publicly expressed arguments for the usefulness of creeds, the Union adopted a statement of the "facts and doctrines of the Gospel" along with a profession on the part of its ministers "to have undergone the spiritual change expressed or implied in them." The "facts and doctrines" involved a list of six assertions: The inspiration and authority of Scripture, "the fallen and sinful state of man," the "Deity, the Incarnation, the Resurrection of the Lord Jesus Christ, and His Sacrificial and Mediatorial work," justification by faith, the work of the Holy Spirit in conversion and sanctification, and the resurrection and judgment. These doctrines had no exposition but were merely spelled out by name.[33] In light of the destructive tendencies of the current theological climate, Spurgeon considered this embarrassingly inadequate.

Such happened to Northern Baptists in 1922. W. B. Riley appealed to the national meeting, in light of "the unquestioned defection from that faith that now endangers the good name and the greater progress of our holy cause," to adopt the New Hampshire Confession of Faith. He presented it as a document of historic sanctity that "rests, in its every sentence, upon the unshaken and unshakable base of Holy Scripture, as an expression of our loyalty to evangelical Christianity." Instead, the Convention adopted, on substitute motion, the suggestion of the liberal Cornelius Woelfkin that "the Northern Baptist Convention affirms that the New Testament is the all sufficient ground of our faith and practice and we need no other statement." This passed by a 1,264 to 637 vote.[34] With "no other statement," persons were given less reasons to be Baptist and statistics show that many decided that it was just as safe to be nothing as to be Baptist. Northern [American] Baptists have struggled to hold their own since. In 1922 the Northern Baptist Convention had 9,109 churches with 1,358,000 members. In 1994 the churches numbered 5,796 with a total membership of 1,516,505.

When conservatives among them, still hoping for redemption, sought to have the Convention recall missionaries who had vital doctrinal deviation and replace them with "equally competent men and women whose evangelical faith and fervor cannot be questioned," they found themselves unable to mount any determinative support to complete the task. In spite of clear evidence that some missionaries denied such doctrines as the virgin birth, the inspiration of Scripture, the deity of Christ, and the necessity of the atoning work of Christ, a roadblock stood in the way of the conservatives' goal. The nonconfessional policy immediately poisoned the doctrinal waters. The Board could claim truthfully: "1. That the denomination itself is constituted of individuals who are allowed a wide degree of theological difference. 2. That the test of membership in the Convention is not put on theological grounds. 3. That representatives of widely differing theological views are members, occupy the platform and take part in the deliberations of the Convention without a theological test being applied. 4. That the denomination appeals to all for support, accepts money from all, thus implying that in some fair way representation should be given to these various groups in the work of the denomination." Though the board claimed not to appoint "non-evangelicals," it had little to no guidance in defining (though they tried), and thus deciding, who fit the category of a "non-evangelical."[35]

May we never suffer from such destructive lack of definition. This book arises from the unshaken conviction that unless one has believed in the redemptive work of Christ as set forth in the Bible, and has been driven to such belief out of an experimental acquaintance with his or her sin and helplessness, he will bear the wrath of God eternally. With less importance, but just as truly, it expresses the conviction that the purest expression of the gospel and its manifestation in church order is found in historic Baptist doctrine and ecclesiology. These testimonies are contemporary expressions of how that conviction has affected the contributors' lives and how they have in turn contributed the personal dimension to what it means to be Baptist.

PART TWO

THOUGHTS FROM THE PAST

2

IN DISREGARD OF CARNAL EASE: WHY I AM A BAPTIST

Isaac Backus (1724–1806)

An early historian and champion of religious liberty among the Baptists, Isaac Backus left a legacy of theological courage and conviction. He was born January 9, 1724, in Norwich, Connecticut, to Samuel and Elizabeth Backus, pure Congregationalists opposed to the Saybrook Platform, Elizabeth being a descendant of the Winslows of Plymouth. When Elizabeth, widowed in 1740, separated from the standing church in 1745, the church took official action against her, suspending her, Isaac, and seven others from Communion. Eventually Elizabeth drew stronger measures on herself, in 1752, by her refusal to pay the minister's tax; she was thrown in prison. From prison she wrote this famous letter to her son.[1]

My Dear Son:

I have heard something of the trials amongst you of late, and I was grieved, till I had strength to give up the case to

God, and leave my burthen there. And now I would tell you something of our trials. Your brother Samuel lay in prison twenty days. October 15, the collectors came to our house, and took me away to prison about nine o'clock, in a dark rainy night. Brothers Hill and Sabin were brought there the next night. We lay in prison thirteen days, and then set at liberty, by what means I know not. Whilst I was there a great many people came to see me; and some said one thing and some another. O the innumerable snares and temptations that beset me, more that I ever thought on before! But, O the condescension of heaven! Though I was bound when I was cast into this furnace, yet was I loosed, and found Jesus in the midst of the furnace with me. O then I could give up my name, estate, family life and breath, freely to God. Now the prison looked like a palace to me. I could bless God for all the laughs and scoffs made at me. O the love that flowed out to all mankind! Then I could forgive as I would desire to be forgiven, and love my neighbor as myself. Deacon Griswold was put into prison the 8th of October, and yesterday old brother Grover, and [they] are in pursuit of others; all which calls for humiliation. This church hath appointed the 13th of November to be spent in prayer and fasting on that account. I do remember my love to you and your wife, and the dear children of God with you, begging your prayers for us in such a day of trial. We are in tolerable health, expecting to see you. These from your loving mother,

Elizabeth Backus

Isaac Backus was converted under the influence of First Great Awakening preaching. The great spiritual revolution of the colonies flowed from the preaching of Jonathan Edwards, George Whitefield, Gilbert and William Tennent, Eleazar Wheelock, and a host of others. Their doctrinal content emphasized that salvation came as a free gift, the effect of sovereign electing love mediated through the substitutionary death of Jesus and brought home to the heart by the effectual working of the Holy Spirit. Alvah Hovey described the effects of the close application of this doctrinal preaching: "These doctrines are very repugnant to the natural heart, and can be received by those only who understand the exceeding sinfulness of sin. Yet they take strong hold of the awakened mind, and when applied by the Holy Spirit, lead it into the presence of God and fill it with peace and strength indescribable."[2] Backus describes the process of his conversion.

> This work was so powerful, and people in general were so ignorant, that they had little government of their passions. Many cried out and fell down in meetings. But I had so much doctrinal knowledge, that I never was overcome in that manner. Neither could I put off my concern, as I had done before, for a more convenient season. No, though I was in good health, I saw that life was forfeited by sin, and that God had a right to take it away in a moment. I saw also that he had now given me opportunity to repent and turn to Him, and that if it was neglected, I was lost for eternity. Time was then taken out of the way, and a vast eternity was directly before me, without any hope of ever having another day of grace, should this be neglected. This moved me to the earnest use of all the means, public or private, within my reach, that I might get a good heart to come to Christ with. For all the sound teaching with which I had been favored had given me no higher ideas than that a good disposition of mind was necessary in order to come to Christ for salvation. But all the awakening preaching that I now heard, and all the books which I read, were so far from producing any such disposition, that my heart seemed to grow worse daily; and I saw seeds of all the evils of the world in me. While others were crying out and falling down in distress, I felt like a stupid beast before God; and nothing was more terrible to me than the fear of losing my conviction and being left of God to a hard heart and reprobate mind; for I fully believed that now was my only time to obtain salvation, that I should never have another day of grace. Neither could I bear to be deceived with a false hope.[3]

NO PLACE TO HIDE

Backus then describes several events in which he was tempted to cast away spiritual concern or, at the opposite extreme, to become settled in spiritual confidence before he had real union with Christ. He fled from these temptations with alarm. God gave him no place to hide.

In the beginning of August, Mr. James Davenport came to Norwich, where he was met by Doctors Wheelock and Pomeroy, and meetings were held incessantly for three days. People were greatly affected and many hopefully converted, while I grew worse and worse in my own view. Powerful preaching, and the sight of many in distress or joy, while I remained a hardened sinner, caused such anguish as words cannot express. Yet hereby God laid open to me the plague of my own heart and the folly of seeking life by my own doings. My tears were dried up, and I could find no good in me. Instead of this I felt inclined to quarrel with the sovereignty and justice of God, and the freeness of his grace, a grace so free that he was not obliged to have mercy upon me after all my doings. A sight of these corruptions increased my distress and filled me with confusion before God. And as I believed this to be my last opportunity, and my convictions seemed to be going off, and the work of God to be abating among us, how awful did my case appear! But God's thoughts are as high above our thoughts as the heavens are above the earth; for He thus drew me off from all trust in myself or any creature, and led me to embrace salvation in His own way.

As I was mowing alone in the field, August 24, 1741, all my past life was opened plainly before me, and I saw clearly that it had been filled up with sin. I went and sat down in the shade of a tree, where my prayers and tears, my hearing the Word of God and striving for a better heart, with all my other doings, were set before me in such a light that I perceived I could never make myself better, should I live ever so long. Divine justice appeared clear in my condemnation, and I saw that God had a right to do with me as he would. My soul yielded all into His hands, fell at His feet, and was silent and calm before Him. And while I sat there, I was enabled by divine light to see the perfect righteousness of Christ and the freeness and riches of His grace, with such clearness, that my soul was drawn forth to trust in Him for salvation. And I wondered that others did not also come to Him who had enough for all. The Word of God and the promises of His grace appeared firmer than a rock, and I was astonished at my

> previous unbelief. My heavy burden was gone, tormenting fears were fled, and my joy was unspeakable.
>
> Yet this change was so different from my former ideas of conversion, that for above two days I had no thought of having experienced it. Then I heard a sermon read which gave the character of the children of God, and I had an inward witness that those characters were wrought in me; such as a spirit of prayer, a hatred of sin, an overcoming of the world, love to the brethren, and love to enemies; and I conclude[d] that I then had the sealings of the Spirit of God, that I was a child of His. New ideas and dispositions were given me; the worship and service of God and obedience to His will were the delight of my soul. I found such happiness therein as I never had in all the vanities of the world; and this I have often experienced since.[4]

Backus gave a statement of his conversion in the church where he had worshiped. Soon, however, the minister began receiving members without a statement of an inward change and taught that the Lord's Supper was a converting ordinance. Backus left and by 1746 had entered the work of the ministry. In 1748 he became pastor of a separate church. When the church refused to pay a subscription imposed on them for the construction of a new building for the local Congregational church, Backus was seized as a prisoner. His diary records: "February 6. This morning I was seized by the officer, and he threatened to carry me to prison for the precinct rate, but glory to God! He gave me a sweet calmness and serenity of soul, not to fear him nor to treat him with any bitterness. I told him that they were going on in an unscriptural way to support the gospel, and therefore I could not do anything to countenance them in such a way. He told me that if I would not pay him he would immediately carry me to jail; but just as he was going to drag me away, there came in a man and called him out and paid him the money; so that he was forced to let me go."[5]

Dispute over Baptism

Soon the church became embroiled in a dispute about baptism, some of the members arguing that only believers should be baptized. Backus studied the issue carefully and with deep distress of mind and came to the conclusion that believers alone were fit candidates for baptism. His diary for August 22,

1751, records this significant event. "Brother Benjamin Pierce, pastor of a church in a part of Warwick, preached among us at Brother Hind's, this day, with considerable power, and then in the evening, concluded to baptize some persons. . . . When I came to see him baptize sundry persons, I having been convinced before that the way that I used to go on in, in baptizing infants, and by sprinkling, was not according to Scripture, and having this opportunity to practice, as I now believed was right, I dared not put it off. Therefore I told some account of my conversion, and then, of my experiences as to these things, which gave satisfaction; then I went down into the water with him and was baptized. And then, and afterwards in the evening, I felt a sweet calmness of mind, and some things opened with special clearness to my soul. Blessed be God."[6]

Immediately trouble emerged in the church over mixed Communion. Separates, who rejected state support of churches but supported infant baptism, and Baptists often worshiped in the same churches and held Communion together. Such a state of affairs, even though they sought earnestly to avoid division and loved one another while they suffered at the hands of the state church, could not long last. Eventually, the Baptists found that the continued practice of infant baptism and holding Communion with such amounted to trifling with the truth.

Backus summarizes the burden of the issue: "And truth so clearly requires baptism before the Supper, that Paedobaptists do never come to the table with any but such as are baptized in their esteem. Neither could we understandingly act in being buried in baptism, until we were convinced that what was done to us in infancy was not gospel baptism; therefore to commune at the Lord's table with any who were only sprinkled in infancy, is parting with truth, by practically saying they are baptized when we do not believe they are."[7]

After years of struggle, therefore, Backus came in January of 1756 to establish a Baptist church in Middleborough because "truth limits church communion to believers, baptized upon a profession of their own faith."[8] His diary makes solemn note of these events.

> January 2, 1756. We had a conference meeting at my house, and brother Hinds was with us. . . . I now declared that I firmly believed that, as none are the proper subjects of baptism but real saints, so every such soul ought to be baptized by immersion before they come to the Lord's Supper. . . .

> And I did solemnly entreat and invite my brethren to arise and build the old wastes; and the most who were present discovered a willingness so to do. So we appointed another meeting next week to labor on these affairs.
>
> January 16. Our people met according to appointment, and Brother Hinds came and preached a sermon from 1 Cor. 5:7–8; and he laid open in many things, clearly, how we ought to purge out the old leaven in order to be a new lump. And my soul had a very weighty sense of the greatness of the affairs before us and of the infinite importance of carefully keeping to the rules of Christ's house both in admitting members, and also in after dealings with them. And had not my soul believed that Christ would go before me, I should not have dared to step forward, but being satisfied of that (after some free discourse with our brethren who do not see with us) I read the Articles and Covenant which I had drawn, and then proceeded, solemnly, in the presence of God and his people to sign them; and the following brothers and sisters signed with me, viz., Timothy Briant and John Hayward, Mary Caswell, Esther Fobes and my dear consort. And there appeared a good degree of solemnity and sense of divine things in acting therein.[9]

Backus had in the meantime published a discourse on Galatians 4:31 "to shew that Abraham's first son that was circumcised was the son of the bondwoman, an emblem of the national church of the Jews; in distinction from regenerate souls, the spiritual seed of Abraham, of whom the Christian church was constituted; into which neither natural birth, not the doings of others, can rightly bring any one soul, without its own consent."[10] In this book Backus showed "the grounds upon which I have changed my principles concerning baptism. May heaven's blessings follow it for the good of the people of God!"

Becoming a Baptist gained neither prestige nor position of favor for anyone in those days. Backus had already investigated the severity of the implications. He challenged his readers with the overwhelming superiority of living, and thus being judged, by truth: "Men who regard carnal ease, or temporal honor and interest, more than truth, cannot be pleased with the forgoing account of things. But their scorn or rage is contemptible, when compared with the divine favor or displeasure."[11]

Following are Backus's articles of faith and church covenant.[12]

ARTICLES OF FAITH AND CHURCH COVENANT

THE CONFESSION OF FAITH AND COVENANT PREPARED BY THE REV. ISAAC BACKUS, AND ADOPTED BY THE FIRST BAPTIST CHURCH IN MIDDLEBOROUGH, AT ITS ORGANIZATION, JANUARY 16, 1756.

ARTICLES OF FAITH

PART I

1. WE BELIEVE THAT THERE IS BUT One Only, the living and true God, who is a Spirit, infinite, eternal and unchangeable in his Being, wisdom, power, holiness, justice, goodness and truth. Deuteronomy 6, John 4:24, Psalms 147:5, and 90:2, James 1:17, Isaiah 40:28, Jeremiah 10:10, Isaiah 6:3, Exodus 34:6, 7.

2. That there are three persons in the Godhead, the Father, Son, and Holy Ghost, who are but one God, the same in substance, equal in power and glory. 1 John 5:7, Philippians 2:6, Acts 5:3, 4.

3. That the Holy Scriptures of the Old and New Testaments, are the Word of God, which he hath given, as our only perfect rule of faith and practice. Acts 20:32, 2 Timothy 3:15, 16, 17.

4. That God who is infinite in knowledge, and perfectly views all things from the beginning to the end of time, hath fore-ordained that whatsoever comes to pass, either by his order or permission, shall work for the eternal glory of his great Name. Acts 15:18, Romans 9:17–23, Acts 2:23, Psalm 76:10.

5. In the beginning, God created heaven and earth, and the sea, and all that in them is, and he upholds and governs all things by the word of his power. Exodus 20:11, Hebrews 1:3, Daniel 4:35.

6. That God made man in his own image, in knowledge, righteousness and true holiness; and made with him a covenant of life, the condition whereof was perfect obedience. Genesis 1:26, 27, and 2:16, 17, Galatians 3:10.

7. Man, being left to himself, soon fell from that happy and glorious estate in which he was made, by eating the forbidden fruit, whereby he brought himself and all his posterity into a state of death. Genesis 3:6, Romans 5:12, 19.

8. Man being thus dead, his help and recovery is wholly in and from God. Hosea 13:9, Ephesians 2:8, John 6:44.

9. God the Father, of his mere good pleasure from all eternity, hath chosen a number of poor lost men, in Christ Jesus, to eternal salvation. Romans 8:29, 30, Ephesians 1:4, 5.

10. Jesus Christ, the eternal Son of God, hath come and taken on him human nature; and in that nature hath yielded a perfect obedience to the laws that we have broken, and suffered death for our sins, and hath brought in a complete and everlasting righteousness; and hath risen and ascended to the right hand of God, and ever liveth to make intercession for us. Hebrews 10:6–10, Daniel 9:24, Hebrews 7:25.

11. The Holy Ghost, and he only, can and doth make a particular application of the redemption purchased by Christ, to every elect soul. John 3:5 and 16:7–15.

12. The Spirit of God applies this redemption by convincing us of our sinful, lost and miserable condition, and then discovering the glorious Saviour, as he is offered to us in the Gospel, in his suitableness and sufficiency, and enabling us to embrace him with our whole souls, whereby he is made unto us wisdom, righteousness, sanctification and redemption. John 16:8 and 1:12, 1 Corinthians 1:30.

13. The life of religion consists in the knowledge of God, and conformity to him in the inward man; which necessarily produceth an external conformity to his law; and brings us to live in obedience to his holy will, in all our ways, and in our several places and relations. John 17:3, Matthew 23:26, Ephesians 2:10, Titus 2d chapter.

14. True believers being united to Jesus Christ by faith, have communion with God; and by his Spirit they are united to each other, and have communion one with another, whereby they are made partakers of each others' gifts and graces. 1 John 1:3, Romans 12:1–13, Philippians 1:7.

15. We believe that the first day of the week, commonly called the Lord's day, is the Christian Sabbath. Matthew 28:1–6, John 20:19, 26, Revelation 1:10, Hebrews 4:8, 9, 10.

16. That God hath appointed the ordinance of Civil Government for the defending of the poor as well as of the rich, in their civil rights and privileges; and the work of the civil magistrate is, to punish moral evils, and to encourage moral virtue, without touching upon anything that infringes upon the conscience, or pretending to dictate and govern in the worship of the Eternal God; which belongs only to Jesus Christ, the great law-giver and head of his

Church. Romans 13:1–4, 1 Peter 2:13, 14, 15, 1 Timothy 1:8, 9, 10, Matthew 23:8, 9, 10, Luke 22:25, 26, Isaiah 33:20, 21, 22, Ephesians 1:22.

17. We believe there will be a general resurrection both of the just and unjust; and that God hath appointed a day in which he will judge the world in righteousness by Jesus Christ; and will reward every man according to his works; when the wicked shall be sent into everlasting punishment, and the righteous be received into life eternal. John 5:28, 29, Romans 2:16, Matthew 16:27 and 25:46.

PART II

CONCERNING CHURCH AFFAIRS

1. WE BELIEVE THAT A VISIBLE CHURCH OF CHRIST is a number of his saints and people, by mutual acquaintance and communion, voluntarily and understandingly, covenanting and embodying together for the carrying on the worship and service of God. 1 Peter 2:5, 1 Corinthians 1:2, Acts 2:42–47.

2. That Baptism and the Lord's Supper are ordinances of Christ, to be continued until his second coming; and that the former is requisite to the latter, that is to say, that those are to be admitted into the communion of the Church, and to partake of all its ordinances, who, upon profession of their faith, have been baptized by immersion in the name of the Father, and of the Son, and of the Holy Ghost. Matthew 28:19, 20, 1 Corinthians 11:23, 26, Acts 2:41 and 9:18, 26 and 8:12, 36–39, Matthew 3:6, 16, Romans 6:4, John 3:23.

3. Since none but saints can rightly partake of these ordinances, therefore the door of the Church should be carefully kept at all times against all such as cannot give scriptural evidences of their union to Christ by faith. 1 Corinthians 11:27, 29, Matthew 7:6, 15–20, Ezekiel 44:7, 9, Isaiah 26:2.

4. A church thus gathered, hath power to choose and ordain those officers that Christ hath appointed in his Church, namely: Bishops or Elders, and Deacons; and also to depose such officers as evidently appear to walk contrary to the gospel, and to discipline their members; though in some such cases it is convenient and profitable to request the advice of neighboring churches of Christ. Acts 1:21–26 and 6:3, Numbers 8:10, Matthew 18:15–18, Acts 15th chap.

5. A Bishop or Elder hath no more power to decide any case or controversy in the Church, than any private brother; yet they having superior gifts

for teaching and ruling ought to exercise and improve the same for the benefit of the church, and the church ought to be subject to the gifts bestowed on the minister from the Lord, while he is rightly acting in his place; whose work is to lead in the acting of the church, and to administer the sacraments, and devote himself to the work of teaching, warning, rebuking and exhorting the people publicly, and from house to house. Matthew 20:25–28, 1 Peter 5:3, Matthew 28:19, Acts 20:20, 28, 31.

6. The Deacon's office-work is, to take care of the poor, and to have the oversight of the temporal affairs of the Church, and to minister at the Lord's table. Acts 6:1–4, 1 Timothy 3:8–13

7. Every saint is commanded to be faithful, to improve every gift and talent that is bestowed on them; in order to which, there ought to be such a gospel freedom that the church may know where every particular gift is, that it may be improved in its proper place, and to its right end; even the glory of God, and the good of his people. And the Church ought to be subject to such improvements. Romans 18:5–8, 1 Peter 4:10, 11, and 5:5.

COVENANT

We do now in the presence of the great all-seeing and most glorious God, and before angels and men, give ourselves up to the Lord Jehovah, Father, Son and Holy Ghost; and avouch Him this day, to be our God, our Father, our Saviour, and our Leader; and receive him as our portion forever. We give up ourselves unto the Lord Jesus Christ, and adhere to him as the Head of his people in the covenant of grace; and rely on him as our prophet, priest and king, to bring us to eternal blessedness. We acknowledge our everlasting and indispensable obligation to glorify our God, by living a holy, righteous and godly life, in this present world, in all our several places and relations. And we do engage, by the assistance of the Divine Spirit, to improve all our time and strength, talents and advantages, for his glory, and the good of our fellow men; promising by Divine help to walk in our house with a perfect heart; and to train up those under our care in the ways of God. And we also give up ourselves to one another in covenant, promising to act towards each other as brethren in Christ; watching over one another in the love of God; and to watch not only against those that are considered more gross evils, but also against all foolish talking and jesting which is not convenient; vain disputing about words and things which gender strife; disregarding promises, and not fulfilling engagements; tattling and backbiting; spending time idly at taverns or elsewhere; and vain and unnecessary worldly conversation on the Lord's days; and whatsoever else that is contrary to sound doctrine according to the glorious gospel of Christ; promising to hold communion—together in the worship of God, and in the ordinances and discipline of his church, according as we are, or shall be, guided by the Spirit of God in his word; expecting that he will yet further and more gloriously open his word and the mysteries of his kingdom; flying to the blood of the everlasting covenant for the pardon of our many errors, and praying that the Lord would prepare and strengthen us for every good work, to do his will, working in us that which is well pleasing in his sight, through Jesus Christ, to whom be glory for ever and ever. Amen.

3

PAINFULLY MORTIFIED, BUT JOYFUL IN THE TRUTH

Ann Judson (1789–1826)

In his introduction to the *Memoir of Ann Judson* in 1829, James D. Knowles wrote: "The Bible, though written in a part of the earth where the female character is undervalued, is full of testimony to the moral and intellectual worth of woman. It is no small evidence of its divine origin, that it thus rises above a prejudice which seems to be universal, except where the Bible has dispelled it." The Bible's impact diffused the leaven of truth so that "Christianity alone teaches the true rank of women; and secures to the loveliest and best portion of our race, the respect and influence which belong to them."[1]

The influence of women in Christian history, and the intense devotion they show to the Savior both in the Bible and in subsequent history, have received greater attention in recent decades. Prior to the recent sensitivity to this task, for several reasons, some quite rational and understandable and some inexplicable and perhaps sinister, the contribution of women to the propagation of the gospel has not been meshed into the historical narratives. Of course, this is not right since the New Testament example gives an unusual amount of attention to the devotion, contributions, and strategic impact of women (for example, Phil. 4:2–3; Matt. 9:20; Mark 5:25–43; Luke 8:1–3; 23:55–56; 24:1–11; John 4), even though it clearly excludes them from the ecclesial position of oversight and teaching authority embodied in the elder or bishop.

Many examples of the power of Christian femininity could be unpacked from the pages of Christian history at large. As moving as any, however, in the story of Baptists in America is the life of Ann Hasseltine Judson. Her testimony of "Why I Am a Baptist" will be told in her own words with brief editorial connections to give continuity to the narrative.

Early Life

She was born December 22, 1789, at Bradford, Massachusetts, into a family esteemed for its social importance, morally upright but, according to Ann's testimony, "ignorant of the nature of true religion." Her early education took place in the academy at Bradford. In her adolescence, peers sought her out for her intriguing conversation, carefree spirit, and social gaiety. She was surrounded with the socially elite who were as "wild and volatile" as she, and in this company she considered herself "one of the happiest creatures on earth."[2]

She encountered some seriousness of thought through contact with Hannah More's *Strictures on Female Education* and John Bunyan's *Pilgrim's Progress.* The first result of these literary encounters was to engender in Ann a legalistic spirit in which she felt that a series of resolutions would put her on the fair way to heaven. She resolved never again to attend a party or engage in frivolous activities. This resolution soon vanished under the strength of two invitations which resulted in her "religious plans" being forgotten. She vowed to make no more resolutions since it was clear that she could not keep them.

Her life in the next months, from December 1805 until April 1806, fell into succeeding periods of "vanity and trifling" in which she far exceeded her friends in "gaiety and mirth." A revival of religion in Bradford brought a series of meetings ("religious conferences"). In this context, though she maintained an exterior of detachment, she felt that "the Spirit of God was now evidently operating on my mind." She lost relish for amusements, felt dejected, and "the solemn truth, that I must obtain a new heart, or perish forever, lay with weight on my mind."[3]

Her disturbance increased. She asked advice from several people whom she perceived to be truly pious and denied her self "every innocent gratification;

such as eating fruit and other things not absolutely necessary to support life." She spent her time in reading and crying for mercy. Her narrative then records the dark night of the soul in her convictions that led to a special working of the Spirit of God.

> But I had seen, as yet, very little of the awful wickedness of my heart. I knew not yet the force of that passage, *The carnal mind is enmity against God.* I thought myself very penitent, and almost prepared, by voluntary abstinence, to receive the divine favor. After spending two or three weeks in this manner, without obtaining the least comfort, my heart began to rise in rebellion against God. I thought it unjust in him, not to notice my prayers and my repentance. I could not endure the thought, that he was a sovereign God, and had a right to call one and leave another to perish. So far from being merciful in calling some, I thought it cruel in him to send any of his creatures to hell for their disobedience. But my chief distress was occasioned by a view of his perfect purity and holiness. My heart was filled with aversion and hatred towards a *holy* God; and I felt that if admitted into heaven, with the feelings I then had, I should be as miserable as I could be in hell. In this state, I longed for annihilation; and if I could have destroyed the existence of my soul with as much ease as that of my body I should quickly have done it. But that glorious Being, who is kinder to his creatures, than they are to themselves, did not leave me to remain long in this distressing state. I began to discover a beauty in the way of salvation by Christ. He appeared to be just such a Saviour as I needed. I saw how God could be just, in saving sinners through him. I committed my soul into his hands, and besought him to do with me what seemed good in his sight. When I was thus enabled to commit myself into the hands of Christ, my mind was relieved from that distressing weight which had borne it down for so long a time. I did not think that I had obtained the new heart, which I had been seeking, but felt happy in contemplating the character of Christ, and particularly that disposition, which led him to suffer so much, for the sake of doing the will and promoting the glory of his heavenly Father. A few days after this, as I was reading Bellamy's

> *True Religion,* I obtained a new view of the character of God. His justice, displayed in condemning the finally impenitent, which I had before viewed as cruel, now appeared to be an expression of hatred to sin, and regard to the good of beings in general. A view of his purity and holiness filled my soul with wonder and admiration. I felt a disposition to commit myself unreservedly into his hands, and leave it with him to save me or cast me off; for I felt I could not be unhappy, while allowed the privilege of contemplating and loving so glorious a Being.[4]

Miss Judson underwent the transforming power of a work of the Spirit of God. She became aware of a remarkable change in attitude toward herself, others, and God. Later she would mention July 6 as the day "I entertained a hope in Christ."[5]

> O how different were my views of myself and of God, from what they were, when I first began to inquire what I should do to be saved. I felt myself to be a poor lost sinner, destitute of everything to recommend myself to the divine favor: that I was, by nature, inclined to every evil way; and that it had been the mere sovereign, restraining mercy of God, not my own goodness, which had kept me from committing the most flagrant crimes. This view of myself humbled me in the dust, melted me into sorrow and contrition for my sins, induced me to lay my soul at the feet of Christ, and plead his merits alone, as the ground of my acceptance. I felt that if Christ had not died, to make an atonement for sin, I could not ask God to dishonor his holy government, so far as to save so polluted a creature, and that should he even now condemn me to suffer eternal punishment, it would be so just that my mouth would be stopped, and all holy beings in the universe would acquiesce in the sentence, and praise him as a just and righteous God. My chief happiness now consisted in contemplating the moral perfections of the glorious God. I longed to have all intelligent creatures love him; and felt, that even fallen spirits could never be released from their obligations to love a Being possessed of such glorious perfections.[6]

RELIANCE ON GRACE

From that time on, Ann viewed her life as the peculiar property of God and pursued her studies in school as a special stewardship. She found greatest pleasure in meditating on the perfections of God and the wonders of his providence and redemption. The closing paragraph of her account of God's dealings with her soul shows her reliance on grace that suffused itself in her thoughts until her death.

> While thus recounting the mercies of God to my soul, I am particularly affected by two considerations; the richness of that grace, which called and stopped me in my dangerous course, and the ungrateful returns I make for so distinguished a blessing. I am prone to forget the voice which called me out of darkness into light, and the hand which drew me from the horrible pit and the miry clay. When I first discerned my Deliverer, my grateful heart offered him the services of a whole life, and resolved to acknowledge no other master. But such is the force of my native depravity, that I find myself prone to forsake him, grieve away his influence from my heart, and walk in the dark and dreary path of the backslider. I despair of making great attainments in the divine life, and look forward to death only, to free me from my sins and corruptions. Till that blessed period, that hour of my emancipation, I am resolved, through the grace and strength of my Redeemer, to maintain a constant warfare with my inbred sins, and endeavor to perform the duties incumbent on me, in whatever situation I may be placed.[7]

Ann continued in her spiritual growth and her meditations built on reading the most profoundly evangelical theological literature she could find, such as Thomas Scott on biblical study and Jonathan Edwards's *History of the Work of Redemption* as well as Joseph Bellamy on *True Religion Delineated.* Typical of the intensity and depth of her theological devotion are the following entrances in her diary.

> Aug. 6. . . . In thy strength, O God, I resign myself into thy hands, and resolve to live devoted to thee. I desire conformity to thy will, more than any thing beside. I desire to have the Spirit of Christ, to be adorned with all the Christian

> graces, to be more engaged in the cause of Christ, and feel more concerned for the salvation of precious souls.
>
> Sept. 2. I have discovered new beauties in the way of salvation by Christ. The righteousness which he has wrought out is complete, and he is able to save the chief of sinners. But above all, his wondrous dying love and glorious resurrection, astonish my soul. How can I ever sin against this Saviour again? O keep me from sinning against thee, dear Redeemer, and enable me to live to the promotion of thy glory.
>
> Nov. 6. I daily make some new discoveries of the vileness and evil of my heart. I sometimes fear, that it is impossible for a spark of grace to exist in a heart so full of sin. Nothing but the power of God can keep me from returning to the world, and becoming as vain as ever. But still I see a beauty in the character of Christ, that makes me ardently desire to be like him. All the commands of God appear perfectly right and reasonable, and sin appears so odious as to deserve eternal punishment. O how deplorable would be my situation, thus covered with sin, was it not for the atonement Christ has made. But he is my Mediator with the Father. He has magnified the law and made it honourable. He can save sinners, consistently with the divine glory. God can now be just, and the justifier of those who believe in his Son.[8]

On her birthday, December 22, 1806, she recounted the events since her last birthday. Her calm assurance, built on biblical categories, gives a sound challenge to any who would desire to have a healthy, informed, and humble confidence before God in the day of judgment.

> Dec. 22. I am this day seventeen years old. What an important year has the past been to me. Either I have been made, through the mercy of God, a partaker of divine grace, or I have been fatally deceiving myself, and building on a sandy foundation. Either I have in sincerity and truth, renounced the vanities of this world, and entered the narrow path which leads to life, or I have been refraining from them for a time only, to turn again and relish them more than ever. God grant that the latter may never be my unhappy case. Though I feel myself to be full of sin and destitute of all

> strength to persevere, yet if I know any thing, I do desire to live a life of strict religion, to enjoy the presence of God, and honor the cause to which I have professedly devoted myself, I do not desire my portion in this world. I find more real enjoyment in contrition for sin, excited by a view of the adorable moral perfections of God, than in all earthly joys. I find more solid happiness in one evening meeting, when divine truths are impressed on my heart by the powerful influences of the Holy Spirit, than I ever enjoyed in all the balls and assemblies I have attended during the seventeen years of my life. Thus when I compare my present views of divine things, with what they were, at this time last year, I cannot but hope I am a new creature, and have begun to live a new life.[9]

COURTSHIP OF ADONIRAM JUDSON

In 1810 she met Adoniram Judson. Judson, born in 1788, had been remarkably converted from deistic infidelity and was part of the Andover group that prompted the Congregationalists to sponsor an effort to propagate the gospel among the nations. Judson soon loved her and wanted her to marry him and accompany him to a "heathen land." His hopes for their marriage did not flatter her with the prospect of a long and materially embellished life. It was filled, however, with the sort of urgency that had already captured her heart. On New Years Day, 1811, he wrote her:

> It is with the utmost sincerity, and with my whole heart, that I wish you, my love, a happy new year. May it be a year in which your walk will be close with God; your frame calm and serene; and the road that leads you to the lamb marked with purer light. May it be a year in which you will have more largely the spirit of Christ, be raised above sublunary things, and be willing to be disposed of in this world just as God shall please. As every moment of the year will bring you nearer the end of your pilgrimage, may it bring you nearer to God, and find you more prepared to hail the messenger of death as a deliverer and a friend. And now, since I have begun to wish, I will go on. May this be the year in which you will change your name; in which you will take a final leave of your relatives and native land; in which you will cross the wide ocean, and dwell

on the other side of the world, among a heathen people. What a great change will this year probably effect in our lives! How very different will be our situation and employment! If our lives are preserved and our attempt prospered, we shall next new year's day be in India, and perhaps wish each other a happy new year in the uncouth dialect of Hindostan or Burmah. We shall no more see our kind friends around us, or enjoy the conveniences of civilized life, or go to the house of God with those that keep holy day; but swarthy countenances will every where meet our eye, the jargon of an unknown tongue will assail our ears, and we shall witness the assembling of the heathen to celebrate the worship of idol gods. We shall be weary of the world, and wish for wings like a dove, that we may fly away and be at rest. We shall probably experience seasons when we shall be "exceeding sorrowful even unto death." We shall see many dreary, disconsolate hours, and feel a sinking of spirits, anguish of mind, of which now we can form little conception. O, we shall wish to lie down and die. And that time may soon come. One of us may be unable to sustain the heat of the climate and the change of habits; and the other may say with literal truth, over the grave –

"By foreign hands thy dying eyes were closed;
By foreign hands thy decent limbs composed
By foreign hands thy humble grave adorned;"

But whether we shall be honored and mourned by strangers, God only knows. At least, either of us will be certain of *one* mourner. In view of such scenes shall we not pray with earnestness, "O for an overcoming faith."[10]

In 1812, Ann and Adoniram Judson sailed for India. They were to meet the Baptist missionaries from England there. In preparation for what they anticipated as a discussion of their instructions to baptize credible believers *and their households,* they restudied the issue of baptism with a view to defending infant baptism. Ann tells the struggle and the results in her diary and in several pieces of correspondence that she wrote on this issue. After relating the growing difficulties that her husband found with this issue, she tells of her own pilgrimage. On August 23, she wrote, "Mr. J. feels convinced from Scripture, that he has never been baptized, and that he cannot conscientiously administer baptism to infants." Then the following:

> I do not feel myself satisfied on the subject of baptism, having never given it a thorough examination. But I see many difficulties in the Pedobaptist theory, and must acknowledge that the face of Scripture does favor the Baptist sentiments. I intend to persevere in examining the subject, and hope that I shall be disposed to embrace the truth, whatever it may be. It is painfully mortifying to my natural feelings, to think seriously of renouncing a system which I have been taught from infancy to believe and respect. O that the Spirit of God may enlighten and direct my mind—may prevent my retaining an old error, or embracing a new one!
>
> Sept. 1. I have been examining the subject of baptism for some time past, and contrary to my prejudices and my wishes, am compelled to believe, that believer's baptism alone is found in Scripture. If ever I sought to know the truth; if ever I looked up to the Father of lights; if ever I gave up myself to the inspired word, I have done so during this investigation. And the result is, that, laying aside my former prejudices and systems, and fairly appealing to the Scriptures, I feel convinced that nothing really can be said in favor of infant baptism or sprinkling. We expect soon to be baptized. O may our hearts be prepared for that holy ordinance! And as we are baptized into a profession of Christ, may we put on Christ, and walk worthy of the high vocation wherewith we are called. But in consequence of our performance of this duty, we must make some very painful sacrifices. We must be separated from our dear missionary associates, and labor alone in some isolated spot. We must expect to be treated with contempt, and cast off by many of our American friends. . . . O, our heavenly Father, wilt thou be our friend. Wilt thou protect us, enable us to live to thy glory, and make us useful in some retired part of this eastern world, in leading a few precious souls to embrace that Saviour whom we love and desire to serve.[11]

In letters to family and friends Ann summarized the events recorded with such pathos in her journal. This letter was written from the Isle of France on February 14, 1813, some five months after their baptism.

I will now, my dear parents and sisters, give you some account of our change of sentiment, relative to the subject of Baptism. Mr. Judson's doubts commenced while on our passage from America. While translating the New Testament, in which he was engaged, he used frequently to say, that the Baptists were right in their mode of administering the ordinance. Knowing he should meet the Baptists at Serampore, he felt it important to attend to it more closely, to be able to defend his sentiments. After our arrival at Serampore, his mind for two or three weeks was so much taken up with missionary inquiries, and our difficulties with government, as to prevent his attending to the subject of baptism. But as we were waiting the arrival of our brethren, and having nothing in particular to attend to, he again took up the subject. I tried to have him give it up, and rest satisfied in his old sentiments, and frequently told him if he became a Baptist, *I would not.* He, however, said he felt it his duty to examine closely a subject on which he had so many doubts. After we removed to Calcutta, he found in the library in our chamber, many books on both sides, which he determined to read candidly and prayerfully, and to hold fast, or embrace the truth, however mortifying, however great the sacrifice. I now commenced reading on the subject, with all my prejudices on the Pedobaptist side. We had with us Dr. Worcester's, Dr. Austin's, Peter Edwards', and other Pedobaptist writings. But after closely examining the subject for several weeks, we were constrained to acknowledge that the truth appeared to lie on the Baptists' side. It was extremely trying to reflect on the consequences of our becoming Baptists. We knew it would wound and grieve our dear Christian friends in America—that we should lose their approbation and esteem. We thought it probable that Commissioners would refuse to support us; and what was more distressing than anything, we knew we must be separated from our missionary associates, and go alone to some heathen land. These things were very trying to us, and caused our hearts to bleed for anguish. We felt we had no home in this world, and no friend but each other. Our friends at Serampore were extremely surprised when we wrote them a

> letter requesting baptism, as they had known nothing of our having had any doubts on the subject. We were baptized on the 6th of September, in the Baptist chapel in Calcutta. Mr. J. preached a sermon at Calcutta on this subject soon after we were baptized, which, in compliance with the request of a number who heard it, he has been preparing for the press. Brother Rice was baptized several weeks after we were. It was a very great relief to our minds to have him join us, as we expected to be entirely alone in a mission.[12]

"I HAVE BECOME A BAPTIST"

On September 7, 1812, the day after her baptism, Ann wrote to a friend, Nancy, and to her parents giving the same basic events but with a few details and perspectives not in the other accounts. The freshness of the experience and the sobering reality of the connections just severed flood abundantly through the lines she writes. To her friend Nancy, she begins the letter, "Can you, my dear Nancy, still love me, still desire to hear from me, when I tell you I have become a Baptist?" She recounted the entire odyssey to Nancy, interspersing her remarks with the overflow of emotion she felt in reliving these traumatic months. The affair was "maturely, candidly, and . . . prayerfully examined for months" she assured her friend, after which she was "compelled from a conviction of truth" to embrace the Baptist view.

They earnestly sought to "count the cost" and prepare for the "severe trials" of such an action, and they anticipated the "loss of reputation" as well as the "affection and esteem" of American friends. More than those considerations, however, the separation from their missionary associates they anticipated as "the most trying circumstance" and that which "has caused most pain." This progression of events urged on by truth, conscience, and providence caused the young Judson couple so recently married and removed from their native country to "weep and pour out our hearts in prayer to Him whose directions we so much wish and need."[13]

The letter for her parents contained virtually the same narrative of events that she included to Nancy. Doubtless she wrote with an intent and hope that they could more easily resolve themselves to the reality that their lovely, intelligent, socially celebrated, personally engaging, and spiritually fervent daughter had become a Baptist, a member of a dissenting sect outside the esteem of the standing order of the established Congregational church.

> Mr. J. resolved to examine it candidly and prayerfully, let the result be what it would. No one in the mission family knew the state of his mind, as they never conversed with any of us on this subject. I was very fearful he would become a Baptist, and frequently suggested the unhappy consequences if he should. He always answered, that his duty compelled him to examine the subject, and he hoped he should have a disposition to embrace the truth, though he paid dear for it. I always took the Pedobaptists' side in reasoning with him, although I was as doubtful of the truth of their system as he. After we came to Calcutta, he devoted his whole time to reading on this subject, having obtained the best possible authors on both sides. After having examined and re-examined the subject, in every way possible, and comparing the sentiments of both Baptists and Pedobaptists with the Scriptures, he was compelled, from a conviction of the truth, to embrace those of the former. I confined my attention almost entirely to the Scriptures, comparing the Old with the New Testament, and tried to find something to favor infant baptism, but was convinced it had no foundation there. I examined the covenant of circumcision, and could see no reason for concluding that baptism was to be administered to children, because circumcision was. Thus, my dear parents and sisters, we are both confirmed Baptists, not because we wished to be, but because truth compelled us to be.[14]

Thus in these providential circumstances, the foreign mission movement among Baptists in America received its first missionaries. Knowing that a renunciation of infant baptism would offend friends at home and incur a loss of reputation, they nevertheless plowed forward. God used these particular struggles of conscience to thrust Baptists headlong into a New Testament enterprise that would increasingly become their passion over the next two centuries. The Judsons entered the Baptist fold in the way each Baptist should: "Because truth compelled us to be."

4

A BAPTIST: PRINCIPLE, NOT SENTIMENT

F. H. Kerfoot (1847–1901)

F. H. Kerfoot served Baptist life as a pastor, professor, and denominational servant. He was born in Clark County, Virginia, on August 29, 1847, at the Kerfoot home place named "Llewellyn." His father was a physician, described as a "warm-hearted, large-minded Christian gentleman." His mother, from the bluegrass section of Kentucky, was known as a "cultured, high-spirited woman of intellectual force and strongly-developed poetic nature."[1] She died when Kerfoot was four.

When the Civil War broke out, Kerfoot's older brothers immediately went into the Confederate army, and his father's services as a physician were needed constantly. The fourteen-year-old, therefore, took the brunt of responsibility for the farm on himself. Just before he was eighteen, Kerfoot joined Mosby's raiders, but the surrender at Appomattox cut short his army career. More hard work on the farm and at neighboring farms operating a wheat thrasher finally secured funds for Kerfoot to attend college.

He entered Columbia University in 1866 and earned the bachelor of philosophy and bachelor of law degrees, normally a six-year program, by 1869. Having felt a compelling call to preach, he chose to enroll at The Southern Baptist Theological Seminary, in Greenville, South Carolina, for the 1869–70 academic year. Poor health brought an interruption to his academic studies. After recovery, he attended Crozer Theological Seminary and graduated in 1872. In that year, James P. Boyce appointed him as an agent for Southern Seminary. After serving in that capacity only briefly, he came into some property and saw an opportunity to travel. He toured Europe, Egypt, and Palestine, and studied for a year at the University of Leipzig. His return to the United States found him moving to Kentucky, where he served as pastor of the Midway and Forks of Elkhorn churches beginning in February 1875. In the Kentucky home of a dear school friend of his mother, he met a Miss Price, who became his bride and his noble and strong companion through life.

The venerable and remarkable pastor and preacher at Eutaw Baptist Church in Baltimore, Maryland, Richard Fuller, died October 20, 1876. The church called Kerfoot as pastor. At the same time the seminary made its move from Greenville to Louisville, Kentucky, and urged Kerfoot to accept a position as an assistant instructor. The faculty, however, as John A. Broadus put it, "yielded to the urgent appeal of friends in the Eutaw Place Baptist Church, Baltimore, who wished him as pastor."[2] From 1877 to 1883 he continued there, and according to George Braxton Taylor, the church was like a "complex, smoothly running piece of machinery," until he was called to Strong Place Baptist Church in Brooklyn.[3] An accidental fall led to protracted lameness and other health problems. Kerfoot soon returned to his former pastorate in Kentucky at Midway.

In 1886 he returned to the seminary to attend a session. According to Broadus, he did "all the class-work with thoroughness and relish" and took his diplomas in the schools attended. At the request of Dr. Boyce, the trustees elected him as coprofessor of systematic theology. Originally Boyce intended that Kerfoot would share the teaching load in theology. Boyce's health and the constant demands for his talent in raising funds conspired to give Kerfoot the full load of teaching. In 1889 he became full professor. During the next ten years he taught and served faithfully in the difficult job of treasurer. This took time, tenacity, grace, tact, and enormous energy and finesse in letter writing.

In 1899, when W. H. Whitsitt's resignation from the presidency took effect, Kerfoot had strong support among the trustees for that position. The reticence on the part of some made the situation untenable, however, and created an opportunity for Kerfoot's graceful exit to a place that needed his administrative skills. In July 1899, he was elected as corresponding secretary of the Home Mission Board of the Southern Baptist Convention. He served only shortly in that position before his death less than two years later, June 22, 1901. He wrote the document below while serving at Eutaw Place Baptist Church in Baltimore.

WHAT WE BELIEVE ACCORDING TO THE SCRIPTURES

It is enjoined upon Christ's people that they be ready always to give an answer to every man that asketh a reason concerning the hope that is in them. (1 Pet. 3:15.) And Paul enjoins upon Timothy, not only that he take heed unto himself, but also unto his doctrines. (1 Tim. 4:16.) We herewith append the leading tenets which we hold, in common with all evangelical denominations, and also those which constitute our distinctive principles as Baptists. It is for the sake of the last, that we are constrained to exist as a separate denomination.

DOCTRINES WHICH WE HOLD IN COMMON WITH OTHER DENOMINATIONS

We believe, in common with all evangelical Christians:

In one God, Maker and Ruler of heaven and earth, revealed as the Father, the Son and the Holy Spirit equal in every divine perfection. Read 1 Corinthians 8:4–6, Matthew 28:19; Jude 20:21.

In the Holy Scriptures as His infallible word, which are able to make us wise unto salvation. Read 2 Timothy 3:16–17.

In the fall of man and his condemnation as a sinner, and God's sovereign grace and love in his redemption.

In salvation in the name of Jesus Christ, who was the "word made flesh," God-man, who obeyed the law, suffered and died for the sins of men, is risen and exalted, a Priest and King. Read Romans 5:12–21; 1 Corinthians 15:3, 4; Acts 5:31.

In the free offer of eternal life in the Gospel to all, and the aggravated guilt of those who reject it. Read Romans 10:11–13; Hebrews 2:3.

In the necessity of regeneration by the Holy Spirit, and of repentance: toward God, and faith in Christ. Read John 3:5; Acts 20:21.

In the justification and adoption of the believer, through the blood and righteousness of Jesus Christ. Read Romans 3:23–26.

In the sacred observance of the Lord's Day for His worship and His work. Read John 5:17; Revelation 1:10; Acts 20:7.

In the present life as man's only day of grace, and, that, when this present life ends, man enters at once into conscious blessedness or woe. Read 2 Corinthians 6:2; Luke 16:19–31.

In the resurrection of the body; the righteous, to eternal life; the wicked, to judgment and eternal punishment. Read John 5:28, 29; Matthew 25:46.

And, in common with a large body of evangelical Christians, nearly all Baptists believe what are usually termed the "doctrines of grace," the absolute sovereignty and foreknowledge of God; his eternal and unchangeable purposes or decrees; that salvation in its beginning, continuance and completion, is God's free gift; that, in Christ, we are elected or chosen, personally or individually, from eternity, saved and called out from the world, not according to our works, but according to His own purpose and grace, through the sanctification of the Spirit and belief of the truth; that we are kept by His power from falling away, and will be presented faultless before the presence of His glory. Read Romans 8, 9, 10, 11; Acts 13:48; Ephesians 1:4–5; Ephesians 2:1–10; 1 Peter 1:2–5; Jude 24; Timothy 1:9; Titus 3:5.

DISTINCTIVE DOCTRINES OF BAPTISTS

I. The Bible is an all-sufficient guide in faith and practice and nothing should be taught for doctrine which cannot be found therein. Read 2 Timothy 3:16, 17; Matthew 15:9; 1 John 2:20, 21, 27.

II. The Bible makes every religious observance a matter of voluntariness, and hence, of individual responsibility or privilege. And while we recognize the right of churches to exercise Scriptural discipline, and the right of governments to impose civil obligations, yet we hold that no church nor government, nor any power on earth, has the right to bind any man's conscience. This principle of voluntariness and individual responsibility also excludes every idea, that religious duty can be done by proxy. Hence, we reject the doctrines of infant baptism and sponsorship, and all efforts whatsoever to perform duties for others. Read John 18:36–37; Romans 14:12.

III. The first religious duty or act which the Bible requires of every person is repentance toward God and faith in the Lord Jesus Christ. Hence, we reject the doctrine of infant baptism, and every doctrine whatsoever which recognizes persons as in any way members of a church of Christ before they have given evidence of personal repentance toward God and faith in the Lord Jesus Christ. Read Acts 2:37–38; Acts 5:19–32; Acts 20:21.

IV. The Bible requires that every person who exercised repentance toward God and faith in the Lord Jesus Christ, shall be baptized into the name of the Father, and of the Son, and of the Holy Ghost. Matthew 28:19. And the Bible teaches concerning baptism:

1. As to the act, it is immersion in water. Read Acts 8:38, 39.
2. As to the design
    (1) It is a confession of Jesus Christ as our Savior and of our allegiance to the triune God. Read Galatians 3:27.
    (2) It is the answer of a good conscience toward God. Read 1 Peter 3:21.
    (3) It is the symbol by the washing of water—inward cleansing. Read Titus 3:5.
    (4) It is the symbol of our having been buried to a life of willful sinfulness, and of our having been raised again to walk in newness of life on earth. Read Romans 6:3–5.
    (5) It is the symbol of our having died with Jesus Christ, and of our having been raised with Him in a life of acceptance before God; and also of our resurrection with Him to life everlasting. Hence, we reject the doctrine of sprinkling and pouring for baptism, as the setting aside of the true ordinance; read as to the act and its signification, and the substitution therefor of human tradition. Read Colossians 2:12[–23].

V. We learn from the Bible concerning a church of Jesus Christ, that it is composed of those who have been baptized into the name of the Father, and of the Son, and of the Holy Ghost, after they have professed repentance toward God and faith in the Lord Jesus Christ. The association of such persons, in order to form a New Testament church, must be entirely voluntary on their part, and must be for the purpose of observing such ordinances and practices as are in accordance with the teachings of the New Testament concerning such organization. Read Acts 2:41–47.

The New Testament recognizes as the proper officers of churches Pastors or Elders, and Deacons. Read Philippians 1:1.

The New Testament shows also concerning churches of Jesus Christ, that every local church has the right to govern itself. It recognizes no right in civil governments to assume control over any church. It recognizes no such thing as priestly or papal domination, nor any authority in its own officers to be in any way lords over God's heritage. It recognizes no ecclesiastical courts or bodies of higher jurisdiction which shall have any right to interfere in the affairs of the churches. Churches may, in mere matters of expediency, associate and co-operate in Christian work if they see fit. Yet no association or council can have any power or jurisdiction, except what the churches see fit to allow. Read Matthew 23:8–11; 2 Corinthians 1:24.

VI. The New Testament teaches concerning the Lord's Supper that it is a memorial ordinance, entrusted to the churches; and that it is to commemorate the offering of the Lord's body and his shed blood till he comes. A careful examination of these ordinances, as appointed by Christ, and of their essential meaning, and of the way in which they were observed by the Apostles, will show that Baptism, which is administered but once and for all time, should precede the Lord's Supper. And, inasmuch as God's Word gives us no warrant whatever for inviting unbaptized persons to the table, which is the Lord's table, we dare not allow our Christian sympathies to lead us into giving such invitations, lest we be found changing the order of God's Word, and ministering to the confusion and obscurity of God's truth. We reject the idea that the Lord's Supper is designed to celebrate love among Christians, or is an ordinance for deciding questions of fellowship either in an individual church or between churches. And in declining to invite members of other denominations, we do not question their piety at all, but only declare that we believe them according to the example and command of Christ to be unbaptized persons and not walking in the New Testament order of ordinances. Read 1 Corinthians 6:17–34.

And for this, as in all things, we appeal to the Bible.
May the Lord give light, and knowledge, and the Spirit of the Covenant.[4]

PART THREE

THOUGHTS FROM THE BAPTIST LEADERSHIP

5

WHAT IS A BAPTIST?

James T. Draper, Jr.

Baptists are people of a remarkable history, a resilient spirit, and a responsible commitment. Many things have been written and spoken in recent years about these people called Baptists. But what is a Baptist? What essentials define the individual and the corporate body of Baptists? Let me suggest some characteristics of a Baptist in today's world that are consistent with what a Baptist has been historically.

1. A Baptist is an individual who has experienced salvation through personal faith in Jesus Christ. Baptists do not believe in proxy faith, where a priest or any other person mediates between the individual and God (1 Tim. 2:5). Every individual must come to the time in life when he or she receives Jesus Christ as personal Savior. This is the basic building block in the making of a Baptist.

2. A Baptist is one who acknowledges the sufficiency of Scripture. Such an individual believes the Bible is God's truth without any error. That is the foundation of all we do and believe. God's Word clearly declares, "All scripture is given by inspiration of God, and is profitable for doctrine, for reproof, for correction, for instruction in righteousness: that the man of

God may be perfect, thoroughly furnished unto all good works" (2 Tim. 3:16–17 KJV).

Baptists have always recognized and often drawn up "confessions of faith." These have been and continue to be guides in understanding the basic beliefs of Baptists, but no confession has a creedal power over any individual or church. God's Word is our final authority and we recognize its sufficiency.

3. A Baptist is one who acknowledges the lordship of Jesus Christ. All of our worship and service centers on him. "He is the head of the body, the church: who is the beginning, the firstborn from the dead; that in all things he might have the preeminence. For it pleased the Father that in him should all fulness dwell" (Col. 1:18–19 KJV).

We also recognize that the Bible testifies of Jesus Christ and is our source of understanding of his person, presence, and relationship with us. All we teach and experience regarding Jesus Christ must be consistent with the revealed truth of God in the Scripture. In *The Encyclopedia of Southern Baptists,* E. Y. Mullins states: "Jesus Christ is the crown of the revelation recorded in the Scriptures. In him all is unified. The lordship of Christ is a fundamental Baptist teaching. In all our doctrine of the Bible we seek to express the meaning of Christ *as disclosed therein*"[1] (emphasis mine). All of our experience with Jesus is validated and confirmed by the truth of the written Word of God.

4. A Baptist is Trinitarian in his or her understanding of God. We believe the Bible teaches that God is eternally one in three persons: Father, Son, and Holy Spirit. Each is fully God, yet God is one. There is no division in the Godhead and no person of the Godhead is less than fully divine. God is Father, who created the world and all that is in it, who planned our redemption from before the foundations of the world, and who has a wonderful plan and purpose for each of our lives.

God is Son, even our Lord Jesus Christ, who became the perfect sacrifice for our sins. He was fully divine, yet fully human. This is a mystery beyond our comprehension, but we know that he was everything man needed in God and everything God desired for man. His virgin birth, sinless life, vicarious death, and promised return is foundational to our faith.

God is Holy Spirit. Jesus Christ said, "I will pray the Father, and he shall give you another Comforter, that he may abide with you for ever; even the Spirit of truth; . . . I will not leave you comfortless: I will come to you" (John 14:16–18). The Holy Spirit is the very presence of God in our midst today. He lives within us and guides us in all we do as he leads us to understand the depths of God's Word. His purpose is to magnify and glorify Jesus Christ, and our experience with him will always be consistent with the Scripture.

5. A Baptist is one who recognizes the autonomy of the local church. There is no such thing as "the Baptist church." There are only local Baptist churches. The local Baptist church is "Baptist headquarters." No individual or entity outside of the local Baptist church has any authority or control over that congregation. Each congregation is free and empowered to minister as it sees the will of God for its ministry and mission. A Baptist church, like first-century New Testament churches, is a local independent body of born-again, baptized believers joined together in Christ for worship and ministry in their community and around the world.

There is no hierarchy in our denomination that has authority over the local church. While Baptists do believe that the New Testament teaches that all the redeemed of all ages belong to the church eternal, we know that the references in the New Testament to the church refer primarily to a local body of believers, who have voluntarily come together to carry out the mission of the church.

To the church God has committed two ordinances, the Lord's Supper and baptism. Neither of these ordinances is sacraments. Neither has power to transmit saving grace. Both are to be preceded by acceptance of Christ by faith as Savior and Lord. Baptism precedes participation in the Lord's Supper. Neither baptism nor the Lord's Supper is essential to salvation, but both are vital to a full and meaningful Christian life. The church is to keep faithfully these ordinances until Jesus comes again. Both the Lord's Supper and baptism are symbols of our faith and testify of the work and ministry of Jesus Christ. As the name Baptist implies, we insist upon baptism by immersion of the body of the believer in water.

6. A Baptist is one who believes in the command of the Great Commission and has a deep commitment to evangelism and world missions. The church exists as a place of nurture and worship, but it is also a place of witness and outreach to the ends of the earth. The marching orders for the church are clearly seen in Matthew 28:18–20. A Baptist is one who has accepted that challenge and assignment from our Lord Jesus Christ. We understand that our Lord Jesus Christ has the world in his heart, and the closer we draw to him, the more missionary we will become.

7. A Baptist is one who fully advocates and supports the cause of religious liberty and freedom for all. We believe that the church and state must maintain separate identities and functions for the good of both. Throughout

Christian history, whenever religion has controlled the state or the state has controlled religion, both have been corrupted and religious and civil liberty have suffered.

We do not believe, however, that this truth prohibits the involvement of Christians in public life. Christians must be involved in public life at every level. Individual Christians and Christian institutions should seek to influence government at every level in the realm of public morals, but they must not seek to control the state. Neither should the state seek to control people's personal religious practices or the expression of organized religion.

Throughout their history, Baptists have stood as guardians of religious liberty and this understanding of the distinctive roles of the church and state. Americans need to know and all of us need to remember that the constitutional rights protecting freedom of religion are due largely to the impact of Baptists from colonial days to the present. Baptists, including John Leland, a preacher from Virginia, and James Manning, the president of a Baptist college—Rhode Island College (later Brown University)—figured prominently in the ratification of the United States Constitution.

James Madison introduced amendments into the Constitution to safeguard religious liberty after conferring with John Leland. When James Madison died, one who eulogized him declared: "The credit of adopting the Constitution of the United States properly belonged to a Baptist clergyman, formerly of Virginia, by the name of Leland."[2]

SOUTHERN BAPTISTS AND COOPERATION

What is a Southern Baptist? This question is a natural outcome of our first inquiry. We as Southern Baptists embrace the uniqueness and essentials listed above, but we move further into the Southern Baptist distinctive of cooperation. We do what we do together. We do what we do together voluntarily. No one coerces us. We are bound together in what my predecessor, James L. Sullivan, called a "rope of sand with strength of steel." To cooperate means that we gather around the essentials listed above and put aside our personal agendas to accomplish the mandate of God for our lives. While there are many other things that Baptists might "believe" or endless convictions we might "hold," those listed above are the bedrock issues that have set Baptists apart through the centuries.

E. Y. Mullins concludes his article in *The Encyclopedia of Southern Baptists* with the following thoughts under the heading "The Only Basis of Unity:" "The one sure and certain road to agreement among all Christians is obedience to the New Testament teachings in all matters of doctrine, polity, worship, and life. To seek unity of view on any other basis is in effect an effort to uproot the fundamental principle of evangelical Christianity—the finality and authority of the Bible. Loyalty to the Bible would very soon destroy any form of unity otherwise established. For Baptists, then, it seems a hopeless undertaking to seek unity of view on any other principle. If the Bible is final and authoritative, why set forth plans of unity based on expediency or mutual concession of vital teachings? They can be only roundabout paths to new issues so long as the Bible remains authoritative and final. Baptists long and pray for complete agreement among Christians of all names. They are second to none in their desires in this direction. They especially desire that it be accomplished on a stable and lasting basis. They firmly believe that the Bible alone is such a basis."[3]

The above essentials compose a tapestry which reveals a pattern that uniquely describes a Baptist. We are a believers' church that voluntarily cooperates around the authority and sufficiency of God's Word in all matters necessary for life "in Christ."[4]

6

BEING BAPTIST MEANS CONVICTION

R. Albert Mohler, Jr.

My very earliest memories of life are Baptist memories. I was born to faithful Baptist parents who made our local church the organizing center of our life outside the home. Simply put, when the doors were open we were there. The sights, sounds, and smells of Baptist life started for me with the Cradle Roll and the church nursery, which was filled with rocking chairs, elderly caregivers with open-toed shoes, and Bible story pictures on the walls. Just imagine a Norman Rockwell portrait of Southern Baptist life, complete with dignified pastor and Georgian architecture. It was warm, wonderful, and where I belonged.

Advancing in years, I was a Sunbeam and a Royal Ambassador, and I was involved in every age-graded choir. Even my Boy Scout troop was sponsored by our church—and my parents would not let me join unless I was first faithful as a Royal Ambassador. The Boy Scouts and the RA's were the same boys, just wearing different uniforms on different nights. The outside world was a mystery.

I had a vague awareness that other denominations existed, but I could not understand why anyone would want to be anything other than a Baptist. At some stage I discovered that my father's parents were Methodists *(Methodists!)* and that he had once been a Methodist as well. I assumed that he was brought to see the light by my mother, who had been raised (thank goodness) in a Baptist family. He must have seen the light quite clearly, for he became a deacon and director of Training Union. Driving across town, I saw evidence of other denominations by name, but those church buildings seemed almost like embassies of foreign faiths.

Attending Vacation Bible School at age nine, I came to a knowledge of my sin and of Christ's provision as my Savior. After talking to my parents, I was taken to the pastor. Dr. T. Rupert Coleman was elegance and dignity personified, but he loved children and talked to me about Jesus as comfortably as he had discussed New Testament Greek with A. T. Robertson, his doctoral supervisor at Southern Seminary. I was baptized at the Southside Baptist Church in Lakeland, Florida, on a summer Sunday night—and left the next morning for Royal Ambassador camp at Lake Yale. If I was eaten by one of the alligators at Lake Yale, at least I was going to heaven.

A major life crisis came at age twelve, when my parents announced that we would be moving to south Florida, where my father would have greater opportunities for advancement in his work. Everything I knew and loved was about to come apart. Both sets of grandparents and all my aunts, uncles, and cousins lived within fifteen miles of our home. I liked my school and our neighborhood, where my friends and I could play in the woods and build forts in the trees.

Most traumatically, we would be leaving Southside Baptist Church—the only place on earth that for me represented spiritual security and transcendent truth. I was not certain that God could be found in the exploding population of south Florida. Worse still, I discovered that Baptists were not a majority in Broward County. Catholic churches named for saints and Jewish synagogues dotted the landscape. The largest church in the area was Presbyterian *(Presbyterian!)*, and no one at my new school looked like a Baptist. Pompano Beach was not Lakeland. I had been thrown out of the "solid South" right into the social experiment of the Gold Coast, where most residents were transplanted northerners. Far more secularized than the culture I had known, the area was a religious cafeteria of denominations, fringe groups, cultic organizations, and bus ministries.

As a family, our first task was to find a new church. For the first time, I visited other congregations (all Southern Baptist, of course) and discovered that not one of them was just like Southside. Eventually, we joined First

Baptist Church, Pompano Beach, a fast-growing and very large congregation. The pace of life was quicker in the culture, and also in our new congregation. The church even had a gymnasium and a bowling alley. Let's just see the Presbyterians try to top those facilities! They did.

Once again, I was involved at every level open to me. We grew to love our new pastor, Dr. Robert L. Smith, a Southwestern Seminary graduate with a polished style and a telegenic personality. I sang in the youth choir, went on all the mission trips, became a leader in the youth group, taught first-graders in Sunday school, rededicated my life to Christ (more than once), was elected youth pastor for youth week, and was involved in weekly evangelism and discipleship meetings. In my spare time I went to school, worked for my father at the store, and played in the school band. There is no intensity like adolescent intensity.

The first rumblings of theological questioning came from immersion in the pluralistic culture of south Florida in the 1970s. An interest in philosophy, politics, and a raging intellectual curiosity led me to ask awkward questions. How could I really be sure that all I had known as true was really true? If our truth claims are true, are all others false? Is the Christian life based on something real, or on mere feelings? In the drug-saturated and sexually liberated world of south Florida, why exactly did we live by a set of ancient commandments delivered in a desert halfway around the world? What is truth, after all?

With these questions troubling my consciousness, I turned to those I trusted—but not to my parents, whom I trusted most of all. Why scare them to death? I was scared enough for all of us. Thankfully, I was surrounded by faithful Christians who held fast to the faith, and eventually led into sources that provided answers they themselves could not give. At this point I was greatly assisted and encouraged by the writings of Francis Schaeffer—a *Presbyterian.* I was also helped by D. James Kennedy, the pastor of Coral Ridge Presbyterian Church and the founder of Evangelism Explosion. His sermons addressed apologetic questions and current issues from a biblical worldview. Going through Evangelism Explosion training gave me further assurance.

I was ambushed by a call to ministry as I was a political science major planning to enter law school. I transferred to Samford University as a religion major and found myself again in the Bible Belt. Being Baptist was no scandal in Birmingham. The questions that had troubled me years back had always lurked nearby. I was determined to follow the truth, even if it took a long time to answer these questions more fully.

At Samford I became president of the ministerial association and participated fully in the "H-Day" program that afforded ministerial students weekly opportunities to preach in Alabama churches, mostly rural. I was eager. The churches were kind. I can hardly imagine how those churches tolerated carloads of "preacher boys" heading up into the hills to preach half-baked sermons illustrated with real-life adventures from college religion classes.

For me, it was an eye-opening experience. My two childhood churches were very large; these churches were small. My pastors had been seminary-educated, polished, urbane, and drove respectable sedans. These pastors were former farmers and machinists, who pounded the pulpit and drove pickup trucks or older cars. Some worked all week in other employment, driving school buses and working in factories, so they could support their families and their ministries. I grew to love them and to see the dignity and dedication of their lives.

They had no time for theological nonsense, and there was not a liberal bone in their bodies. These churches were Baptist to the core, even though their cultural setting was far different than what I had known. But what made them Baptist?

At Samford University, and especially at Southern Seminary, I was immersed in the culture of Southern Baptist aristocracy. I flourished in its context and found myself at home. Yet I also noted a sense of discomfort among some professors and Baptist leaders who were embarrassed by the "backwoods" conservatism of Southern Baptists. Their disdain for this conservatism was often masked by terms like "Southern populism" and "uncritical evangelicalism," but the effect was to dismiss conservative evangelicals as uneducated, unsophisticated, and backward—unenlightened by studying the works of Bultmann, Tillich, Moltmann, and Niebuhr.

For some time I bought the argument that "intellectual integrity" demanded the reconsideration of every cherished doctrine. But I was repulsed by seeing the Christian faith cut down to size with the pruning shears of modern thought. Modernism was giving way to postmodernism in the larger academy as I studied for the Ph.D. in theology. Modernist rationalism and existentialism were supplanted by postmodern relativism and deconstructionism. The reality and objectivity of truth were denied. Only the words remained.

I came to see that for some persons, even some Baptist leaders and seminary professors, Baptist identity had been reduced to a set of "distinctives" all revolving around libertarian notions of the sovereign self. Concepts like the priesthood of all believers, soul competency, the autonomy of the local church, and religious liberty were recklessly employed to argue, as a tract of the times put it, *Being Baptist Means Freedom*—nothing more.

The controversy in the Southern Baptist Convention was now fully underway, and every issue was a matter of heated debate and furious argument. It was a strange and volatile time to be a seminary student, and I was a staff member of the institution as well. I dearly loved Southern Seminary, and I loved the school even more as I came to cherish her history and heritage.

The crisis in the Southern Baptist Convention forced the question of Baptist identity, and it forced deeper questions as well. I came to see that the issues of debate in the controversy pointed to more urgent questions and foundational truths. As a young theologian grappling with the chaos of modern theology, I began to see the foundations crumble.

The question of Baptist identity cannot be separated from the prior question of Christian identity and the authenticity of Christian truth. I heard persons describe themselves as Baptists even as they systematically dismantled the Christian faith and abandoned its most essential truths. The noble name of the Baptists was in danger of becoming a license to reformulate Christianity in radical terms, to leave nothing but a bare notion of religious experience devoid of doctrinal content.

And yet, the more I observed this pattern, the more I saw it as an aberration from the Baptist heritage. Baptist confessions of faith bore witness to the robust orthodoxy of Baptists throughout their history. Substantial theological content, the confessional structure of doctrinal parameters, congregational discipline, and bold witness to the truth of God's Word were hallmarks of the Baptist heritage.

As a Christian theologian, I am a Baptist by conviction. Baptists often claim a list of "distinctives" as our defining marks. I would argue that few, if any, of these doctrinal principles are truly distinctive. Other denominations practice believer's baptism, organize their polity by congregationalism, and affirm the necessity of personal Christian experience. Furthermore, Baptists share in the great evangelical inheritance, standing in the Reformation heritage and seeking to hold fast to the faith "once for all delivered to the saints" with our evangelical brothers and sisters of other denominations.

What makes Baptist identity truly distinctive is the unique manner in which we hold these truths together in symphonic wholeness and seek to apply them to our congregational life. Baptist identity is rooted in the Baptist congregation.

Several key convictions form the pillars of our Baptist identity. Among these are the integrity of the gospel, the authority of the Bible, and the New Testament vision of the Church.

THE INTEGRITY OF THE GOSPEL

Baptists are a gospel people. We cherish the gospel of Jesus Christ as the means of salvation to all who believe. We know that there is salvation in the name of Jesus and in no other name. Sinners come to Christ by faith, and are justified by faith alone. Grace is our theme and the gospel of Jesus Christ is our message. As the 1644 London Confession stated: "The tenders of the Gospel to the conversion of sinners is absolutely free, no way requiring, as absolutely necessary, any qualifications, preparations, terrors of the Law, or preceding ministry of the Law, but only and alone the naked soul, as a sinner and ungodly to receive Christ, as crucified, dead, and buried, and risen again, being made a Prince and a Savior for such sinners."

Believer's baptism is essential to our understanding of the gospel, for it is our public profession of faith in Christ. It underscores the necessity of personal confession of Christ as Savior and Lord, and denies any faith by proxy. Our rejection of infant baptism is rooted in the clear and normative New Testament witness to the baptism of believers by immersion. But we are also chastened by the knowledge that millions of persons, baptized as infants, consider themselves Christians while never confessing Christ as Savior. I am a Baptist because we defend the integrity of the gospel.

THE AUTHORITY OF THE BIBLE

Every denomination operates under some concept of spiritual authority, however vague or unbiblical it may be. Baptists often describe their churches as "spiritual democracies." This is a true statement, but it can be dangerously misunderstood. Christ rules in his church, and he rules through his Word.

The Bible, and the Bible alone, holds ultimate authority in a Baptist congregation. The Second London Confession of Faith (1677) put the issue plainly: "The whole counsel of God concerning all things necessary for his own Glory, man's Salvation, Faith and Life, is either expressly set down or necessarily contained in the Holy Scripture; unto which nothing at any time is to be added, whether by new Revelation of the Spirit, or traditions of men."

Baptist congregationalism is an exercise in bringing ourselves under submission to the Word of God—not in exercising our own authority in the place of Scripture.

THE NEW TESTAMENT CHURCH

Congregationalism is more than a system of church polity; it is the Baptist vision of the visible church as revealed in the New Testament. The core of congregationalism is the affirmation of our responsibility, under the lordship of Christ and the authority of Scripture, to come together as believers under a covenant of faithfulness to Christ. No one is a Baptist alone.

Seeking to define the church, the New Hampshire Confession of Faith (1833) states that a visible church is "a congregation of baptized believers, associated by covenant in the faith and fellowship of the Gospel; observing the ordinances of Christ; governed by His laws; and exercising the gifts, rights, and privileges invested in them by His Word." Every word of this definition is essential to the New Testament vision of the church.

In a Baptist congregation, every believer is in covenant with brothers and sisters in Christ. Believer's baptism by immersion, faithfully following the example and instruction of our Lord, is the sign of that covenant, and is prerequisite to membership. We are a congregation of believer priests, serving the Lord in the preaching of the Word, the observation of the ordinances, discipline in accord with God's laws, and the proclamation of the gospel.

I cannot reconcile any other form of church government with the New Testament. Believer's baptism is so central and essential to our understanding of the church that we can see no church without this ordinance and can recognize no other baptism as true baptism. We came by our name honestly.

Baptist by family heritage, I am a Baptist by conviction. With thankfulness to God, I claim this heritage as my own and pray that the Baptists of this generation will stand in faithful obedience before God. By God's grace, this is why I am a Baptist.

7

SHOOT-OUT AT THE AMEN CORRAL: BEING BAPTIST THROUGH CONTROVERSY

Paige Patterson

EARLY INFLUENCES

In 1952, Methodist scholar Franklin Hamlin Littell released *The Anabaptist View of the Church.* I was only ten years old, but I later read the book as a sixteen-year-old boy upon the recommendation of my father. Franklin Littell's book and my father's recommendation converged as the central influences in my early life regarding my choice to be and remain a Baptist. Littell's book, though not the first influence, did provide my earliest seriously reflective convictions about remaining a Baptist.

Above all else, the family and the church in which I was reared must be considered. My father and mother, Dr. Thomas Armour Patterson and Honey (as Mother was popularly known), were both intensely interested in theological and ecclesiastical matters. Hence, my father served as the pastor of the First Baptist Church of Beaumont, Texas, with my mother by his side. She wrote the history of the Woman's Missionary Union of Texas, entitled *Candle by Night.* They provided the foundation I needed to embrace my Baptist heritage.

My father received his doctor of theology degree at Southwestern Baptist Theological Seminary. He wrote under W. T. Conner concerning the impact of the theology of J. R. Graves on Southern Baptist life, an important consideration later in my testimony.

My conversion experience at age nine was sufficiently vivid that I remember it to this day with much greater clarity than I do many events that have happened within recent days. Of course, by the age of nine I had already been taught the importance of believer's baptism by immersion. Therefore, my conversion on Good Friday night was followed by my baptism at the hands of my father on Easter Sunday night. Almost immediately my father and mother intensified my theological training. When I started preaching at age fifteen, my father began to purchase books for me to read.

By age sixteen, I had come into sufficient contact with people of other denominations (many of whom I considered to be born-again believers in Jesus) that my Baptist heritage was inevitably challenged. Challenges to comfortable notions continued through high school and college. I had opportunity to be exposed to other writings that answered my questions and reconfirmed my earliest intellectual considerations. My reading of Littell's *The Anabaptist View of the Church* established clearly in my mind that the New Testament church and the Anabaptists of the Radical Reformation in Europe were right in defining a true church as being made up of those with a new-birth experience who had followed Christ in faith-witness baptism by immersion.

Soon I became aware of the debate on Baptist origins. Barry White in England rejected any organic connection between the Baptists of England, and hence of America, and the Anabaptists of South Germany and Switzerland. Robert Baker and William R. Estep of Southwestern Seminary seemed convinced of a connection: "The rapid appearance of Anabaptists over a wide area lends confirmation to what reliable historians have asserted:

small communities of pious Christians, rarely appearing in historical records but endeavoring to reproduce the New Testament in simple, anticlerical, nonsacramental purity, were interspersed throughout the length and breadth of Europe in the centuries before the Reformation. It would have been impossible for them to leap full-grown into the focus of history had this not been true."[1]

But I also knew that to some degree the debate concerning whether or not there was a connection between modern Baptists and the Anabaptists of the Reformation was purely academic. I had read enough to know that I believed essentially what Anabaptists believed, and most contemporary Baptists I knew believed the same.

Gradually across years of study, I read other books with increasing commitment to Baptist theology. Leonard Verduin's 1964 publication, *The Reformers and Their Stepchildren,* underscored everything I had come to believe. While Luther, Calvin, and other magisterial reformers were shining stars in the theological firmament, nonetheless they had been inconsistent with their *volkskirche* concept. The Anabaptists had acted as a much-needed corrective to call Luther, Calvin, and others to a theology consistent with their expressions of *sola gratia* and *sola fide.*

Albert Henry Newman's *Manual of Church History,* published in 1902, came into my hands as did his *History of Anti-Pedobaptism,* which was first published in 1896. The former volume assisted me in distinguishing clearly among the various Anabaptist groups—some with whom I felt little identification and others with whom I felt instant affinity. *History of Anti-Pedobaptism* helped me to understand the important point made by Landmark Southern Baptists—namely, that the Roman Catholic Church was hardly a monolithic institution in any century. By the same token, that book helped me understand that rejection of infant baptism did not necessarily identify a group as Baptist. Hence, I avoided mistakes that some Landmark Baptists made.

The latter book also awakened an interest in the precursors to the Reformation. Matthew Spinka's book on John Hus published in 1968 and Murray Wagner's biography of Petr Chelcicky published in 1983 led me further to see that there were people who were remarkably baptistic in some of their conclusions even before the Reformation.

Still later Arnold Snyder's *The Life and Thought of Michael Sattler* in 1984, and William Klassen and Walter Klaassen's *The Writings of Pilgram Marpeck* in 1978 were invaluable. I found many of the works of the incomparable Anabaptist theologian Balthasar Hubmaier, published by W. R. Estep in

Anabaptist Beginnings 1523–1553 in 1976. Although I reveled in the writings included in that volume, Hubmaier's *On the Sword, On the Christian Baptism of Believers,* and *Concerning Heretics and Those Who Burn Them* made the greatest impact and led me to embrace many of his views. I also read Andrew Fuller on *The Atonement of Christ and the Justification of the Sinner.* I may be one of the few to read every entry in William Cathcart's *Baptist Encyclopedia* of 1881. As still a further influence, *Covenant and Community* by Walter Klaassen explored the life and writings of Pilgram Marpeck.

College years added a different emphasis. Attending Hardin-Simmons University in Abilene, Texas, I was in the heart of the most rigid of the Church of Christ domain. Its adherents wished to debate *ad infinitum* the necessity of baptism for salvation and the possibility of losing salvation. All of this in a healthy way forced me back again to the New Testament. In college I began to manage an elementary level in Greek. The more I read and studied, the more I became incontrovertibly committed to Baptist principles.

Particular ministers also influenced and guided my life, adding to my resolve to continue being a Baptist. At Hardin-Simmons, Zane Mason, a precious saint of God who taught history, and Ray Ellis, who intimidated me into learning Greek, encouraged me profoundly. In seminary, Wayne Ward, my cousin by marriage and professor of theology at Southern Seminary, was still at the pinnacle of his service to the seminary. Wayne Ward, in addition to my father, was one of the most influential men in my life. At that time, he had not abandoned many of the aspects of evangelicalism he unfortunately later abandoned.

Others who contributed were evangelist Angel Martinez, who convinced me that one could be both an evangelist and a scholar. During my Ph.D. work, William Mueller, who had studied with Karl Barth, forced me to become more thorough in my investigations. Dr. James Mosteller, who taught church history and who was wonderfully interested in Anabaptists, opened the way to new materials about the Radical Reformation that I had not yet discovered. Dr. Clark Pinnock, who had just come to New Orleans Seminary, introduced me to philosophy as not necessarily a negative or heretical discipline. He taught me both philosophy and methods of public discussion.

In all of this time, I had read carefully the various members of the Landmark triumvirate, including *Theodosia Ernest* by Amos C. Dayton, all of J. R. Graves's available works, and William Pendleton's contributions on the subject as well as his short systematic theology. I read John T. Christian and even J. M. Carroll's *The Trail of Blood.*

While I was profoundly influenced by the Landmark tradition in my view of the importance and independence of the local church, I did not follow the Landmarkers in some of their more questionable conclusions. Nevertheless, I dare not fail to acknowledge my indebtedness to them.

REFORMED THEOLOGY

Another influence impressing me to remain a Baptist were encounters that I frequently experienced with proponents of Reformed theology through college and seminary days and even afterward. At first, I felt myself drawn to Reformed theology for reasons that make it appealing to me until this day. For the most part, I observed that those who embraced Reformed theology tended to live remarkably saintly lives, an interesting reversal of what, according to Arminians, should have been the case. Arminians of various stripes, who believed that you could lose your salvation, seemed never to tire of accusing Calvinists of believing that once you were saved you were always saved and hence you could live like the devil. In fact, the lives of those espousing Calvinism seemed to me, on the whole, to exhibit more of the holiness of God and fewer of the moral lapses than I found in the lives of their opponents.

Second, you never had to wonder where someone of the Reformed persuasion stood regarding Scripture. He would endorse Scripture as being the inerrant Word of God.

Third, undoubtedly full-blown biblical Trinitarianism would be espoused by those of a more Calvinistic persuasion. Fourth, the same is true of the emphasis on salvation by grace alone. Nothing in the Bible is any more certain to me than this fact: All human effort to make oneself acceptable with God is not only a failure but is reprehensible. All of our righteousnesses are like filthy rags (Isa. 64:6). My Reformed friends believed this and taught it clearly. Salvation was permanent for those in the Reformed tradition. The nature of the new birth itself is sufficient to establish beyond any shadow of a doubt the keeping power of the Lord.

In addition to this, all of my Reformed friends saw the dangers in untethered experientialism that was so often found among many of the Arminians and certainly among the Charismatics. Though most of these non-Reformed groups seemed to believe in the authority of Scripture, their experience in fact seemed to take precedence. Personal experience would frequently claim authority equal to or beyond holy Scripture. My Reformed friends all saw that every experience had to be adjudicated by the standard of God's revealed Word.

But while I felt then and still feel a certain affinity with Reformed theology, my Baptist commitments were actually further deepened by an examination of what I thought then and now to be inherent mistakes in the Reformed system. First, the abandonment of the congregational form of government was a significant mistake. Though Congregationalism frequently had tragic results and some ominous weaknesses, seemingly for me it came closest to reproducing the New Testament pattern.

A far more serious problem was the acceptance of pedobaptism. I find no support for this in Scripture. The more lengthy the attempt to defend the practice, the more absurd and plastic the arguments seem to be.

Third, I found among my Reformed friends many cool heads but few hot hearts. Of course, I recognize that this is a judgment of the heart, which only God can really see. Therefore, my judgment here is not definitive but only how things appeared to me. My Calvinistic friends then and now talk a lot about evangelism and have their favorite examples. Spurgeon, Carey, and several contemporary pastors are inevitably presented as proof that Calvinists have both cool heads and hot hearts.

But, in fact, to me for some reason God seemed to be favoring those who were less Reformed. Their churches tended to grow faster, and even if you dismissed 75 percent of their new converts as being not genuine, the 25 percent about whom one could be fairly certain usually constituted about 80 percent more than those who found Christ in and through the witness of more Calvinistic communities. Again, this is a judgment based on personal observation, but it is hard for me not to conclude that Reformed teaching in its essence, while correct on many things, did not have it right on some very important matters. The system is remarkably tight, but the more I examined it in the light of Scripture, the more I found that things are not quite so simple. Calvinists, like Arminians, had some unconvincing explanations about biblical passages which seemed to contradict the tight system they had created.

In addition, I did not find the Reformed tendency to avoid evangelistic invitations and appeals to be convincing. The argument that we owe such to Finney or some other relatively modern proponent seems, for starters, to contradict rather clearly Joshua 24:15 and what happened on the day of Pentecost in Acts 2. One could argue, of course, that at Pentecost nobody sang *one* verse of "Just As I Am," let alone twenty verses and that there was no evidence that any sawdust trails were available in the temple or that anyone had decision cards. Nevertheless, it seemed to me some kind of invitation was given, since three thousand people were added to the church on the day of Pentecost.

Therefore, in the final analysis, my decision was made. I would adopt the many helpful insights provided by Reformed theology, but I would never allow myself to be called "Reformed" or a "Calvinist." I could not embrace infant baptism. I could not justify the persecutions in which some reformers had participated, and I could not abandon Congregationalism and the general consistency of a thoroughgoing Baptist theology. Certain of the traditional five points of Calvinism, specifically limited atonement and irresistible grace, seemed always to lack sufficient scriptural evidence, and indeed, to be unable to explain much Scriptural evidence to the contrary. I find myself more in harmony with the beliefs of Reformed persuasion than of Arminian positions. But I also find that I am increasingly comfortable just being called a Baptist until this hour.

THE SHOOT-OUT AT THE AMEN CORRAL

My son loves to sit around Tombstone, Arizona, and watch the tourists as they come to see the reenactment of the shootout at the O. K. Corral. He reminded me one day that whether I liked it or not (and I did not particularly like it), I had been involved for the last twenty years in a shoot-out at the Amen Corral. He referred, of course, to the twenty years of redefinition of which we have been a part, the conservative revival in Southern Baptist life. A number of events influenced me heavily during this period to reaffirm my conviction that I was right to associate myself with the people called Baptists.

First of all, I developed close friendships with Robert Preus of the Missouri Synod Lutheran Church and with James Montgomery Boice, James Kennedy, and Francis Schaeffer of the Presbyterian Church. I also became a friend and correspondent with Tom Oden and Charles Robb of the Methodist Church. Oden wrote in a delightful style in *Agenda for Theology* and *Requiem,* a funeral dirge for all Methodist education. Charles Robb has long been involved in an effort to bring a revival of Bible-believing values within the Methodist Church. No one encouraged me in my efforts at reform among Southern Baptists as often or as intensely as Schaeffer.

These friends, I learned, loved Jesus just as I did. There was no doubt in my mind that they knew the Savior and that they were prepared to give their lives for the gospel if necessary. I loved them profoundly as brothers. However, as I listened to them, I realized that the ecclesiastical systems rendered it ultimately impossible for them to effect a lasting return to the faith of their fathers. The Missouri Synod Lutherans under Preus succeeded initially, but in my estimation that initial victory is at least in jeopardy. The Methodists and the larger group of the Presbyterians in America have found themselves, if not on a slippery slope, then surely on a wild toboggan ride to the bottom of the course. Their ecclesiology does not allow them much of a chance to turn it around.

All of this is to say that I find in Baptist ecclesiology and polity the possibility for a grassroots referendum. Because Baptists rejected all forms of connectionalism, and Baptist churches, associations, state conventions, and national conventions are independent, autonomous entities, the people in the churches find it possible, though not easy, to rise up and say, "We do not approve of the direction that our denomination is going, and we want this corrected." The primacy of the local church has been crucial. I knew from studying Baptist history as well as Southern Baptist bylaws that such a referendum was possible. But, in 1979, I did not know for sure whether that was merely a technical matter or whether a referendum was genuinely possible. As it turned out, that which was technically possible resulted in one of the great reformation movements in modern time.

At this time I also read with fascination and great profit the story of the Downgrade Controversy among British Baptists. I was astonished at how the Southern Baptist Convention controversy mirrored the Downgrade Controversy, even to the selection of language and methods. I took heart from Spurgeon's courage and faith.

Ultimately I concluded out of the controversy that my early judgments based on Franklin Littell's book *The Anabaptist View of the Church* and substantiated particularly by the writings of Marpeck and Hubmaier were exactly correct. I traveled to sixty-five countries and examined almost all possible expressions of Christianity to conclude what would be considered ecumenical by some—namely, that genuinely born-again believers are found in almost any Christian communion. I saw them as my brothers and sisters in Christ and rejoiced with them.

But by the same token I came increasingly to believe in the voluntary associations of born-again believers who had witnessed that experience of grace by a public believer's baptism by immersion and who had gathered themselves together under the lordship of Christ and the authority of the Bible to take the gospel to their own communities and to join hands with others of similar persuasion to get the gospel to the end of the earth. I was persuaded that the position of Baptists on both of the ordinances—baptism and the Lord's Supper—were the only positions that grasped the New Testament teaching on those subjects.

Consequently, I have remained and doubtless will remain until the day of my translation a Baptist—not a proud Baptist, just a Baptist grateful to God beyond anything I could possibly say for his grace and mercy. I am also grateful to my fellow believers in Baptist churches around the world who have sacrificed much to hold high these standards and principles.

PART FOUR

THOUGHTS FROM ACROSS THE SEAS

8

WHERE I BURIED OLD ERROLL HULSE: A JOURNEY IN BELIEVER'S BAPTISM

Erroll Hulse

I was born in South Africa. My father was Anglican, and so in the usual way I was christened. My parents did not attend church unless we happened to be on my grandfather's farm for Christmas, in which case we attended a Christmas service. This was our alpha and omega of church attendance.

My knowledge of the Bible came through five years of senior education at Marist Brothers, a well-known Roman Catholic school in Johannesburg. I was a boarder for five years from age twelve to seventeen. The government of South Africa legislated that Protestants in Roman Catholic schools be separated from Catholics for religious instruction. In our class we were required to memorize whole chapters from the Bible. In that class it was implied that the Bible was the very Word of God. There was nothing better, therefore, than to memorize it. Even though I did not know the gospel, this was very important preparatory work for me, and it has helped me from that time to the present.

After matriculation I began a six-year course in architecture in the Pretoria University (Afrikaans language). Apart from an evangelical aunt whose godliness impressed me and whom I knew prayed for me, I had not been exposed to evangelical Christians. At the university I was soon impressed by the outright manner in which some fellow students witnessed to their faith. One of them befriended me and invited me to his Baptist church. I agreed, but insisted that he come first to "my church." This was hypocrisy because I never attended. However, we went to a local socially acceptable church together. After the service I asked, "Well, what do you think of that?" "Dreadful!" was his response.

I then attended his church, a Baptist church. This happened to be during an evangelistic campaign led by a Welsh evangelist, Ivor Powell. I responded to the appeal and "decided for Christ." But this was no passing emotion. For me this was a transforming faith union with Christ. Follow-up was poor and my faith would have lingered long in the doldrums had it not been for my fiancée who, without outside agency, had been deeply convicted of sin, turned to the Bible and found peace with God. It was a Saturday night when she told me this. I said, "Right, from tomorrow we will attend the Baptist church morning and evening every Lord's Day!" That was in 1953. Forty-seven years later we sustain that practice with the same conviction.

We applied for baptism and church membership. In preparation we were introduced to the basic disciplines of the Christian life: commitment to the weekly prayer meeting, tithing, the importance of personal witness, the dangers of worldliness, and the importance of missionary outreach.

Baptism for us was based on the Great Commission and on the examples described in the Book of Acts. As I look back, I see that infant christening did nothing for me. Infant christening and believer's baptism are two completely different things. Christian baptism is for those who enter consciously into a faith union with the three persons of the holy Trinity. It is an event that calls for an action commensurate with the wondrous change that is wrought in a person who is called out of darkness and brought into light. Immersion in water suitably illustrates union with Christ in his death, burial, and resurrection. Plunging into water is a perfect symbol for the washing away of sin.

It is noteworthy that while in high school I attended classes and was confirmed. I remember the bishop laying hands on me. He was a large man with huge hands. My understanding of what it was to be saved was nil. It is easy to assent to a few items of Christian doctrine. It is quite another to be challenged about the guilt of personal sin and the necessity to trust in Christ for forgiveness. Multitudes have been confirmed, but they have no notion of any saving faith in Christ.

I often recall Pretoria Central Baptist Church where I was baptized. There could be a gravestone there to mark the spot: "Here lies buried the old unregenerate Erroll Hulse, thankfully never again to appear—and from here rose the new Erroll Hulse to walk in newness of life, a citizen of the New Jerusalem" (Col. 3:2, 9).

In spite of the many qualities of the church, we felt a lack of teaching, particularly in respect to church history. For this reason, following my graduation, we decided to find work in London that would enable us to study extramurally at the interdenominational London Bible College. At that time, 1954, a theological renewal was underway. My wife and I benefited from the weekly preaching ministry of D. Martyn Lloyd-Jones as well as from the lectures at the London Bible College under such tutors as John Waite and Donald Guthrie. But it was the teaching of principal Ernest Kevan, professor of systematic theology, that influenced our thinking the most.

THE CHALLENGE OF INFANT BAPTISM

In 1957 I was asked by Iain Murray to join him in pioneering a publishing house, the Banner of Truth Trust, which was based on the Westminster confessional standards. The Westminster Confession is, of course, Presbyterian and hence pedobaptist. Our aim was to republish the works of the sixteenth-century reformers and the sixteenth- and seventeenth-century English Puritans. Here I was, a Baptist, with a leading role in a pedobaptist publishing house! If the Reformers and Puritans were right about the great central doctrines of Scripture, what about baptism? If they were correct in so much, why not in the matter of infant baptism?

Working closely with Christians of Presbyterian conviction meant that I needed to have a firm basis for my doctrinal position. In this I was helped by the writings of theologian John Murray. In his exposition of the covenant of grace, Murray showed the development of the covenant from Noah to Abraham to Moses to David to Christ. The decisive issue is the question of continuity and discontinuity of the covenant, and the crucial passage is Hebrews 8:7–13.

In the old covenant administration the whole nation was included. It is noteworthy that Abraham circumcised all the males in his household, including those bought from a foreigner (Gen. 17:27). This represented a considerable number. We read of 318 trained men in Abraham's household

(Gen. 14:14), which is more than is customary for a family picnic. The administration of the Abrahamic covenant points forward to the Mosaic covenant made with the entire nation of Israel. In the old arrangement, the inclusion of all meant inevitably that they did not all know the Lord. It often seemed that only a remnant knew the Lord; hence they broke that covenant. This led to judgment, which came to a climax at the time of Jeremiah and Ezekiel, both of whom announced the promise of a new and better covenant to come.

In the new covenant, only those who have the writing of God's law on their hearts are included. The new is a better covenant because all members, from the least to the greatest, know the Lord. Inclusion is not therefore by natural birth. It is by new birth (John 1:12–13). The passing of the old covenant is emphasized in Hebrews 8:13. It has vanished away. It is no longer the basis of church membership. Covenant teaching, far from weakening Baptist doctrine, actually endorses and strengthens it.[1]

From 1957 to 1967 I worked full time with the Banner of Truth publishing house. It was midway through that period that I accepted a call to a part-time pastorate of a village church. This work grew and needed a full-time pastor. I accepted this position in 1967. Moving into pastoral work called for further clarity in which leading questions require clear answers.

I am a Baptist by personal experience. But was that experience biblical? Can my position stand the test of Scripture? I now face some of these searching questions.

CAN THE BAPTIST POSITION STAND UP TO CRUCIAL QUESTIONS?

Have you ever felt there is something compelling about the case for infant baptism? No! I have never felt there is a case for baptizing infants, not even remotely so. We had four children, and I understand well the feelings of parents. I have seen the importance of noting the difference for children brought up in the homes of believers. This privilege is clearly referred to in 1 Corinthians 7:14 where children of believers are described as "holy." The advantages of children born into and brought up in a Christian home are enormous.

Yet such advantages do not entitle any infant or child to baptism. Each person must come personally into the new covenant relationship with the Lord by repentance and faith. To qualify for baptism, each one must personally evidence the testimony of new birth. Each one must be justified by a faith of his or her own and not rely on the faith of parents, however godly they may be.

Baptists are misrepresented in the notes of the *New Geneva Study Bible* where it is stated that Baptists exclude believers' children from the visible community of faith.[2] That is not the case. Our children enjoy the full benefits of teaching, worship, and prayer within the fellowship of the church. When they come to personal faith, they apply for baptism and church membership, which will also bring them to the Lord's Table. In pedobaptist churches, the ordinance of confirmation is invented to bring young people into the privileges of formal membership.

Have you ever felt the weight of the argument that so many great Reformers and Puritans advocated infant baptism? No. I have always seen infant baptism as the antithesis of believer's baptism because in the minds of those who practice infant baptism, it nullifies the need for baptism when a person, baptized as an infant, later comes to faith. Of course, there are many like myself baptized as an infant (actually not baptized at all; better to call it sprinkled or "christened") who on conversion apply for believer's baptism and church membership.

In my view the most influential work on infant baptism is that of John Calvin in his *Institutes of the Christian Religion.* In the edition I own, Calvin devoted fifty-six pages to baptism. In the first five he touches on what baptism signifies but is not systematic in coming to grips with the Great Commission, which requires that all those disciples are to be baptized—the way it works in the Book of Acts. He then devotes fifty pages to a defense of infant baptism. His arguments are weak.

Calvin resorts to bullying and abuse, bluster and invective. He belittles and ridicules those who hold to believer's baptism. He accuses Baptists of slandering Christ and of shameful untruth in pointing to the fact that infant baptism was unknown in the early years of the church. He accuses us of wickedness in withholding baptism from our infants. He suggests that the Lord punished the arrogance of those who disagree with Calvin's reasoning. In fact, Calvin declares that we who disagree with him are raving insane![3]

Finally, Calvin takes on the weakest possible advocate of baptism in the person of Servetus, who was burned alive as a heretic in Calvin's Geneva. Calvin refutes Servetus in six pages. This is pointless, since Servetus is feeble. What counts at the end of the day is biblical exegesis, particularly of Matthew 28:15–20; Hebrews 8:7–13; Romans 6:1–10; and Colossians 2:11–12. It is these passages of Scripture that decide the issue of baptism.[4]

Calvin's argument that baptism takes the place of circumcision has prevailed with generations of Presbyterian denominations. I am not a Barthian, but I do understand why some have so much respect for Karl Barth, who had an exceptional grasp of the sixteenth-century Reformation. Barth pointed out that Calvin is exceedingly unclear in his reasoning on baptism and resorts to scolding. I love Barth's eloquence when he says: "Do I deceive myself when I suspect that the real and decisive ground for infant baptism, beginning with the Reformers and continuing to the present day, very simply is this: Men at the time would not renounce, for love of money, the existence of the Evangelical Church in the form of the Constantinian corpus Christianum, and they will not today under any circumstances and for any price, give up the contemporary form of the People's Church? When the Church breaks with infant baptism, People's Church, in the sense of a state church or a mass church is finished."[5]

I have been inspired by the testimony of the Anabaptists of the sixteenth century who suffered terribly for their faith. They were unreliable in a number of ways, but in their grasp of the nature of the New Testament church and their rejection of the national nature of the church advocated by the magisterial Reformers, I believe they were correct. Ulrich Zwingli moved clearly in the direction of the "gathered church" concept and led his followers in that way. Sadly, however, he then drew back when it became apparent that it would be impossible, without severe persecution, to follow the gathered church principle.

Do you think it is important to insist on immersion for baptism? I have never doubted that immersion is intended to symbolize union with Christ or that immersion was the method used in the New Testament. The word *rantizo* means to sprinkle and the word *baptizo* means to dip or to immerse. The Holy Spirit could easily have used *rantizo* if he meant us to sprinkle. The Greek Orthodox Church uses immersion when baptizing infants because they grasp their own language.

I have always rejected the argument that there could not be enough water in Jerusalem to baptize three thousand converts in one day. As an architect, I know that no city can exist without adequate water supplies and water conservation. Furthermore, the issue was settled by a Presbyterian, Murray Adamthwaite of Australia, who was involved in archaeological work in Israel. He testified that in the 1970s and 1980s no less that forty-eight purification pools (built to meet the requirements of the laws in Leviticus 15 and Numbers 19) were unearthed in the temple mount area. The specification of rabbis was that a minimum of forty-seven inches depth was required and a minimum of six steps down into the water.[6]

How important is believer's baptism? Salvation is first; baptism is second (1 Cor. 1:13). Making disciples is first; baptism second (Matt. 28:18–20). believer's baptism is God's appointed way of entrance into church membership. Practiced with discernment on the basis of genuine credible profession of faith, believer's baptism safeguards the nature of the church and preserves her from being nominal in character. In pedobaptist churches it is noteworthy that there is often struggle with this issue. For instance, when the church in the Netherlands changed from Roman Catholicism to Protestantism, it was soon discovered that it was impossible to maintain a "holy church" with such a high proportion of evidently unregenerate members.[7]

There is a problem when the Lord's Table is not related to believer's baptism. If those baptized as infants have a right to the table irrespective of evidence of a saving change and holiness of life, a quandary follows. Jonathan Edwards faced this dilemma. He sought to guard the Lord's Table from evidently unregenerate members. There may have been other reasons for his unpopularity, but this was the primary reason that led to his dismissal from his church in 1750 by a vote of 230 to 23.

How can you reject infant baptism when it was the practice of the post-apostolic church? I do not accept that it was the practice of the post-apostolic church. With regard to that question, a fine work has come from H. F. Stander and J. P. Louw of the South African Dutch Reformed Church. They show that infant baptism first appeared in the third century.[8]

Do you believe that church membership should be confined only to those who have been baptized as believers? Yes, I do, and for three reasons.

My first reason has to do with the apostolic command to baptize. We see in Acts 2 that the apostles required all converts to be baptized without exception. "Be baptized every one of you," commanded Peter on the day of Pentecost. There may not be two standards, namely believer's baptism for new and another wholly different baptism for infants.[9]

Some object to this on the grounds that the practice of believer's baptism divided families. Note the radical new covenant position stated by our Lord: "Do not suppose that I have come to bring peace to the earth. I did not come to bring peace, but a sword. For I have come to turn a man against his father, a daughter against her mother, a daughter-in-law against her mother-in-law. A man's enemies will be the members of his household" (Matt. 10:34–36).

Apart from Micah 7:1–6, this radial teaching is nowhere to be found in the Old Testament, where the unity of the nation of Israel as the standard bearer of God's revelation was the primary consideration. Micah suggests that scandalous sin, bribery, and corruption cause deep family division for those who refuse to compromise holiness. But in the new covenant era, union with Christ (which is the main significance of baptism) results in inevitable cleavage in families. Our Lord is faithful to warn of this. This dramatic teaching about family division is new. Taking the side of Jesus is something quite radical. It involves turning away from the status quo. In our Western culture it is turning away from the world and, in many cases, from nominal, self-righteous, nonsaving religion. It is not acceptable for a convert to say that he cannot be baptized because members of his family will be offended.

In Islamic nations, believer's baptism can be extremely costly. It is rightly interpreted to mean that there is no salvation in Islam but only in Christ. This results in resentment, anger, and often severe persecution. Believer's baptism focuses on union with Jesus, which can spell the loss of everything in this world.

Believer's baptism can also be costly for those who have grown up in pedobaptist denominations. For instance, the pioneer missionary to Burma, Adoniram Judson, on his way to that country for the first time in 1812 gave himself to an in-depth study of baptism. The sea voyage took five months. When he was persuaded of believer's baptism, this spelled the end of all his support. Ann Judson fiercely resisted this change, but after searching the Scriptures for herself came to the same position as her husband.[10]

My second reason has to do with church history. The truth of believer's baptism and the reality of the gathered church symbolism have been recovered at the cost of much suffering and martyrdom. We are required to provide clear guidelines for future generations. It is said that churches often begin in a revival, and those converted in such a revival are zealous for the truth throughout their lives. The next generation takes the truth for granted. The third generation abandons the truth. That may be cynical, and it need not be so. At least we can leave landmarks for future generations. It is encouraging to observe that there are churches in England that have remained faithful for over three centuries.

A death is represented in believer's baptism. In my baptism I died to the world. Now I live in newness of life with Christ. The old unregenerate self is dead (Col. 3:9). This is parallel to our Lord's teaching, "If anyone would come after me, he must deny himself and take up his cross and follow me.

For whoever wants to save his life will lose it, but whoever loses his life for me and for the gospel will save it" (Mark 8:34–35). Baptism represents that point of taking up daily self-mortification. As Paul says, "I die every day" (1 Cor. 15:31). I look back on my baptism as a historic event displaying, as Paul says, "In him you were also circumcised (aorist tense) . . . not with a circumcision done by the hands of men but with the circumcision done by Christ (a reference to new birth), having been buried with him in baptism and raised with him through your faith in the power of God, who raised him from the dead" (Col. 2:11–12).

My third reason is practical. To accept infant baptism is to deprive those who come to faith of an ordinance that is practical in its administration. While baptism does not save, as we have seen, it exemplifies something momentous—union with Christ and the washing away of sin. The ordinance is intended to have a powerful testimony, for the candidate as a seal of his or her faith, and to the gathered church as a congregation.

Do you believe that Baptists are perfect? I have sought to state the case for the Baptist position and am aware that in doing so there is the danger of dogmatism and even arrogance. Baptists are never perfect. Baptist churches in various countries where I have had the privilege to preach—in Indonesia, Brazil, Australia, Cameroon, and the Philippines—are beset with the sins and divisions of believers who are subject to the gradual and often painful process of sanctification.

It seems the most common shortcoming of Baptists, when it comes to the ordinances, is to administer baptism prematurely, for example in the case of children or young people who have not had their faith put to the test. In our family, our oldest daughter was the first one baptized, but we persuaded her to wait two years—from age twelve to age fourteen.

Adequate time should be allowed for maturity. In the case of Christian homes, it is not always easy to assess conversion as our children are saturated with Christian teaching. Even in the cases of those who profess conversion from the world, there is danger of proceeding to the pool too quickly. It is no honor when a church is known for many false professions. A fine balance and much discernment are needed. Pentecost is often cited to endorse hasty baptism, but we must not forget that those in Jerusalem were well-taught, seasoned believers, in the Old Testament sense. They knew well the books of Scripture cited by the apostle Peter. Can that be said of our pagan postmodernsociety?

Conclusion

Believer's baptism marks the greatest change that exists for a sinner. He is brought from the kingdom of Satan to the kingdom of God by new birth. He is justified. He is set apart. A work of progressive sanctification is begun in his heart. He is adopted into the family of God. Believer's baptism is the ordinance designed to mark this transformation. He has been baptized by the Holy Spirit into Christ and into the body of Christ (Gal. 3:26; Rom. 6:1–7; 1 Cor. 12:13). All this refers to something that has taken place.

With our infants, we pray fervently, teach, and demonstrate the gospel to them as they grow in understanding. We hope that one day all this will bear fruit, but we have absolutely no right to attest these things before they are confirmed in reality. Believer's baptism not only declares the wondrous grace of God in conversion; it also demonstrates to the person who now walks in newness of life that all his resources lie in the triune God with whom he is now united. He does not look to secret formulas or gimmicks in his struggles and temptations. His baptism tells him that he is in Christ for time and eternity and that in that union he must and will persevere to the end.

9

WHY I AM A BAPTIST—AGAIN: CONFESSIONS OF A FORMER, FORMER BAPTIST

Michael Lawrence

Why am I a Baptist? Not finally because I was raised in a Southern Baptist family, though I was; and not finally because I became a Christian in a Southern Baptist church, though I did. In fact, I am a Baptist today not because of my background but in spite of it.

I grew up in South Carolina in the early 1970s in a family whose Southern Baptist roots stretched back several generations and across several state lines. I can't remember a time when we weren't in church. By the time I was seven or eight years old, I knew without anyone coaching me that I was a sinner, and that Jesus had died for me on the cross. And with both a child's faith and a child's understanding, I walked down the aisle one Sunday night during the invitation, shook the preacher's hand, and asked to join the church on profession of faith. A few weeks later I was baptized. And that was that. I had made a decision for Jesus that took care of my eternal future. It not only seemed the sensible thing to do, but the right thing as well.

Later I would come to see and experience both the errors and the dangers of turning gospel conversion into a mechanical system. But to this day I am thankful that my Southern Baptist pastor and Sunday school teachers took the authority of the Bible seriously and so taught me about sin, the cross, the resurrection, and the necessity of personal faith in Christ. And I'll be forever grateful to them, along with my mother, as the human instruments of my conversion.

In my child's mind, Christianity was about the past and the future. In the past Jesus had died on the cross for my sins so that I might be forgiven and in the future live in heaven. But as I grew up, I learned in my Sunday school classes that there were all sorts of rules to be kept as a Christian in the present. This wasn't too much of a problem for me as a child in a churchgoing family, but during my teenage years it was a different story. By the time I graduated from high school and headed off for college, I found that my behavior and my faith were often at odds. I knew Christ was my Savior, and that "once saved, always saved." But increasingly I found my Christian faith isolated from much of my life.

HELD BY GOD'S GRACE

Eventually, the dissonance between my faith and my life took its toll. Soon after arriving at Duke University as a freshman, I decided to rush a fraternity, which mainly involved drinking large quantities of cheap beer. And as many freshmen do, I began to question the beliefs and assumptions that I had grown up with. I even began to wonder if I wanted to be a Christian at all. But try as I might, my conscience, formed as it had been through my Baptist upbringing, would not let me go. The moralistic approach to Christianity which I had learned was inadequate to bring me to maturity in Christ. But by God's good providence those "rules" provided an important hedge I had to jump if I were to pursue the growing attractions of the world. In the end, by the grace of God, it was a hedge I could not clear.

But looking back, I see that it wasn't only my Baptist conscience that held me back from the world. Far more important was the fact that Jesus wouldn't let me go. At the same time as my dalliance with the world, I had also become involved with InterVarsity Christian Fellowship through a dorm Bible study. There I encountered peers whose Christianity wasn't simply defined by a decision they had made as a child to walk the aisle and shake the preacher's hand. Instead, I saw in them a faith that was genuine and incredibly attractive. This is not to say that I had never met a genuine Christian in my Southern Baptist churches back home, but simply that Jesus used these Christians at that particular moment to impress upon me what previously I had been blind to: the fact that faith was more than a decision. And in response I decided that the faith they had was the kind of faith I wanted.

When I shared this with my Bible study leader, he suggested that I attend a weekend retreat sponsored by InterVarsity Christian Fellowship. In that context, the connection between being a Christian and living like one became clear. Christianity, it turned out, was not just fire insurance for the future or a set of rules to be followed, but a relationship with Jesus which had implications for my life in the present. Of course, Baptists have historically taught just such a view of faith and the lordship of Christ. Moreover, this view was probably embodied in the teaching and preaching I had grown up under. But only now was I ready to hear. When I went into that weekend, thanks to the Baptist church, I already knew what it meant to call Jesus my Savior. But when I left that weekend, I saw that my Savior must be sovereign and I knew more fully what it meant to call Jesus my Lord. That weekend, my childhood faith grew up.

Somehow, I had never heard of the lordship of Christ in the Baptist churches of my youth. In the midst of weekly evangelistic sermons and Sunday school lessons which focused on the rules of the Christian life, the message of a personal relationship with Jesus had gotten lost. I don't mean to imply that this was the case in all Southern Baptist churches everywhere; and it is possible that the fault lies entirely with me, for I may have missed hearing what was there all the time. Still, in retrospect it seems that other consistent emphases, many of them good, smothered the teaching of Christ's lordship in salvation, rendering it a virtual omission. I almost abandoned the faith because of that omission. Now, I was more than a little angry and perplexed that I had not learned about the lordship of Christ in my Baptist experience. I don't claim that my anger was righteous, but it was real and it was to have an important effect on decisions I was about to make.

I didn't realize it at the time, but what I encountered my freshman year at Duke was evangelicalism, a transatlantic, interdenominational movement within Christianity united around the essentials of the gospel. But that was not all. I was also confronted by the theology of the Reformation. My newly grown-up faith was hungry for sound, Bible-based teaching. Soon I was reading books such as J. I. Packer's *Knowing God* and Sinclair Ferguson's *Know Your Christian Life.* I also wanted to hear preaching that did more (though not less) than present an evangelistic sermon each Sunday. As a result, I found myself in a local Presbyterian church with strong expositional preaching.

As I studied my Bible, I also found myself increasingly dissatisfied with the free-will theology I had learned in the Baptist church. Instead, what I saw on the pages of Scripture was a human will enslaved to sin and a work of salvation finished on the cross. When I looked back on my own experience, it was clear to me that left to myself I would never have come to Jesus. Thankfully I began to trace in my own life God's grace in calling me to and preserving me in faith. No longer could I define a Christian as someone who had made a decision for Jesus and who tried hard to live a good life. A Christian, I came to see, was a sinner whom God sovereignly rescued, whose faith was a gift, and whose life of obedience was a response to grace.

These weren't easy conclusions to reach. They grated against my pride and self-sufficiency. But by the end of my freshman year, I couldn't deny the truth of the doctrines of grace, though I still thought of myself as a Baptist.

A RICH THEOLOGICAL HERITAGE

But that summer, back in my local Southern Baptist church, I felt like a fish out of water. Both my concern for discipleship and my new theological convictions at best were thought a distraction from evangelism, and at worst considered a hindrance to it. The only thing we agreed upon was that you couldn't be a Baptist and Reformed at the same time. Ironically, we were both wrong. Both my home church and I were unaware of the rich and profound theological heritage to which we as Baptists were heirs. In the confessions, sermons, commentaries, and doctrinal writings of three and a half centuries of Baptists, there was abundant proof that zeal for God's sovereign glory and zeal for the salvation of souls could happily and consistently reside in the same heart. Nevertheless, by the time I returned to Duke in the fall, I was convinced that I was going to have to become a Presbyterian in order to live out what I thought the Bible taught concerning the Christian life.

I even expressed this thought to a new friend, Mark Dever. He assured me that I didn't have to take such a course of action, that Baptists had historically believed and cherished all the things I now did, and could do so once again. He encouraged me to stick it out in the Baptist fold, and I did, after a fashion. I continued to hold firm to my belief in congregational government and the appropriateness of baptism for believers only. But try as I might, I couldn't bring myself to be a part of a church that seemed to ignore or disregard so much else of what the Bible taught. The next eight years I either attended or was a member of a local Presbyterian church.

In the intervening years I married and served on staff with InterVarsity Christian Fellowship. I also seriously considered whether God was calling me into pastoral ministry. Repeatedly I turned down requests to stand for election as an elder in my Presbyterian church because I didn't believe in infant baptism. Nevertheless, two Presbyterian ministers in particular strongly encouraged me to enter the ministry. I too felt God's call, and agreed with them that seminary would be a good place to sort out whether I was going to be a Baptist or a Presbyterian.

Secretly I was rooting for the Presbyterians. Theologically and personally I felt comfortable there. The only thing standing in the way was my conviction concerning believer's baptism. I even told my wife that if in the end I was convinced of believer's baptism I would go into teaching rather than the pastorate, so averse was I to returning to a local Baptist congregation. So I left for Gordon-Conwell Theological Seminary desperate for someone to convince me that infant baptism was biblical. I found that person in Dr. Meredith Kline.

Previously, the arguments for infant baptism that I had encountered revolved around either some form of presumed election of Christians' children or what I took to be a blurring of the distinction between the old and new covenants. Infants were baptized under the first argument on the assumption that they would become Christians eventually. The second argument simply assumed that since infants were circumcised in the old covenant, they were to be baptized in the new. Both arguments I found incompatible with the New Testament.

But Dr. Kline advanced what for me was a new approach to the question. According to Kline, circumcision as given in Genesis 17 was a sign of both blessing and judgment, of being set apart or of being cut off. It thus signified that everything of Abraham's, even his own children, stood under the lordship of Yahweh. Circumcision was a sign, not of the child's faith, but of the parents', and so was appropriately given both to Isaac, the child of the promise, and to Ishmael, the child of the flesh. Baptism, argued Kline, was the new covenant parallel to this old covenant act of discipleship, an interpretation based in part on Paul's parallel of baptism and circumcision in Colossians 2:11–12.

Like circumcision, the waters of baptism symbolized both blessing and judgment. To baptize one's child was to acknowledge that the child would experience either the salvation of God by keeping the covenant through faith or the judgment of God as a covenant breaker. Like the water of the Red Sea, which was a path of salvation for Israel, but a means of judgment against Egypt, so was the water of baptism. Thus, to baptize one's children was not a presumption upon God's grace. Rather, it was a profound expression of one's submission to the lordship of Christ and an acceptance of his judgments.

That was all I needed to hear. My past frustration and present hope lent an emotional strength to his argument that biblically it didn't deserve, and I plunged into Presbyterianism wholeheartedly. It wasn't long before I was licensed in the Presbyterian Church of America and was working as an assistant pastor in a church not far from the seminary. The weekend before I graduated I accepted a call to be the associate pastor of that same church. My wife and I had just had our first child, and I was looking forward to performing my first baptism as a Presbyterian minister, that of my own son. It seemed as if I had finally left Baptists for good.

But God's providence is a mysterious thing. Soon after completing my ordination exams and gaining the approval of the presbytery and the congregation, I found that my installation as associate pastor was blocked. According to the constitution of the PCA, senior and associate pastors are to be elected by the local congregation and approved by the presbytery. Likewise, a pastor can only be removed from office by those who placed him there: the congregation and/or the presbytery. But to my surprise, I found that one man, without the knowledge or consent of the congregation or presbytery, was preventing me from taking up my ministry. It was the senior pastor, a man who had been my friend and mentor for nearly four years. The reason was a change of heart on his part. I was devastated. The timing could not have been worse. I was unemployed with a two-month-old baby. It seemed as if my life was falling apart.

BACK TO GOD'S WORD

Yet God was at work. In the midst of what was one of the most painful periods of my life, God met me and drew me back to his Word. Rarely does a pastor get the opportunity to reconsider his fundamental theological positions once he has entered the ministry. The busyness and pressures are often too great to allow the kind of time that is needed for reflection and study. But time and opportunity are exactly what God gave me. Given the circumstances of my departure, my thoughts were first taken up with questions about what the New Testament had to say about church government. I considered the implications of Acts 6:1–7 and 13:1–3; 1 Corinthians 5; and Matthew 18:15–20.

Without abandoning the Bible's teaching that a plurality of elders is to lead the local church, I came to see that the New Testament placed the final authority, both for discipline as well as the recognition and setting apart of officers, with the assembled congregation. My own experience was simply a poignant confirmation of God's wisdom. The result was a new appreciation for the Baptist understanding of congregationalism, an appreciation that has grown into a conviction.

But biblical church government was not all that I reconsidered. The issue of congregationalism inevitably raised a more fundamental question, and that was who was rightly to be considered a member of a New Testament church. As a Presbyterian I was accustomed to thinking of two categories of church members: Christians and their baptized children. When I was first introduced to covenant theology, Dr. Kline had pointed out the dual nature of the family in God's plan of salvation. Under the old covenant, the family was a common grace institution for the propagation and preservation of the human race. But it was also a channel for saving grace though the Abrahamic covenant. Simply by being a descendant of Abraham, a child was counted a member of the covenant community.

So it continued, Kline maintained, under the new covenant, pointing to such texts as Acts 2:39, Romans 9 and 11, Colossians 2:11–12, and 1 Corinthians 7:14. As a result, the children of a Christian parent were to be considered members of God's new covenant community and given the sign of baptism. This is not to say that infants were to be considered regenerate. Evidence of faith was required for that. Rather, the covenant community on earth, both old and new, was designed by God to be a mixed community of the saved and the unsaved; the church was in fact to be a church within a church.

But as I considered the implications of such passages as John 1:12; 3:1–8; and Mark 3:31–35, I began to see that the natural family itself was but a type and a shadow in the old covenant, a picture of the true family of God, born of the Spirit through faith in Christ. And throughout the New Testament, this spiritual family was equated with the church. The inclusion of physical descendants within the old covenant pointed forward to the inclusion of the spiritual seed of Christ in the new (Gal. 3).

Moreover, according to Jeremiah 31:29–30, 34, the old covenant mechanism of inclusion in the covenant through lineal descent would specifically not carry over into the new. While children were to be cherished and brought up in the instruction of the Lord, they could not biblically be considered members of the new covenant community apart from their own professed faith in Christ. And if they were not members of the covenant community, then they had no business receiving the sign of that covenant in baptism. As it turns out, my son was not baptized as an infant. I still hope to perform that baptism, but on the basis of his faith in Christ, not mine.

THE CHURCH AS GOD'S FAMILY

Ironically, it was an understanding of the church as the family of God, something I learned as a Presbyterian, that finally served to make me a reconvinced Baptist. The process has not been easy and has taken nearly two years of study, reflection, and prayer. Along the way I've had to face my sinful resentment toward the denomination of my youth and to repent of allowing that resentment, rather than the Word of God, to guide my choice of a church in which to minister.

But it hasn't only been humiliation. I've also been surprised by a sense of joy and thanksgiving for the grace of God. For surely it was by his grace that I heard so young that God does indeed save sinners through his beloved Son, Jesus Christ. And surely it was by God's grace that the Baptist congregations of my youth gave a prominent position to the authority of the Bible. My gratitude and joy in these things now far outweighs any uneasiness I feel about current Baptist church culture. Culture, even that of the Baptist church, changes, but God's Word remains the same. I know that many Southern Baptists share both my uneasiness about our culture and my confidence in the Word of God and are working to see life and truth more congenially, consistently, and clearly united. I am pleased to be able to throw my lot with theirs.

Moreover, I am convinced more fully than ever that the fundamentals necessary for proclaiming the gospel and making disciples are present: a conviction that Jesus Christ alone is God's salvation for his people; a belief in the Word of God alone as the sole rule of our faith and practice; a commitment to see Christ alone rule his church through the local congregation of believers; the expression of Christ's saving work through personal submission to baptism; and finally, a desire to live out our faith together as members of God's spiritual family. Having come full circle, I find myself a Baptist, not by heritage or convenience, but by conviction under the Word of God.

10

FLYING THE FLAGS HIGH IN AFRICA: BAPTIST HOPE FOR A RAVAGED CONTINENT

Conrad Mbewe

I agree with Charles Haddon Spurgeon. The great nineteenth-century Baptist preacher did not worry about the offense some "thin-skinned" members of other denominations might take by the explicitly Baptist witness of his Metropolitian Tabernacle. He said that the strongly Baptist peculiarities of the Tabernacle's history might offend some "thin-skinned" member of other denominations. Spurgeon said that he and his people "have no desire to sail under false colors, neither are we ashamed of our principles: if we were, we would renounce them to-morrow."

Had I been asked to write my testimony of why I am a Christian, I would gladly have left out the Baptist emphasis in the present testimony. Yet my task is that of declaring why after twenty years in the trenches of the Christian life, I am satisfied to work for the glory of God in the Baptist fellowship. It is only fair that my reader will allow me to be plain on my subject without being offensive. I have seen how my spiritual forebears struggled for the truth and suffered for liberty of conscience in former times, and I must also nail my colors to the mast. So much that crosses the oceans as news from the African continent is negative and depressing. I have no doubt that it will cheer the hearts of many around the world to know that the convictions that make them serve as Baptists in their part of the world are also espoused dearly by a son of the African soil. God is at work here as well.

CONVERSION AND MEMBERSHIP

If all that were meant by the title of this book was how I found myself in the family of churches called Baptist, then my answer would be that I was brought into this circle by a few providential happenings in the 1970s. There was very little analytical thinking at that stage. When my mother died in 1971, my two sisters and I left Lusaka, the capital city of Zambia, to be fostered by my mother's elder sister in Ndola, a town some three hundred kilometers north of Lusaka. We began to gravitate back to Lusaka one by one, as each of us finished high school and commenced university studies, since the only university in Zambia then was in Lusaka. My elder sister was the first to return in 1978.

It was the tradition of the Lusaka Baptist Church to hold special evangelistic meetings for freshmen in the first few weeks of each academic year. My elder sister attended the meetings in September that year and was, by the Lord's grace, soundly converted and subsequently baptized in the same church. I also gravitated down to Lusaka the following year for my university studies. I got converted through my sister's testimony and the witness of a friend soon after my return to Lusaka. Upon commencing my university studies, it was natural that I would follow my sister to her church. That is how I found myself attending the Lusaka Baptist Church.

In March 1980 I was baptized there and joined its membership. Humanly speaking, then, if my sister had been converted in the local Presbyterian or Pentecostal church, I probably would have ended up there too. So, in so far as the question of how I found myself joining a Baptist church upon my conversion goes, I could have been anywhere. I was a very young Christian at that stage, and my spiritual senses had not yet been trained to differentiate truth from error.

However, no sooner was I settled in the Lusaka Baptist Church than I began to feel my way through the maze of Christendom. The University of Zambia had students from every part of Zambia and every religious inclination—Moslems, Hindus, Christians, animists, etc. It also had all the groups and sects that call themselves Christian—Liberals, Roman Catholics, evangelicals, Seventh-Day Adventists, and Jehovah's Witnesses. Then, to get closer home, there was an evangelical Christian fellowship that brought together evangelical Christians from every conceivable background and denomination—Episcopalians, Presbyterians, Congregationalists, Pentecostals, Baptists, etc. It was therefore not unusual to find students from these varied backgrounds in locked horns over who was in the right religion or church. This was the red-hot crucible in which, for five years, my convictions were tested, tried, and confirmed.

I graduated from the University of Zambia in 1984, convinced that the Baptist expression of the church is the most biblical one—whether it is labeled "Baptist" or not. And so, although I became a Baptist by an act of sovereign providence, I have been content to stay a Baptist for over twenty years now. This is because of my settled conviction that it best expresses the teaching of Scripture on what a church should be. I now proceed to outline a number of facets of this conviction.

BELIEVER'S BAPTISM

I became a Christian on Friday, March 30, 1979, but only got baptized exactly one year later on Sunday, March 30, 1980. Why this one-year delay? It was because I had been sprinkled as an infant in the United Church of Zambia and felt no need to go through the same ordinance, until the Lord convinced me through the Scriptures. I noted from the Bible that repentance and faith were necessary before a person could be baptized (Acts 2:38). I also saw that baptism signified dying with Christ, being buried with him, and rising together with him in newness of life (Rom. 6:4). It was an outward physical expression of an inward spiritual experience. Since all these were not in my experience at the time I was sprinkled as a child, I saw the need to be baptized in the biblical way. My father was not happy with this. Although I invited him to the happy occasion of my baptism, he did not come. Oh, what a blessed day that was! I recall coming out of the baptismal waters saying a silent prayer to the Lord in my ecstasy, "Lord, from this day onward, I'm gonna fly all my flags high!"

BIBLICAL AND DOCTRINAL EMPHASIS

Baptists have always been known as the people of the Book. The Bible has had the center stage in the life and worship of Baptists across history. In a number of churches calling themselves "Baptist," preaching is at a discount as more time is being given to singing and testimony sharing. Yet history has shown that whenever this has happened, the churches have lost their spiritual strength and vitality. This is inevitable because sanctification, that is, the Christian's spiritual growth, is primarily through the instrumentality of the Word (John 17:17). There can be a lot of excitement and cheers in a home where children live on candies and cookies, but malnutrition is soon to set in. There may not be as much excitement in the home where full-cereal and rich-protein meals are served, but you can be sure that in a few years' time this home will produce society's strong and reliable workers. That has been the story of Baptists in Zambia and the world over.

I thank God that he led me not only to a Baptist church but also to one whose pulpit emphasized expository and doctrinal preaching. The pastor then was Joe Simfukwe, and he was certainly in no hurry to get us through the Bible. Neither was he content merely to rush us to the practical applications. Having reminded us of the context, he squeezed all the soul-nourishing doctrinal juice out of each passage of the Bible and applied it pungently to our lives. When I joined the church, I found the pastor in Romans 5 and, by the time I graduated from the University, he had reached Romans 8. Coupled with that, he took us through the Ten Commandments, John 3, 1 Corinthians 11–14, Malachi, Hebrews, and Ephesians. My understanding of the order of salvation was formed as we went through Romans and Ephesians.

Sitting under the same pulpit, I ended up with a majestic understanding of God's work in creation, providence, redemption, and final judgment. It has been like sitting on the sun and watching all the planets going around it in perfect symmetry. Everything in God's world is now tied together into one entire biblical system. My respect for the Bible and knowledge of how to let it speak for itself was primarily learned there.

Is this not what has made our Baptist heritage so rich? Our spiritual forebears kept the place of preaching central in the church's worship. As long as the centrality of the pulpit has been maintained, Baptists have continued to know God's presence and power. And whenever this has been sacrificed, the power has in due season been lost. Confessions of faith have been of the very warp and woof of Baptist church life in its most glorious times. The famous Second London Baptist Confession of Faith of 1677 and 1689 has been a real doctrinal bulwark for the Baptist churches. Charles Haddon Spurgeon republished it in 1856, soon after commencing his long pastorate in London and even wrote a preface for it. He admired this summary of what the "fathers" of the denomination believed.

Twenty years later, as I look at the leaders of almost all the churches in Zambia that have stability and maturity, I see individuals who sat with me under the sound of that pulpit. At one time, I would have doubted the wisdom of a perennial pulpit diet of the pure milk and strong meat of God's Word when others were boasting of having an exciting mixture of popular psychology and anecdotes. But when today I look for those who boasted thus in our student days, their spiritual malnutrition is evident for all to see. One well-known leader in a non-Baptist church in Zambia who has witnessed this recently said to a friend of mine, "One thing I admire about you Baptists is your consistency. We have jumped from church to church over the last decade or two and are still feeling dissatisfied, but you have continued in the same course where you were twenty years ago." The reason is obvious: We have found the truth!

BAPTIST CHURCH POLITY

Baptists have a lot in common with other Protestant churches. This is especially true in terms of a return to the final authority and total sufficiency of holy Scripture in all matters of faith and conduct. However, Baptists go one step further. They apply this principle of the Protestant Reformation to the realm of the nature of the church, without giving tradition the place of a sacred cow. Hence issues of separation of church and state, regenerate membership, believer's baptism, and autonomy of local churches under the direct oversight of Christ have been the insistence of Baptists across history, even at the price of their own blood. Other Protestant churches have failed to reach this far in their application of biblical teaching.

Thankfully, during my formative years at Lusaka Baptist Church from 1979 to 1984 the application of God's Word did not end with general doctrines about life in this world and in the world to come. Being in a Baptist church, I was able to see the truths of God's Word on the nature and organization of the church applied before my eyes. The Lusaka Baptist Church was governed by elders, under the direct superintendence of Christ, through his Word and his Spirit. It related to other like-minded churches in an "association" rather than a hierarchical denominational structure. With respect to its membership, it accepted only those who had a credible profession of faith and had been baptized. The Lusaka Baptist Church elders kept the church clear of any entanglements with the state. Instead, they kept the church's commission of world evangelization through the preaching of the gospel and the planting of like-minded churches constantly before us.

What a glorious foundation this was for me! I never had to wrestle with any discrepancies between what the Bible taught about the church and what I was seeing in the local church. My fellow university students, who belonged to Protestant churches which were not Baptist in church order, had the task of seeking long denominational explanations to justify clearly unbiblical church practices. But I was content simply to appeal to the Bible. The subsequent years in the trenches of pastoral ministry have only confirmed this experience, as we have gone to the Bible again and again to seek light in handling various ecclesiastical issues. There has been no need for a human "appendage" to the Bible to explain the way ahead. It is all there in the Bible!

THE PRESENT AND THE FUTURE

I am a Baptist today, not because of pride in a denominational tag, but because of the biblical, distinctive traits of Baptists across history. I would gladly serve under a different name if that church held on to these biblical truths. Having been the pastor of the Kabwata Baptist Church in Lusaka, Zambia, for the last thirteen years, it has been my joy to see all the Scriptures being applied to all of our church's life. Although I received all my education in Zambia and never saw the outside world until I was at least five years in the ministry, the exposure of my worldwide preaching trips in recent years has only confirmed these convictions.

The Reformers' definition of the church is certainly biblical. The church is the place where the preaching of God's Word, the ordinances, and discipline are exercised. I cannot help but add regenerate church membership, believer's baptism, rule by elders, and local church autonomy to this definition. Consequently, we have sought to apply all these seven characteristics of biblical ecclesiology as conscientiously as is humanly possible at Kabwata Baptist Church. With all due respect to my ministerial colleagues in non-Baptist churches, I cannot with good conscience go about God's calling in my life in any other context. I have seen the light!

The winds of change are blowing on the African continent. Many of our nations are in bloody civil wars that have continued for decades. Famine has taken its toll in various countries. The AIDS epidemic is wiping out entire families and villages. Corruption, in both high and low places, is eating away at the pillars of society. No doubt, the church is also growing at an unprecedented rate, but religious pluralism is gripping the popular mind among the intelligentsia.

As I stand in the midst of all these tragic realities as a preacher of the gospel and as a church pastor, I often feel like Ezekiel in the valley of dry bones. I hear the voice of God saying, "Can these bones live?" I know they can. It is not by forming a huge church denomination that can coerce the state or work in formal partnership with it in the political arena. It is not by campaigning for Christian presidents who can declare their nations Christian. These bones can live through the instrumentality of God's saving and sanctifying Word. These bones will live as God's pure church grows in quantity and quality and becomes salt and light in Africa.

Therefore, as I enter the twenty-first century, I thank God for my Baptist heritage. In it I see the only hope for this ravaged continent. To me, therefore, being a Baptist is not just a fruit of providential guidance but the only place I can conscientiously serve the head of the church and the governor of history, the Lord Jesus Christ, in today's Africa and today's world.

11

FROM A WELSH REVIVAL TO A BAPTIST PULPIT

Geoffrey Thomas

Why am I a Baptist? The question seems stark, but it has the advantage of concentrating the mind. Actually, before I am a Baptist, I am first a Christian. So the question must first be asked, "Why am I a Christian?"

I am a Christian because God chose me in Christ before the creation of the world (Eph. 1:4), and because two thousand years ago the Son of God loved me and gave himself up for me (Eph. 5:25), and because in 1954 the God who had "set me apart from birth and called me by his grace, was pleased to reveal his Son in me" (Gal. 1:15).

EARLY CHRISTIAN INFLUENCES

I am a Christian because of my mother, who was born in 1906. In 1904 a religious awakening took place in Wales that changed the life of her mother's brother, Oliver Bown. He was then a twenty-two-year-old living with my grandparents. He had a special affection for my mother and her older sister. Uncle Oliver involved himself in all kinds of Christian activity for many years. He organized children's meetings and wrote religious doggerel:

Come to the children's meeting
  Held in the Gospel Hall
Come every Friday evening,
  Come and welcome all.
The meeting is at half past six,
  And it finishes at half past seven.
Come to the children's meeting
  And the way to heaven.

My mother sang it to me. It was in these meetings some time before the first world war that she "gave her heart to Jesus." When she and my father were courting in the late 1920s, they would be walking home hand in hand on a Saturday night through Merthyr Tydfil, often hearing the sound of someone preaching in the street. It would be Uncle Oliver. They would try to creep by without his spotting them for fear that he would have them stand in the circle with them, or give out some tracts.

I once asked Dr. Martyn Lloyd-Jones if he had ever met my uncle Oliver Bown, mentioning that he had kept an antique shop under the railway arches in Pontypridd for years. Of course he knew him. There were few men of evangelical convictions in Wales that Dr. Lloyd-Jones did not know. "Wherever I would preach around Cardiff he would be there in the congregation, and I would hear that deep 'Amen,'" Dr. Lloyd-Jones said. "He would generally be there with that boxer." What an elusive picture. Uncle Oliver was dead by the time I had grown interested in his early history, his influence over my mother, and his contact with the Doctor. Who was the boxer? Maybe some day I will learn that.

So I was privileged to grow up in a home characterized by my mother quietly singing hymns. These sounds accompanied all her activities, the memory of which evokes even today a lump of nostalgia in my throat. How favored I was to have that humble, gentle, self-denying, jolly, affectionate lady to nurture me, her only surviving child. What an unwelcome change senility brought to her life in the battles of her last years. In her 80s, she lived with us, and I was her pastor.

Unlike my mother, my father was not a Baptist but a Welsh Congregationalist. That is, he was raised in a Welsh-speaking congregation of some size and evangelical consciousness, that of Bethania, Dowlais. It was also affected by the revival of 1904. I heard as a boy its men speaking of the older men they could remember who would come straight from the Dowlais iron foundry in their leather aprons to the prayer meeting before going home to eat, and how they would pray with great earnestness for God's blessing to fall on the church. After the evening service there was always a second meeting, and there such men would have opportunity to stand and exhort the congregation about the word they had heard preached, some of them speaking eloquently.

My father's twin brother became a preacher, and his sister married a preacher, but my father became a stationmaster with the Great Western Railway and also was the treasurer of that church. Religion was very important to my father. Twice a Sunday he would be in his place, and also at the midweek meeting. But one could not say that Jesus Christ and the Bible were central to him. I cannot remember seeing him reading the Scriptures. He knew little about experiential religion. Its decline among the Congregationalists was rapid, more so than with the Baptists who in isolated congregations maintained the centrality of the Word and gospel in those churches.

My mother and father kept their memberships in their different churches, attending sometimes together and also separately. The Baptist church in High Street, Merthyr, was near our home. I went there with my father and mother's father for the morning service while the women stayed at home and cooked the Sunday dinner for their men—a South Wales tradition. I cannot say that I heard the gospel there, or that there was an impression of earnestness from the pulpit, that the preachers were longing that everyone in the congregation should trust in Jesus Christ and become Christians. Then in the evening we three went to the Welsh church in Dowlais where I understood nothing of the brief sermons but loved singing the great hymns, taking the men's tenor parts naturally.

> Doed y rhai sy'n llesg eu meddwl,
> Doed y rhai sy'n galon drist;
> Fe a llawer gofid heibio
> Wrth was'naethu Iesu Grist
> Os Efe gaiff Ei le,
> Daw y ddaear fel y ne'.

In 1951 a move took place that made things clearer, spiritually speaking. My father became stationmaster a dozen miles or so from Merthyr, to Nelson, and we moved a little farther than that to a village in the Rhymney Valley called Hengoed, but still in the county of Glamorganshire. I was initially devastated by the move from a town which for me had become the center of the world, a town with a wonderful Carnegie library five minutes from home, four cinemas, and a theatre with a repertory company that put on a new play each week. All my friends lived there, and I was to move to a village without even a chip-shop!

TABERNACLE BAPTIST CHURCH

But a hundred yards from the station house, along Raglan Road, was Tabernacle Baptist Church. It had been founded as a result of the 1904 revival in Wales. The Mount Pleasant Baptist Church across the valley in Maesycwmmer in Monmouthshire had known a work of the Spirit of God and a number had been converted. But many of the older members had resented this emphasis on an experience of the new birth. The church became characterized by friction and mutual allegations—"fanatics!" "unspiritual!" This was a conflict repeated across Wales. Those who had "received the blessing" left the church and scraped and saved and finally built the Tabernacle on the hillside in Hengoed.

There my mother and I found our home, while my father went to a Congregationalist church on the other side of the valley in Maesycwmmer. Some of the older members who had gone through that split forty-five years earlier were still alive, but there had been a national religious decline. The church had been characterized by a series of brief pastorates. There was respect for the ministry, but little discernment. There was delight when the message of the cross and the call to salvation were preached, but such sustained ministry was rare. The social gospel had taken its grip on the Welsh pulpit in every denomination. The people heard the staple themes of little discourses on the brotherhood of man and the universal fatherhood of God. People now looked to the state to become their shepherd so they might not be in want. "They ought to do something about it," became the standard mentality for the whole nation. Caesar was more real than Jehovah Jesus.

Our arrival in Hengoed was swiftly followed by a young preacher whose mother had been converted and influenced by the 1904 revival at the very geographical heart of that movement, the area around Gorseinon and Loughor near Swansea. His zeal in exhorting the congregation to come to Christ was irresistible, and they called him to become their pastor. He preached earnestly, and numbers of people professed faith. There was the "second meeting" after the evening service at which most if not the entire congregation remained. That always began by testing the meeting. "Has anyone received Christ as their Savior? If so, let the congregation stand while they remain seated." If anyone did sit down the minister would walk up the aisle and shake them by the hand, saying "God bless you." It was a dramatic moment and certainly helped focus the preacher's sermon on what would happen after the sermon. Would he be preaching for a response? Was his gospel one that demanded a change of life? Did he believe in conversion?

But there were certain negatives also in such a call to immediate public profession. It took the discretionary initiative out of the hands of the preacher, and considerable congregational pressure was brought to bear on him to baptize and bring into membership these people who had been moved that night. However much he might instruct them in the next month, it would not be much longer before the church expected them to be brought into membership. The majority of those who made such a profession, known to me then and still today, had blossom but no fruit. They did not continue in church attendance. There was a great falling away among those who sat down and were subsequently baptized.

CONVICTION AND CONVERSION

During the winter of 1953 and into the spring of 1954, I came under the gentle convictions of the Holy Spirit. I would walk along Raglan Road on a Sunday night and I would think, *I wonder if God will call me to himself tonight?* I never took a step with the determination that this would be the night I would sit down. I knew my heart first needed to be opened and I had to be given a birth from above. Then one night, as the Word was being preached, that assurance that God was indeed my Savior through Jesus Christ flooded my life, and I remained seated. A few weeks later, dressed in black—like a monk for all the world—I was baptized.

Then the witness to Christ, and the quest for fellowship and the growth in grace began in earnest. A couple of us began a Christian union in school. We asked any minister with any doctrine to come and speak to us. We knew no better. I remember one young, thin, dog-collared Baptist came along excited about the World Council of Churches Assembly in Evanston, Illinois. "What would you give up for a united worldwide church?" he asked us. "You Baptists, would you give up baptism? How many of you are Baptists?" I raised my hand and looked around. The whole group of boys had raised their hands. We were all Baptists and we had not known it. The custodians of experiential religion in that area of west Monmouthshire and the Rhymney valley happened to be the Baptist churches.

It was in Christian camp that I met the Presbyterians. They were a great crowd of men. They loved hymns like "A Debtor to Mercy Alone" and "Come Ye Sinners Poor and Needy," sung to the minor harmony tunes. "What a gem!" they would say after we had sung one such hymn. They spoke of Dr. Martyn Lloyd-Jones and how they had heard him, and what his texts had been. "Did you hear him on that passage? And on this passage?" I longed to hear this man. September 1958 came and I had my first opportunity to hear the Doctor preaching at a building now demolished in Cardiff, Memorial Hall Forward Movement. It was an important occasion as much for what I did not understand as what I did. There was a solemnity about it all. In those days every man wore a dark suit, and most of the women had hats. The hymns were Toplady's and Wesley's and Watts' sung with voluminous sincerity. Then he preached, and I remember nothing about his words at all, just the impression of the difference of this kind of ministry, and its importance. I then understood why those men in camp spoke of him as they did, and how I had to find out why, and soon, and hear more preaching like that.

It was a month before university at Cardiff and a biblical studies course. A friend told me that I would find two religious groups at the university, the Inter-Varsity Fellowship and the Student Christian Movement and that if I were to decide which one to join I would be wise in reading a representative book of each. Gabriel Hiebert had written *Fundamentalism and the Church of God,* published by the SCM Press. It declared that authority for what we believe is to be found in the church's teaching. *Fundamentalism and the Word of God* was written by another Anglican, J. I. Packer, and published by the Inter-Varsity Press. It claimed that the authority for what we believe is to be found in the infallible Bible.

I read these two books in the order in which they were written and thought then, as I do today, that Packer's arguments were unanswerable. The one whom I profess had saved me, whom I had taken as my infallible teacher from God, taught that the Scripture cannot be broken. For me he can say nothing wrong, and his submission to the Word of God had to be mine also if I were to go on calling him Lord. I had never heard a sermon on any doctrine throughout my life, and now I knew I could trust in a book that would be my foundation for the next fifty years.

JUSTIFICATION BY FAITH

The ministry of the speakers who came to the Inter-Varsity Fellowship group at the University College of Wales, Cardiff, over the next three years was life-enriching. In January 1959 across one weekend conference the IVF traveling secretary in Wales, Elwyn Davies, taught in three sessions the doctrine of justification by faith. God has constituted a righteousness by the incarnation of his Son, Jesus Christ, and he imputed that righteousness to the sinner who believes in Christ, and God declares him to be righteous in an act of justification. It was thrilling stuff. I had been justified for almost four years, but did not understand this. I knew more joy in that truth gripping me then than at the time of my conversion, though I knew I was not converted then. It was one of those spiritual fillings that God gives us under his Word throughout our lives.

Books also were God's kind gifts to me, and they produced the same extraordinary elevations. I borrowed J. C. Ryle's *Holiness* from the local library. I bought the first volume of Lloyd-Jones's *Studies in the Sermon on the Mount.* I wanted to live like that and preach like that. I could not imagine a greater life. A friend taking the same course as myself gave me her copy of the *Banner of Truth* magazine, which her future father-in-law, I. B. Davies, had passed on to her. I subscribed to the magazine and steadily learned the great truths of the Protestant Reformation. I read Iain Murray's *The Forgotten Spurgeon* and John Murray's *Redemption Accomplished and Applied.* I discovered the historical writings of J. C. Ryle, the journals of George Whitefield, and Jonathan Edwards's *Religious Affections.*

Except for Charles Spurgeon, these men were not Baptists, but three of the four lecturers who taught us biblical studies were Baptists. Kindly men, they all had the liberal view of Scripture, believing it contained the Word of God but was not itself the Word of God. Still, they could give no key to the mystery of which bits of the Bible were the Word of God and which were the mere words of man. It ultimately depended on our own attitudes. How easy it might have been for the professing church if there had been such an entity as the "assured results of modern criticism" which could highlight the words of the Bible with a special pen, and so illuminate the inspired parts, and we could then discard the rest. No such understanding exists. Once the inspiration of the Bible has gone, then everyone believes what is right in his own eyes. So the liberal has no authority, and his religion is usually an extension and confirmation of his own better nature.

WESTMINSTER THEOLOGICAL SEMINARY

From those years of blessing and buffeting I sailed on a cargo boat from Liverpool in September 1961 to Westminster Theological Seminary in Philadelphia for three years of divinity study, to sit at the feet of John Murray,

Edward J. Young, Ned Stonehouse, Cornelius Van Til, John Sanderson, Edmund P. Clowney, Edmund Palmer, Norman Shepherd, Meredith Kline, and others. I started the course with fellow students John Frame, Will Metzger, and Robert den Dulk, and we were later joined by Gary North. In the seminary ahead of us there were students like Walter Chantry and Palmer Robertson.

These were privileged years, especially because of the privilege of meeting John Murray. He was the man who was most full of God of any Christian I have known. When you saw him, and thought you had the opportunity to speak with him, your heart beat faster. There was a transparency of life and a depth of affection that drew you to him like a magnet. What a blessing to spend some minutes with him, to walk around the woody campus and have his arm encircle yours. But with what care did you converse with him because the holiness and righteousness of God which also was manifest in him. He drew, and yet he warned too, quite without any self-consciousness. At the same time, one rejoiced at being with him, and was grieved when that time together was over, but how carefully one spoke and acted.

Westminster Seminary was a Presbyterian seminary of conservative men in contrast to the department of biblical studies at Cardiff, staffed as it was mostly by liberal Baptist men. What struck me instantly at Westminster was the transcendent intellectual power of its teachers. Edward J. Young was more widely read than Aubrey Johnson. For the liberal scholar, biblical exegesis began a century ago, but the conservative scholar is fascinated by the opinions of church fathers, the Reformers, and the nineteenth-century men of Princeton and Edinburgh. God has not begun to shed light on his Word during this last century alone. Ned B. Stonehouse's breadth of learning excelled the New Testament men in Cardiff. The questions raised in Cardiff in the philosophy and biblical studies departments were answered in Philadelphia by Dr. Van Til.

How, as a Baptist, did I find the challenge of Presbyterianism? Dr. Lloyd-Jones once asked me that question publicly at a discussion meeting of the Westminster Conference. How did I not become a pedobaptist? Certainly I viewed their understanding of the Scriptures with the utmost respect. Just as I squirm when I hear Baptists make a few jibes at infant baptism during a baptismal service, I squirm when I hear Baptists speaking with disrespect of the theological contributions of these pedobaptist brothers. Any system of doctrine that has produced men of the caliber of Thomas Bilney, Samuel Rutherford, Jonathan Edwards, Robert Murray M'Cheyne, J. Gresham

Machen, and Cornelius Van Til merits respectful engagement. To understand their teaching is more than a courtesy; it is a basic requirement. Baptists who knew those men loved them fervently. It is humbly stirring to read their confessions of adoration for Christ.

What kept me a Baptist was the fact that (in the words of Presbyterian Louis Berkhof), "there is no explicit command in the Bible to baptize children, and that there is not a single instance in which we are plainly told that children were baptized."[1] That parents brought children to Christ for his blessing is an encouragement for every parent continually to do the same in prayer. That the promise of the Holy Spirit is to men and women and their children and to everyone called of God merely asserts that the promise of salvation is not merely to the generation alive at Pentecost or to the dwellers in Jerusalem. That Paul refers to holy children in 1 Corinthians 7:14 I gladly acknowledge as a reality of my own experience. I was set apart by the artless devotion and love for Christ manifest in my mother. Would that my boyhood friends had had such mothers. I had a Christian witness at home and access to gospel ministry in the church. Through her prayers she brought me into the orbit of the great High Priest's intercession.

The teachers at Westminster Seminary began their courses in biblical, historical, and systematic theology in the Book of Genesis. That was their mighty strength. They helped give me a Genesis I had to believe in. The little niggle we students might have had is that some of them hardly came out of the Book of Genesis! The covenants of God are the foundation of our hope, and baptism does have reference to spiritual circumcision, the circumcision of the heart, just as physical circumcision does. The Abrahamic covenant in its New Testament form, however, requires only the spiritually circumcised to receive the sign of that circumcision. To baptize the physical seed of believers is to introduce an Old Testament covenant procedure into a new covenant arrangement. For this reason during my ministry in our congregation in Aberystwyth since 1965, I have baptized believers and not their infants. I believe that the weight of scriptural evidence is on the side of this practice.

PART FIVE

THOUGHTS FROM THE PASTOR'S STUDY

12

WHEN OUR SENSES GET IN THE WAY: FROM CATHOLIC SACRAMENTS TO BAPTIST CONVICTION

Andrew Davis

Sometimes our senses get in the way. I remember well the sensory nature of my years in the Roman Catholic Church: the sight of the stained glass windows depicting the various "Stations of the Cross" of the final hours of Christ's life; the sound of the bells I rang as an altar boy the moment the priest lifted the eucharistic host toward heaven as a sacrificial offering for our sins; the pungent aroma of the incense crystals the priest spooned into the incenser; the feel of the droplets of holy water; the taste of the eucharistic wafer that was supposed to minister saving grace to me simply by virtue of having eaten it. For those twenty years in the sacramental system of the Roman Catholic Church, my senses were saturated.

But I never heard the Word of God. It's true that the priest read from the Old and New Testaments every week, and he usually took a few minutes to give us a moralistic homily. In later years, after I came to personal faith in Christ and read the Scriptures daily for myself, I was amazed to notice how much of the Mass had been steeped in scriptural language. But I never *heard* the Word of God, for it was never clearly preached, explained, or applied. The Holy Spirit did not use the sensory display of the Catholic sacramental experience to bring me to Christ. That would come later with a simple explanation of the gospel from the words of the Bible.

I later learned that God has ordained that it is by faith that we are justified before his throne (Rom. 3:28) and that this faith comes from hearing the Word of Christ (Rom. 10:17). It is not hearing itself, for the mere vibrating of the eardrum does not channel eternal life. I heard, saw, smelled, touched, and tasted many things, but I never really *heard.* I was walking by sight and not by faith. My senses were in the way.

The purpose of this essay is to give glory to God for the transformation of my heart through the words of Scripture which led me to walk away from Catholicism into simple biblical Christianity, then into Protestantism, then into baptistic convictions, then ultimately into the Southern Baptist Convention, in whose fellowship I now pastor a church. The differences between being Catholic and being Baptist center on passages of Scripture which the Holy Spirit has interpreted in me directly, without the mediating influence of the Catholic Church. In short, I am a Baptist simply because I believe Baptist doctrine and polity best conforms to biblical truth. Let me tell you my story.

A LIFE OF SACRAMENTALISM

Of course, I don't remember the first time my senses were stimulated by the "means of grace" the Catholic sacraments purported to be. After all, I was an infant being "baptized." However, I do recall the day I received my first Communion, along with my sister and brother. We were dressed in white and paraded around St. Jeremiah's church in Framingham, Massachusetts, with faces beaming and hearts swelling. We knew nothing of the complexities of the unholy marriage of Aristotelian philosophy and Christian theology that supported transubstantiation. I assume we were told that the little wafer we ate that day actually was Jesus Christ's own flesh, but I never understood the significance of that fact. I would find out later that it mattered not what I believed, but only that I partook in the sacrament. The "grace" worked on me no matter what was going on in my mind.

The next step was to make my first confession, and that day was a good deal darker and more somber. None of us was dressed in white, and none of us was joyful. When my turn came, I walked to the confessional booth with my heart pounding. I knelt on the velvet cushion as the priest slid open the small screen in the wall separating us. "Bless me, father, for I have sinned," I stammered, as I had been instructed. For the representative collection of transgressions I presented, I got off easily that day: ten "Hail Mary" prayers and five "Our Fathers." And so a transaction occurred that established in my mind the "business" aspects of forgiveness—this sin is worth that good deed. Little did I realize what an ancient history that idea had. It fit nicely into a part of my brain and became the way I dealt with sin from then on, until I understood the grace of God in Christ.

About this time, when I was ten or so, I became an altar boy. I was truly excited to have the honor of wearing the surplice assigned to me, and I diligently and carefully went through the training in order to learn all my duties. I still tend to think of the whole Mass in terms of those specific duties. The high point of the Mass occurred when the priest held the wafer up to God as our sacrifice. We jingled the bells signifying the mysterious transformation that had just taken place in the wafers, the same wafers that had earlier been taken from a large plastic bag in the sacristy.

As the people stepped forward to "receive Christ," we held a small copper palate under their mouths lest any of the sacred wafer should fall. As each of these people ate, the priest would say, "The body of Christ," and they would reply "Amen," meaning "Truly!" Catholic theology taught that they were receiving grace *ex opere operato,* simply by partaking physically. I knew little of this. That's the whole point, for the foundational principle of *ex opere operato* is that the people don't need to understand in order to benefit. The Word of God works so differently, for Jesus said about his words, "Consider carefully what you hear!" (Mark 4:24). There was not much of a call for consideration during the Mass.

My final sacramental step in Catholicism occurred when I was confirmed. I went through CCD classes (instructions given primarily to prepare children for whatever sacrament came next), and did so joyfully, without any hesitation. According to Catholic theology, when the bishop anoints us with oil, we will be filled with the Holy Spirit *ex opere operato,* whether we understood what that "filling" meant or not. But I was not filled with the Spirit. According to Scripture, the Holy Spirit did not enter me until the moment I was justified by faith, when I truly heard the gospel and believed it. It didn't happen that day, no matter how much I seriously wanted it to happen. "It does not, therefore, depend on man's desire or effort, but on God's mercy" (Rom. 9:16). God's mercy came to me a different day.

I now had experienced gladly everything the Catholic Church's sacraments had to offer me for my salvation, and I was still "dead in transgressions and sins" (Eph. 2:1) and "without hope and without God in this world" (Eph. 2:12). My salvation waited for a simple explanation of the Word of truth, the gospel, applied directly to my soul by the powerful Spirit of God. The ornate sensualism of Roman Catholic life had effectively veiled the powerful Word of God from my understanding, a veil every bit as impenetrable as that which covered the minds of Jews whenever Moses was read to them (2 Cor. 3:15).

THE SPIRIT RIPS THE VEIL

The momentous event occurred during my third year at the Massachusetts Institute of Technology. Despite the glad willingness of my earlier participation in the Roman Catholic path of sacraments, I had not attended a Catholic church at all in three years of college. I had no hungering or thirsting after the things of God, clear evidence of the fact that I did not have the indwelling Spirit and was still lost. God used a friend who was involved with Campus Crusade for Christ to lead me to Christ, though it took a year for the call of the Spirit to take hold of my heart. Eventually I saw the need for repentance from sin and faith in Christ. In October of 1982, I trusted in Christ alone for my salvation. The finished work of Christ on the cross had become my righteousness. All my achievements in Catholicism meant nothing, because I was saved by grace alone. At that moment, the Holy Spirit finally entered my heart and began opening Scripture to me. The journey of discovery in God's Word had now begun in earnest. I had now come to a simple biblical Christianity. The Bible would soon lead me further.

The first major step for me was to begin a discipleship relationship with a mentor through Campus Crusade for Christ. Since that group is a parachurch organization, my mentor had to lead me to a church for Sunday. Crusade was not sufficient. He brought me to an independent Bible church that was baptistic in its doctrines and polity. Without recognizing the Rubicon I had crossed and all that previous generations had paid to make that crossing, I had become a Protestant. The simplicity of the worship service and the centrality of the Bible were clear to me. I made feverish notes all over my worship bulletin, and the Spirit opened my eyes to passage after passage of Scripture.

I was also studying the Bible for myself, and it wasn't long before I began to repudiate the errors of Catholic theology by the simple power of the Word of God. Martin Luther had said that the plowman with the Scripture was better than all the popes and councils without it. I was now that plowman, and the very soil under my feet was being overturned. In the years before and during the Reformation, the Roman Catholic Church had vigorously opposed the translation of the Bible into the common language of the people, specifically because they denied the perspicuity of Scripture. They believed the Scriptures were not clear, too obtuse for the untrained reader to comprehend properly. All kinds of doctrinal errors would come from such a widespread dissemination of the Bible to the unlettered.

It wasn't until I wrote a seminary paper on this topic three years later that I understood fully how much the Catholic Church repudiated the perspicuity of Scripture, especially at the Council of Trent with its lists of banned books, including the Scriptures in the vernacular. I was already behaving as though the Scriptures were clear. By the power of the indwelling Spirit, the words were changing everything. This clear light caused me to rethink each of the sacraments the Catholic Church had bestowed upon me.

The Lord's Supper was one of my first doctrines to be transformed by the Bible. I could find no justification whatsoever for the doctrine of transubstantiation. Instead I came to see the Mass as a denigration of Christ's completed work on the cross. The Book of Hebrews was particularly devastating to the Catholic "sacrificial system," since it portrayed Christ as both the final sacrifice and the final priest. Hebrews 7:26–27 spoke to me powerfully: "For it was fitting that we should have such a high priest, holy, innocent, undefiled, separated from sinners and exalted above the heavens; *who does not need daily, like those high priests, to offer up sacrifices,* first for His own sins, and then for the sins of the people, because He did this *once for all* when He offered up Himself" (NASB).

What, then, was the significance of that moment when the priest offered up the eucharistic wafer while I rang the bells? I had learned to see the Lord's

Supper as a deeply spiritual memorial of the sacrifice Jesus paid for my sins and as a promise that He will return for me some day. I was thoroughly Protestant on this matter. I would soon become a Baptist.

BECOMING A BAPTIST

My involvement with Campus Crusade for Christ did not address the issue of baptism, because this organization was an eclectic evangelical group with no denominational ties. As is frequently the case, my own convictions were shaped in the crucible of doctrinal controversy. As we sought to evangelize in the Boston area, we ran into an aggressive group called the Boston Church of Christ. They taught that a person had to be baptized by their group in order to go to heaven. My mentor with Campus Crusade and I spent most of a night looking at all the verses on baptism in the New Testament.

Three things came clear: (1) the doctrine of the requirement of baptism for salvation was clearly unbiblical—the thief on the cross didn't need baptism to join Christ in paradise (Luke 23:43), and Christ did not send Paul to baptize but to preach the gospel (1 Cor. 1:17); (2) infant baptism was never clearly exemplified in the Bible, but always only believer's baptism; (3) baptism was commanded by Christ in the Great Commission (Matt. 28:19) and demonstrates the new life in Christ for every disciple (Rom. 6). The Holy Spirit began to work on my heart that, though the Boston Church of Christ was wrong in requiring baptism for salvation, I was wrong in rejecting it for myself. It took another year of working it through biblically, but I finally relented and was baptized in the Ipswich River in Topsfield, Massachusetts.

The full implications of believer's baptism would not come for many years, especially the ideals of a believers' church: a high view of church membership as a covenant fellowship committed to one another's growth in Christ and to the corresponding need for church discipline. All I knew at the time was that the simplest teaching of the Bible was of believer's baptism. I found out later that my own personal journey to Baptist convictions through the scouring of the New Testament had been traveled again and again in the past—by the Anabaptists in sixteenth-century Switzerland, by John Smyth in seventeenth-century England, by many converts of Anglican evangelist George Whitefield during the First American Great Awakening, by Adoniram and Ann Judson en route to Burma in the nineteenth century. Just as the Bible led all these people to

Baptist convictions, so also was I led. The unchanging Word speaks the same truth generation after generation.

A FINAL STEP: SOUTHERN BAPTIST COOPERATION

Within a year after my conversion to Christ, I spent a summer on an evangelism project with Campus Crusade at Hampton Beach, New Hampshire. There, in addition to doing beach outreaches, we spent the evenings learning about Christ's Great Commission (Matt. 28:18–20). We read a book entitled *In the Gap* by David Bryant in which he argued that every Christian must be a "world Christian," whose central purpose in everything was the fulfillment of that Great Commission.[1] I immediately began to pray that God would lead me into overseas missions. Even more significantly, a filter was established in my heart. Every decision would be made based on whether or not it tended maximally toward the fulfillment of the Great Commission. It was this filter which originally led me to be involved with a Southern Baptist church-planting effort in Topsfield, and which has caused me to rejoice in a continued fellowship in the Southern Baptist denomination. The central principles which keep me united with the Southern Baptist Convention are, first of all, their commitment to the divine authority and perfection of the Scriptures and, secondly, their cooperation among local churches for the purpose of fulfilling the Great Commission.

Congregational church polity is the principle Baptists cling to as best exemplifying the way New Testament churches were governed. The possible weakness of this approach is that churches could tend to be anything but "world Christian" in their outlook. The global could get sacrificed to the local concerns. However, many other local Baptist churches saw that their field of concern was the world, and that they could never do much at all toward world evangelization if they did not cooperate with other local bodies of Baptists in tangible ways.

In the same way, my own call to labor toward the fulfillment of the Great Commission has been tangibly supported by the SBC Cooperative Program. This has come in three specific eras in my life. First, as we were planting a Southern Baptist church in the rocky soil of eastern Massachusetts, we received financial assistance for six years. This enabled our pastor to be full-time, rather than bivocational. We also received assistance in many other ways from Southern Baptists. That church in Topsfield survived, and even thrived, in part because of the Cooperative Program.

Secondly, when God called my family and me to go to Japan as missionaries, we were fully supported by the Cooperative Program. Most missionaries have to raise their own support by going from Christian to Christian, referral to referral, church to church. It can take a year or more of full-time fund-raising to finish this process. Furthermore, once we were on the mission field in Japan, there was a fully developed mission team waiting for us, to educate us and enable us to be maximally effective. They included language experts, cultural experts, mentors, and mission strategists.

Perhaps for me the clearest example of the financial power of the Cooperative Program was seen in the context of the dramatic plunge of the value of the American dollar against the Japanese yen from 1993 to 1995. When we arrived in 1993, one dollar was worth 118 yen; at one point in 1994, the dollar was worth 82 yen; this was more than a 30 percent drop in the value of our money! Many "faith missionaries," who had raised their own funds themselves, had to leave their Great Commission work to go home and raise more money. The Cooperative Program enabled us to stay put, for the International Mission Board guaranteed our budget in yen, not in dollars.

Thirdly, I saw the benefits of cooperation for ministry when we returned from Japan and enrolled in the doctoral program of The Southern Baptist Theological Seminary in Louisville, Kentucky. Because the Cooperative Program subsidized all the housing and tuition costs, I was able to get an advanced degree at a top-notch institution with no new debts. By contrast, independent seminaries cost between three and ten times as much for a Ph.D. Best of all, because of the clear stand the Southern Baptist Convention had taken in the previous fifteen years on the inspiration and authority of the Scripture; the education available at Southern Seminary was doctrinally pure and helpful for the furthering of my ministry. It was not a tool in Satan's hands to cause me to doubt the very Scripture that had brought me from Catholicism to Baptist convictions.

CONCLUSION

There is a certain sensory majesty to the Roman Catholic sacramental system and its heritage and tradition. No one can miss the beauty of that heritage when gazing at the Sistine Chapel, when listening to the ancient Gregorian chants, when smelling the rich spices of the incense smoke during an Easter Vigil Mass. In recent years some evangelicals have rejected the supposedly sterile worship of their own traditions to return to Rome.

However, there is a far greater majesty in the perfection of Scripture than in anything humanity can do to reach toward God. Scripture's light is more pure and beautiful, its sound richer and more powerful for the transformation of a sinner's soul, its food more delicious and nourishing by far. No worship compares with the exultation of a heart over the majesty of God in Scripture and over the perfect salvation that Christ offers in his Word. Baptists can have their own worship styles and traditions that appeal to the senses and veil Scripture as well. The lessons I have learned in my journey from Catholic to Baptist convictions serve as an encouragement to the "simple plowman" to keep reading and meditating on verse after verse of the Bible, and to "taste and see that the Lord is good" (1 Pet. 2:3). Because God is sufficient for our joyful worship in heaven, his Word is sufficient for our joyful growth on earth.

13

ALL THINGS CONSIDERED . . . A BAPTIST

Mark E. Dever

THE DECISION

I am a Baptist because in the spring of 1982 in a seminar taught by David Steinmetz at Duke University I researched Zwingli's and Calvin's positions on infant baptism expecting to be convinced and was not. I found their arguments far better and more sophisticated than those I had yet heard; yet I did not find them finally persuasive.

Jesus commanded in Matthew 28 that the disciples should baptize those who are taught and who are obedient. Every letter in the New Testament that mentions baptism presumes that those who have been baptized are regenerate. And since belief and not baptism is presented as saving, this presumes that each person baptized had believed. Every example of baptism in the New Testament was of believers, even the so-called "household baptism" in Philippi, recorded in Acts 16. The one place in the New Testament that mentioned baptism and circumcision together (Col. 2) specifically paralleled physical baptism not with physical circumcision (as the pedobaptists were arguing) but with the circumcision of the heart—regeneration.

I could go on, but suffice it to say that when I considered everything from the realities of the Old Testament covenant, to the importance of the family, to the way we should regard our children, to the dangers of a merely subjective understanding of baptism, I found the arguments set forth in order to justify infant baptism challenging, instructive, full of good cautions, but not finally persuasive in the light of the clear teaching of Scripture.

This was a hard reality for me, because I was attending a Presbyterian church that I very much enjoyed. I think I may have simply assumed that this would mean I would end up as a Presbyterian because of theological commitments I had made completely apart from that church.

Having a Southern Baptist background, I had first attended a few different Baptist churches when I went off to college. And yet there was something that seemed so culturally insular and self-referential about them. I remember turning up at one of these churches and being greeted again and again by a minister of music (or of something) who always said, "We want to give you a big Baptist greeting this morning."

Looking back, I can see that the minister issued that greeting with all the naïve, cultural pride that is part of what is both so endearing and dangerous about America, and especially about the South. At the time, however, this seemed like nothing so much as a barrier to my non-Christian friends whom I was bringing to church not to hear about being Baptist, but to hear about being Christian.

By contrast, this Presbyterian church was in so many ways a wonderfully Christ-like picture of Christocentricity. They centered on Jesus, and on following him. He was who they talked about. The messages were serious, and seriously from the Bible. The entertainment factor was less; the gospel factor was heavier, more acknowledging of the unbelieving world, and yet more doggedly Christian for it.

I happily settled in there for three years of fruitful evangelism, discipleship, and service. I preferred Bach to Gaither, exposition to mere exhortation, and simple Christian truth to denominational particularities. I myself had been a teenage agnostic for a few years, so I was particularly sensitive to how clearly gospel-centered a church should be. I did not bring people to church to introduce them to my culture, but to Christ.

Imagine my shock then when confronted with this truth about baptism: the Bible does not command—explicitly or even implicitly—the baptism of infants. I could not in good conscience be a member of the church where I had been laboring for three years.

I immediately realized this meant that I must be some kind of Baptist, whether or not the word was there in the name of the church I joined. It might be a Bible church, or an Evangelical Free church, an American Baptist, or Conservative, Southern, or General Conference Baptist church. It might be one of the burgeoning "non-denominational" churches, yet most of which practiced exclusively believer's baptism. But it could not, in good conscience, be a pedobaptist church. I had become certain that though you could get a baby wet, you could never baptize it.

PROLOGUE

Back of all these self-conscious decisions was my family. They had raised me in a Southern Baptist church in western Kentucky. Two uncles were Baptist preachers. My great-grandfather (who died before I was born) had been a student at The Southern Baptist Theological Seminary in the early 1900s. He and his brother were both Baptist ministers (he, as I later found out, staunchly Calvinistic, his brother staunchly Arminian).

My own immediate family had little church involvement by the time I became a Christian, but I had been well-rooted in a large and loving community that intended to study the Bible and win the world for Christ. The pastor I knew throughout my early years was a faithful expositor of Scripture, a man full of the Spirit of Christ, a combination of personally irenic and yet doctrinally careful.

After becoming a Christian I preached everywhere: the Church of the Nazarene up the road (the minister's daughter was in my class); the Church of God (his daughter was, too); the Methodist Church (his son was); the Assembly of God, little country Baptist and Christian churches. My teens were a veritable travelogue of southern Protestant piety.

In college, I came into a rude awakening that the world was wider than my town. I looked for the Methodist fellowship on campus only to be warned that it was not evangelical. I was shocked. My experience of Methodists was that they were always and very evangelical. I asked my new friend what he was. He answered, "Presbyterian." And I asked him, with innocent surprise, "And you're a Christian?"

The Baptist Student Union was led by a woman (an adjustment for me). When I was talking to her early on, I found that she considered the bodily resurrection of Christ at least unimportant, and perhaps even fictitious. So I ended up in what I first had taken to be a sports meeting—the Inter-Varsity Christian Fellowship—where I found numerous evangelical Christians, agreeing on Christ, never really considering much about those issues which separated the evangelical denominations.

That was the context for my coming to self-consciously own credo-baptism, the baptism of believers only, as the clear teaching of the Bible.

EPILOGUE

All of that is why I became a Baptist. Why I have and still do remain one is a question requiring a bit more reflection. I went to an interdenominational seminary for my master of divinity degree, in part because of its academic reputation, but also because a number of its faculty were known to be both Reformed and baptistic. This intrigued me.

Once we moved to live near the seminary, my wife and I began attending an American Baptist church that was known as evangelical, but we found the sermons fairly consistently were on nuclear disarmament. I had taken a number of classes on this topic at my undergraduate university, and I didn't find these sermons too accurate or helpful. Besides, though my wife and I had our share of fights in our first year of marriage, we had no nuclear weapons, and so were not being personally challenged from the Word as we came to church Sunday by Sunday.

A ministry opportunity opened up for us at a church in our own town. (The American Baptist church was in another nearby town.) This church was a Congregational church and, though theologically liberal itself, had an evangelical youth group. For three years, I worked with that youth group. In my second year there, in part because of conversions we had seen and the consequent need for teaching, and in part because of the desire of the few evangelicals among the adult members, I got permission to begin a Sunday evening service with expositional preaching. (At the time, there was no evening service.)

After a couple of years of this, and of growing frustrations with the Congregational church (e.g., Unitarian deacons, sermons preached against the idea that people are sinful and need saving), I agreed with the forty or so Sunday evening attenders that an evangelical church should be planted.

It was at this point that I made my most self-conscious denominational decision. I considered leading the young group to be independent, Conservative Baptist, Baptist General Conference, or Southern Baptist. As I looked around, at least three things drew me to the Southern Baptists. The first was their commitment to missions. They were aggressively church planting in our greater metropolitan area already. The second was the battle over inerrancy they were then embroiled in. The Southern Baptists cared enough about the truth to fight for it. And the third was the depth of their theological history. The BGC and the Conservative Baptists had solid evangelical commitments, but nothing more. The SBC had a richly evangelical, Protestant, confessional, and theological history.

After a little over a year with this church, having completed my M.Div., I left this church in the care of another brother and went to The Southern Baptist Theological Seminary in order to do a master of theology degree. At that time, the heresy at Southern was worse than even the conservatives were publicly saying. At the same time, I found many dedicated brothers and sisters with a desire for biblical truth to be known and for God to be loved and served and made known. Reentering traditional Southern Baptist church life was, honestly, difficult. What had discouraged me eight years before (the insularity and self-referential qualities) remained, but so did the good things.

After only a year and a half there, I took my degree and headed over to Cambridge, England, to pursue a doctorate. For four years I worked on my degree, researching and writing on Richard Sibbes (an Anglican Puritan) and becoming more and more involved in a Baptist church there which was clearly Christian, deeply committed to teaching truth and which had a wonderful evangelistic ministry. For two additional years I stayed on after my Ph.D., teaching in the university and preaching at this church.

In early 1993 a letter came from a member of the Capitol Hill Baptist Church, back in Washington, D.C. I did not know the church, although I knew a couple of its members. They were in need of a pastor, and they inquired about my interest. After much prayer and almost a year of back and froing, in December of 1993 I accepted this invitation and actually began the ministry in this, my current church, in September of 1994. (They were very patient.)

CONGREGATIONALISM, TOO

It has been in the regular discipline of expositional preaching in a local church setting that my baptistic understanding of Christianity has been reenforced and sharpened. Preaching through John's Gospel and the Johannine Epistles, I felt that I was confronted again and again with the congregational nature of Christianity. Love of God that does not evidence itself in love of brother was mere notional Christianity. It was all in the head. It was false. The Letter of James, too, provided a striking reminder of the importance of living out the words we spoke and of the dangers of self-deception.

It began to become clear to me why our Baptist forebears had championed believer's baptism (and of people about ten years older than so many Baptist churches baptize today!). It began to become clearer to me why church memberships of Baptist churches had been smaller than their attendances, and why discipline had figured so largely in the life of the congregations. I began to believe that Scripture's clear teaching on discipline had to be not simply ideal, but practical, and that it must be able to be implemented without abuses. Understanding that membership matters—that it is to make visible the witness of the body of Christ—made historic Baptist polity come alive to me. Collecting such polities became a pastoral passion which led to the publishing of the book entitled *Polity: Biblical Arguments on How to Conduct Church Life.*[1] Jesus' promise of John 13:34–35 that our loving one another would be a great witness to the world has become central to my understanding of the church.

I desire to do nothing to make the distinction of the church from the world fuzzier than it needs to be. Such compromised, undisciplined membership roles leave the erring sheep in sin, the weaker sheep confused, the older, more mature sheep wrongly irresponsible, and the watching world clueless about what it really means to be a Christian. The greatest evangelistic tool that God has given us—the church—is left largely unused. At most, the church becomes a platform for our individual evangelism, rather than being the community of life and hope that God designed it to be—its very life bearing witness to the light in a dark world.

As I have continued to preach and teach through the New Testament, even the congregationalism of traditional Baptist polity has come alive to me. I never liked the coercive nature of Episcopalian or Presbyterian polities, but Bible churches' varieties of independent Presbyterianism seemed less problematic. Certainly the New Testament conceives of a plurality of elders in local churches. And certainly most Baptist churches do not have a plurality of people they call by that name. In our church, therefore, we have worked to recover this New Testament office of elder, recognizing qualified men beyond the pastoral staff of the church.

At the same time, this should not be confused with the kind of elder-rule in which the elders rather than the congregation act as the final court of appeal. There is too much in the New Testament that actually supports the classically held (though today rarely articulated) view of polity among Baptists known as congregationalism. For years we have been too lost in the twentieth-century efficiency of our programs and pragmatism of our committees to look carefully at Scripture on this matter.

But as I have looked through Scripture—with all respect to brothers and sisters who disagree—I find Jesus in Matthew 18 teaching not that the pope or a bishop, not that a conference or the elders, not that a general assembly or a pastor is the final court of appeal. Rather, the *ecclesia,* the gathered congregation, is. In Acts 6, who do the apostles appeal to in order to solve a problem in the congregation? The congregation. In 1 Corinthians 5, who does Paul lambast for failing to exercise discipline? The congregation. In 2 Corinthians 2, how does Paul say that the congregation had finally acted to excommunicate the sinning brother? By a vote of the majority. In Galatians, to whom does Paul appeal to correct serious doctrinal error, invoking the clarity of the gospel to them regardless of appeals to apostolic authority or angelic visions? The congregations. In 2 Timothy 4, who does Paul blame for the false teaching that will be endured? The congregations.

SUMMATION

I could go on, but you get the point. I am, as my Baptist forebearers were, a convinced congregationalist, understanding elders to function within that, and only by the delegation of the congregation. This does not, of course, mean that congregational decisions are inerrant. I think the congregation that fired Jonathan Edwards as their pastor back in 1750 was wrong. But I also think they had every formal right to do so. And each congregation—yours and mine included—will bear responsibility before God for the decisions we intentionally make, and those that we simply allow to be made by neglect.

A careful reading of the Gospels shows that Jesus clearly intends us to follow him together. Christian discipleship is an individual affair, but it is not only an individual affair. Foreshadowed in the Old Testament in a nation, spelled out in the Acts and the epistles in examples and instructions, the congregation is how God has always intended to show himself in his glorious characteristics.

The Creator of the universe has revealed himself in space and time, most fully in history in the incarnation of the Lord Jesus Christ, inerrantly in the written Word of God. He has answered our sin with mercy. His Spirit calls us to salvation from our sins through the preaching of the Good News of Jesus Christ, backed up by the changed lives of Christians. We are saved by grace alone through faith alone in Christ alone; our lives are to point to the truth of our faith. Baptism is to mark off those who have been spiritually raised to new life. And the local congregation of such forgiven, reborn men and women bear responsibility for the expression of this great gospel. The certainty that God teaches all of this in his Word is why I am a Baptist.

14

A BAPTIST ON THE HOT SEAT

Tom Elliff

It may have been cool outside that day, but I was on the "hot seat." It was early in the fall of 1962. I sat before the ordination council in the East Main Baptist Church, El Dorado, Arkansas. A few months earlier, while serving as a youth pastor in that same church, God had distinctly called me into the gospel ministry. Now, as an eighteen-year-old freshman at Ouachita Baptist University, I had answered another call, this time to the pastorate of the Southside Baptist Mission of Warren, Arkansas. With that call, both the mother church (First Baptist Church, Warren) and the new mission requested my ordination.

ONE HUNDRED QUESTIONS

My grandfather, A. P. Elliff (who would preach until the week of his death at age ninety-two) was the "questioner." In his hands was a list of over one hundred questions, complete with Scripture references; questions he had developed in the early 1900s as a means of determining whether potential preachers had any grasp of systematic theology. Also sitting in the council was my father, a Baptist preacher and the one who delivered the "challenge sermon" at my ordination.

Others present included my mother's father, T. A. Carter, who, though over ninety years of age, was an active and faithful leader in his rural Baptist church; my uncle, J. G. Murray, and my future brother-in-law, Bailey Smith, both Baptist pastors; my two brothers, Bill and Jim, who would subsequently enter the ministry as Baptist pastors. Other relatives of mine who were Baptist preachers had sent their regrets for being unable to attend.

The questioning was friendly but intense. Two other men were being ordained as deacons in that same service, yet it seemed that, other than their having to share their testimonies and verify that they tithed, the questions were mostly directed toward me. My grandfather had preached up and down the Arkansas-Oklahoma border, having originally settled with his family in southeastern Oklahoma when it was still "Indian Territory." He had become known as quite an "exhorter" in protracted, brush-arbor meetings, coming to town weeks in advance to debate the "Campbellites" as a way of setting the stage for revival. As such, he was thoroughly schooled on the unique aspects of Baptist doctrine. (In one meeting, four angry "Campbellites" broke a seat to the floor and were subsequently arrested for disturbing the peace!) Now my grandfather wanted to know if I embraced and could adequately "defend the faith."

I shared with the council my personal testimony of faith in Christ, recalling with joy each detail I could remember. From 1947 to 1952, my father pastored the First Baptist Church of Fordyce, Arkansas. There, in the summer of 1951, I came to know Christ during an outdoor crusade sponsored by our church. I recalled having been particularly excited about that crusade, riding around town on my bicycle and nailing announcements to fence posts and telephone poles. Little did I know that, by midweek, I would be under deep conviction, having started down a literal "sawdust trail" on three consecutive nights but not finding the courage to "go all the way."

Late on Thursday evening, after waiting for my father to come home from the crusade, I knelt with both my parents, repented of sin, and trusted Christ. I could (and I still can!) remember the incredible sense of peace that flooded my heart. And later, lying in bed and looking out the window up at the stars I said, "Dear God, I believe I must be the happiest boy in the world!" I was not baptized until the following fall, after my father assumed the pastorate of the Bethany Baptist Church in Kansas City, Missouri.

It was while living in Kansas City that I first became aware not all Baptists—indeed not even all Southern Baptists—believed alike regarding the integrity and authority of the Bible. A new seminary, Midwestern Baptist Theological Seminary, had been founded in our area. One of its professors had written a book indicating his conviction that the Bible was neither inerrant nor infallible. He believed that while some of the Bible was God's word to man, other portions were simply adaptations of ancient myths and legends and, as such, were just man's words about God. The furor that erupted over the writing of this book and the discovery that some other professors in our Baptist institutions believed similarly, ultimately birthed our 1963 *Baptist Faith and Message.*

INERRANCY OF THE SCRIPTURES

As a teenager, the significance of this issue was not lost on me. I have clear memories of my father standing toe-to-toe with seminary students and professors in defense of the integrity and authority of the Scriptures, much as my grandfather must have done in earlier years. As a young witness to these opening salvoes in our Southern Baptist battle for the Bible, I came to appreciate that the inerrancy of the Scriptures was foundational to all our beliefs. I heard then, and in later years read for myself, the accounts of previous times in our Baptist history when the Bible was under attack.

In the days that followed, I found that a certain reverence for God and respect for his Word was growing in my heart. And I determined that a high view of the Scripture was one to which I would give myself without compromise. I wanted to have the same view of God's Word as my Master. I understood then, but did not fully appreciate until later and through personal experience, the price that must be paid so successive generations might have the same privilege as I—the privilege of hearing the "old, old story" in its purest and unadulterated form.

So there I was, nervously answering my grandfather's questions. But he seemed to be asking for something more than a simple comprehension of the doctrines so near to the heart of Baptists: God's triune nature and sovereignty, the inspiration of the Scriptures, the reality of Satan, man's sinful nature, the incredible miracle of the virgin birth, blood atonement, the bodily resurrection of Jesus, the absolute sufficiency of Christ, eternal security, salvation's evidence through "separated" life, the autonomy of the local church, the priesthood of all believers, the purpose of the ordinances, the Great Commission, the imminent return of Christ, the judgment seat of Christ for believers, the great white throne judgment for unbelievers, both heaven and hell as eternal realities . . . on and on he pressed. What was he seeking?

Now I realize he was looking for me to be a Baptist by something more than mere comprehension or convenience. He was seeking in me the evidences of an unwavering conviction. And really, that's why I am a Baptist! I am a Baptist by conception, by conversion, by confession, by calling, by commission, by combat . . . but ultimately, by conviction. And, like Paul of old, I rejoice to claim that "I am what I am, by the grace of God."

15

MISERY LOVES COMPANY? A PRESBYTERIAN PASTOR COMES HOME

Fred A. Malone

At least my Aunt Grace began to hug me again.

After having been raised a Southern Baptist, I became a Presbyterian in 1972. After seven happy years as a Presbyterian minister, I became a convinced and sometimes miserable Baptist. "Miserable?" you ask? Yes, miserable. Not that I was a miserable Baptist in the sense of being a poor Baptist or being a Baptist without personal joy. It's not even that I am miserable because it has cost me a great deal to be a Baptist, although it has. Aunt Grace, devoted as she was to the Woman's Missionary Union, might have been glad to have me back, but some Baptists were a bit suspicious of my theological commitments. In the process, I lost many Presbyterian contacts and opportunities.

My long, hard journey back to Baptist life causes me to be miserable in heart when I see other Baptists demonstrate a lack of conviction about the things that make us Baptist. The name *Baptist* is being removed from many church signs. But even worse than that, distinctive Baptist beliefs have been removed from some churches that still bear the name. Some Baptist churches are in danger of surrendering to liberal ecumenism, while others are in danger of being swallowed up by well-meaning church growth strategies.

Southern Baptists have been right to appeal to our Baptist forefathers in defense of biblical inerrancy, while liberals deceitfully shout "no creed but the Bible!" We are in danger, though, when conservatives begin to shout "no creed but the Bible!" as the discussion turns to what the inerrant Bible teaches about God, salvation, and church life.

Why do so many Baptists leave? From the 1950s to the 1990s, some Baptist churches failed to major on expository preaching, family life, and personal holiness. As a result, many Southern Baptist youth, influenced by the Jesus Movement and parachurch ecumenical ministries, have left SBC churches for the seemingly warmer waters of independent Bible churches and conservative Presbyterian congregations. As a former Presbyterian, I am convinced that the Presbyterian Church in America has been built largely from searching and frustrated Baptists. These former Baptists may hear more Bible in these other churches when compared with the endless stories, illustrations, jokes and "exciting" (a tired word) denominational promotions in their local Southern Baptist churches.

Some former Baptists have even been saved through good Presbyterian Bible teaching. To them, accepting infant baptism was a small price to pay for finding eternal salvation. As Southern Baptists, we should grieve when we lose some of our most committed people to our Presbyterian and Bible Church brothers. Sadly, many other Southern Baptists have left us for charismatic churches, finding the Bible more often referred to there, even if it is erroneously interpreted.

MY PERSONAL JOURNEY

I was baptized at age nine in my Southern Baptist church. My parents always brought me to all services on Sunday and on Wednesday nights. I will always be grateful that they did so and that they made sure I participated in such things as the Bible drill. However, our youth group meetings contained little Bible study. Our dear pastor, a godly man, did not preach expository messages through the books of the Bible, so I received only piecemeal instruction from the Bible. Because of this, I didn't understand much more than "Jesus died for our sins" and "we should be dedicated Christians." The latter concept was defined by the Sunday School Board offering envelopes—present, on time, brought Bible, brought tithe, and read lesson.

I walked the aisle seven times in various meetings, trying to get rid of guilt for my sins and failures. After emotionally cathartic experiences of feeling cleansed, I would find myself in old ways within a week or two. I sang in the choir and in quartets and even played a trumpet in church, but I led a double life of profane language, immoral behavior, and evil thoughts. Those who knew the "real Fred" must have thought me a hypocrite then, but only because I was.

In college, I rejected Christianity in favor of sociology and psychology, believing church people were ignorant. My evolutionary philosophy led me to believe that we were just animals. "Survival of the fittest" justified the most wretched behavior, as long as one could get away with it. My marriage was in shambles. I soon became afraid, however, of what the world would be like should my selfish "survival of the fittest" attitude be applied to any society.

As I searched for meaning, I began to read the Bible again. I attended some meetings of Campus Crusade for Christ. For the first time in my memory, I heard a real Bible exposition. A Presbyterian minister, Frank Barker, preached the message from John 15. After examining the evidence for Jesus' resurrection, I prayed for God to give me faith if he were real. God saved me in 1969. In doing so, he healed my marriage and granted me an insatiable thirst for his Word. Debbie and I joined Lakeview Baptist Church in Auburn, Alabama, and I became the summer youth worker under my beloved pastor, Rex Dickey.

As I taught the college class, I came across some doctrines in the Book of Romans that I had never been taught. The apostle Paul was teaching that God was sovereign in all things, including my salvation. The Sunday school lesson, however, summarized Romans 9–11 in just a few short paragraphs, neglecting its main teachings. I was stimulated to study these questions that I could not find answered in the Sunday school literature. I found that Presbyterians emphasized God's sovereignty and human depravity, but so did the early Southern Baptists. In fact, so did the 1963 *Baptist Faith and Message.* I wondered why some Baptists seemed to have forsaken what they once believed while building our denomination.

Called to the ministry of the gospel, I knew that I must go to seminary to satisfy my thirst for biblical knowledge. I visited the Baptist Student Union director at Auburn University for guidance. He cursed a couple of times and recommended The Southern Baptist Theological Seminary in Louisville, handing me a book by a professor there. This book denied the Mosaic authorship of the Pentateuch, making me suspicious of Southern. I looked for other seminaries, finding Southwestern Baptist Theological Seminary in Fort Worth to be the most conservative. On my way there, however, I visited Reformed Theological Seminary in Jackson, Mississippi, because I had heard of its clear stand on biblical inerrancy. I felt at home there, so much so that I decided to enroll.

When the Alabama Baptist Convention's executive secretary visited Lakeview, I told him why I chose Reformed over Southern. He became angry and told me I was not really a Southern Baptist. When I asked the deacons to recommend me to this non-SBC seminary, most agreed. An older deacon, however, stood up angrily and said, "This is of the devil!" Only the encouraging attitude of my beloved pastor Rex Dickey kept me a Baptist.

At Reformed, I continued to learn about the common theological heritage between Presbyterians and early Southern Baptists on the doctrine of salvation. After we moved there, however, two Southern Baptist pastors visited me, harshly warning me that the things I was learning were, again, "of the devil." I could not see how, since I found more biblical knowledge and personal godliness at Reformed Seminary than I had ever experienced in Southern Baptist life up to that time.

So, in the face of warm acceptance by the Presbyterians at my seminary and harsh rejection by the Southern Baptists in my home denomination, I did what many other Southern Baptist students and ministers have done before and since. I accepted infant baptism and became a Presbyterian. At the time, infant baptism did not seem such an important consideration compared to the Presbyterian dedication to biblical inerrancy and the grace of God in salvation. In addition, I found the Presbyterians in the middle of Evangelism Explosion, a curriculum used by the Lord to bring scores of sinners to Christ, without high-pressure altar calls.

After serving happily for seven years in Presbyterian churches, I was unsettled when reading Exodus 12. This text revealed that the household children partook of the Passover meal. Since I believed baptism was a continuation of circumcision and the Lord's Supper was a continuation of the Passover, then did this mean that Presbyterians should allow children to take communion from their earliest years? I found that Presbyterian theologian Louis Berkhof decided against such a notion. The reason he gave, however, was that the New Testament requires partakers of the Lord's Supper to examine themselves first (1 Cor. 11).

Then it hit me. The New Testament also requires baptismal candidates to repent first. If one is hermeneutically consistent, one must accept both pedobaptism and pedocommunion, or one can accept neither. This discovery uncovered many inconsistencies in my position, leading me to adopt the position that only disciples should be baptized. I was a Baptist, again.

When I subsequently met with the Alabama Baptist ministerial placement representative, he questioned me on the Cooperative Program, not on my theology. After learning that I could support the Cooperative Program, but that I had reservations about liberalism at Southern Seminary, he told me there was no place for me in SBC life. Thankfully, Ernest C. Reisinger, a Baptist pastor who shared my theological commitments, had been given a copy of a journal I had written about my theological journey.[1] God overruled misdirected, paternalistic denominationalism as Pastor Reisinger called me to be his associate at North Pompano Baptist Church in Florida.

When Ernie decided to republish James P. Boyce's *Abstract of Systematic Theology*, he asked me to write the introduction. We distributed the volume on seminary campuses. The response was overwhelming, as students were confronted with the theology of the Southern Baptist founders. Many of them asked, "Why weren't we taught this in seminary?" Thankfully, now hundreds and thousands of young Southern Baptists are rediscovering the biblical faith of our forefathers.

A DOCTRINAL FOUNDATION

As I have stated before, I am a Baptist by *conviction* and by *choice*. As a Presbyterian, I believed that the Abrahamic circumcision of infants gave Christians, as the children of Abraham, the right to baptize their infants. It made sense to me. After all, the Presbyterians at Reformed Theological Seminary strongly affirmed this, and they were more committed to biblical inerrancy than many Southern Baptists.

What I did not understand was the following:

1. Jesus Christ is the only final physical seed of Abraham (Gal. 3:16, 19).
2. Only those "of faith" are the seed of Abraham through their faith relationship to Jesus Christ (Gal. 3:14, 26–29; Rom. 4), not the offspring of believers.
3. The new covenant of Jesus Christ is defined as including regenerate forgiven members alone, not believers and their children (Heb. 8:8–12).
4. Infant baptism is based by inference on a final Old Testament authority over the New Testament.

5. Infant baptism violates the regulative principle of worship, cherished by Presbyterians and Baptists alike, which maintains that ordinances must be instituted by revelation, not by inference from the Old Testament.

The baptism of disciples alone is the only instituted baptism of Jesus Christ in the New Testament (Matt. 28:19–20). That is why I am a Baptist.

PRACTICAL IMPLICATIONS

There are various practical implications to this belief in the baptism of disciples alone. First, the New Testament church is called repeatedly "the disciples" (Acts 6:1–7; 9:26; 11:26). This means that the local church must be composed of baptized disciples who give evidence of their regeneration by their repentance and faith in Christ before their baptism. That is why Peter commanded the people to "repent and be baptized" at Pentecost (Acts 2:38). There is no room in the New Testament for a church made up of "believers and their seed" as members.

Second, the baptism of disciples alone affects evangelism. It means that candidates for baptism should have adequate understanding of the person and work of Jesus Christ and the gospel of repentance and faith. They should be committed followers of the Lord Jesus Christ. Jesus "made" disciples first; then they were baptized (John 4:1–2). This is "lordship salvation," a prerequisite to baptism. The candidates must know what they are committing to—a submission to Christ and his commandments as Lord of their lives. This requires that the faith and salvation experience of an individual must be examined before baptism.

This Baptist distinctive means that, instead of baptizing immediately anyone who "walks the aisle" or "raises a hand" or "prays a prayer," the pastor must meet with the baptismal candidate to examine his beliefs and commitment. This practice would remedy greatly the problem of inflated church rolls of uncommitted members. At the same time, it would help to ensure that we do not mislead one precious eternal soul into thinking he is saved when he does not understand the gospel.

Third, to understand the church as an assembly of baptized disciples demands that the worship and teaching ministry of the church on the Lord's Day be geared toward disciples, not "seekers." The Great Commission requires that baptized disciples be taught "to do all that [Christ] commanded [his disciples]." In short, systematic expository teaching and preaching is a commandment of the Great Commission. This is what is missing in many of our Baptist churches today, even though it is so clearly commanded by Jesus

Christ. I believe that the expository preaching of pastors in the Presbyterian Church in America has attracted many former Southern Baptists who are hungry for the Word of God. Expository preaching will edify the saints and evangelize the sinner at the same time.

Fourth, if the church is an assembly of baptized disciples, the priority and autonomy of the local church must be emphasized over denominationalism. The local church is the only earthly organization that has Jesus Christ as its head, carrying his authority. In chapters 2 and 3 of Revelation, Jesus is seen as the head of each of the seven churches. No church was more important to him than another because it was bigger or richer or had fewer problems. They all had problems, and he dealt directly with each one as head.

This means that each local church has Christ as its head and has all the authority of his Word to govern its life, without being dictated to by another church or association of churches. If churches choose voluntarily to associate with one another, however, they must agree on the doctrines and practices concerning the purposes of their association in missions, literature publishing, ministerial preparation, and so forth (Acts 15).

Fifth, the church, as an assembly of baptized believers, must recognize the priesthood of the believer as he or she approaches God through Christ alone. Every Christian is a disciple of Christ, not of the church. This does not mean, however, that one can believe anything he wishes and still be a member of a local Baptist church. It simply means that individuals approach God through Christ, not through the church. The church must examine the beliefs of potential members, making sure they believe the gospel of Christ as stated in the Scriptures and in that church's articles of faith. Neither a Mormon, nor a Jehovah's Witness, nor a Muslim can be a member of a Baptist church, no matter how sincere he may be.

Sixth, the fact that it is an assembly of baptized believers requires that a congregation practice church discipline. Besides the fact that Jesus commanded this of each local church (Matt. 18:15–17), it is obvious that a person who professes to be a disciple of Jesus Christ, yet who stubbornly refuses to live by his teachings, is not really a disciple (Matt. 7:22–23). For a local church to confront and to discipline baptized members is an act of love and obedience.

Seventh, the church as an assembly of baptized disciples means the church must practice biblically regulated worship. Again, the Great Commission calls the church to teach baptized believers to do whatever Jesus commanded. Therefore, worship must be "in spirit and in truth," not "in spirit and in creativity." To invent new forms of worship other than the worship instituted by Christ and his apostles in the New Testament is for professed disciples to disobey his commandments. The approved elements of worship in the New Testament are the reading of Scripture, the preaching and teaching of the Bible, prayer, baptism, the Lord's Supper, collections, and the congregational singing of psalms, hymns, and spiritual songs.

Such additions as drama, dance, rock bands, puppets, gospel monkeys, high-wire acts, power-lifting demonstrations, and so forth are violations of the biblical regulative principle of worship, which Baptists have historically believed. Furthermore, such unbiblical practices push out time given to commanded practices. An assembly of baptized believers must follow their Lord's commandments, not their inventions, in his worship.

CONCLUSION

In a postmodern and post-Christian world, absolute truth with exclusive divine authority from Scripture is denied, sneered at, or added to the list of equally valid truth systems. Under such hostility to (or ecumenical ignoring of) absolute biblical truth, I believe that those brave souls of sincere Baptist conviction who dare to declare "thus saith the Lord" will experience both opposition and success.

The opposition will come from those who, from sincere postmodern relativistic and pluralistic convictions, oppose those who have exclusivist convictions. According to postmodern ideology, pluralism should give respect to all views. The pluralists, however, often intentionally exclude the exclusivist claims of the Christian (and Baptist) worldview. This is a danger even in Baptist life, coming from those so-called Baptists who oppose historic Baptist theology.

The success will come when searching souls who have suffered shipwreck on the hidden reefs of postmodern nihilism begin to seek solid answers from God's written Word. Success will come also when sincere Christians who are tired of seeking emotional highs find direction for life's issues in the same divine truth. These tired people may travel the circuit from profligate living to failed promises of emotional deliverance from sin and self until they finally plop down in relief in the pews of those churches that read the Bible, teach the Bible, and are willing to say "thus saith the Lord" in matters of faith and life.

I believe the Baptist faith has the answers for such people, both for salvation and for daily living. I am a Baptist by conviction and choice. I am a

Baptist by the force of Scripture upon my conscience. It is my hope and prayer that others will join me as a joyfully convinced Baptist. After having described myself as a "convinced and sometimes miserable Baptist," I might be tempted to say this is because misery loves company. But this would not be true.

My journey toward Baptist convictions might be a miserable one at times, but nothing makes me happier than finding ranks of committed Baptists united in a missionary spirit to build biblical churches. As such, I suppose you could say that I am a Baptist for the least miserable of all possible reasons: for the glory of God on earth.

16

A BAPTIST—TESTED BY FIRE

Al Meredith

When a gunman intent on destruction and murder gave our church, Wedgwood Baptist Church in Ft. Worth, Texas, international notoriety, my convictions as a pastor came under immediate worldwide investigation. By God's grace I also did some sober and edifying reflection, on all that it meant to be a Christian minister, a part of the world family of Christians, the power and wonder of the comfort and strength that is in the gospel, and what it means in particular to be the minister of a Baptist church. I want to share with you my pilgrimage in faith and how certain convictions have stuck with me, through thick and thin, and make me a Baptist.

MY PERSONAL JOURNEY

My mother came from a family of believing, but only nominally involved, Congregationalists in the small town of Gaylord, Michigan, where her father was a salesman, small-time farmer, and owner of the local hotel. She was converted as a teenager there, finished college in the height of the Depression and went to Chicago to find work. There she found my father.

He had been raised on a farm in central Iowa. His family had deep roots in the Quaker movement and he grew up in the local Friends church. Desperately seeking to distance himself from the farm, he rode his motorcycle to Chicago in 1932 to seek his fortune. What he found was "far above rubies"; he found a godly wife.

When I was born in Detroit, Michigan, in 1946, my parents were attending a Methodist church where they had me christened. Soon afterward they joined the Ebenezer Baptist Church (a Swedish General Conference church) where my father consented to being immersed. As my mother later explained to me, the pastor called our home, patiently explained the meaning and significance of believers' immersion and concluded by asking my father, "Now can you think of any reason why you would NOT want to be baptized?" When my father could not, the issue was settled.

At six and a half years of age I fell under the convicting power of the Holy Spirit. Aware of my "lostness" and deeply burdened by it, I cried myself to sleep for weeks. I would cry out to God my desire to become a Christian, but I did not know how. Why I did not ask my parents or Sunday school teachers I do not know, but the burden of my sin grew increasingly oppressive. Finally, on a Sunday evening in April of 1953, a different preacher was in the pulpit. For once, I did not fall asleep. I felt he was speaking directly to me. Who he was or what he said, I cannot recall, but when he concluded with an invitation for those who wanted to become a Christian to come forward, I pulled on my father's sleeve and, together, we walked the aisle. I and several others were taken to a prayer room for counseling as the evangelist explained to us Acts 16:31, "Believe on the Lord Jesus Christ and thou shalt be saved" (KJV).

I prayerfully entrusted my life and eternal soul to the one who died for me and the burden of my sin was gone! I slid down the banister and ran out the door to tell my friends. "How precious did that grace appear the hour I first believed."

Several months later my family moved to a small town north of Detroit where I would spend the rest of my childhood and adolescence. Located on the beautiful St. Clair River (part of the Great Lakes system), Marine City boasted the second oldest Catholic church in the state. The populace was 85 percent Roman Catholic, so Protestants were in the minority, but Baptists were considered part of the lunatic fringe.

My family joined the Fellowship Baptist Church and, upon my baptism, I soon followed. They belonged to the General Association of Regular Baptist

Churches, God-fearing people who had pulled out of the American Baptist Convention in 1932 because of the alarming growth of liberalism in that body. We relished the role of "fundamentalists" and lined ourselves up against the prevailing culture. Like most of the fundamentalists of that day, our dispensational eschatology taught us that the world and its institutions were in the hands of the wicked one, and things would continue to deteriorate until the rapture of the church ushers in the great tribulation. As the people of God, our chief concern was to witness to a lost and dying world and to keep ourselves separate and undefiled from its contamination. As a Baptist, I knew I was different from the world.

Unfortunately, at times the Christian life was portrayed as a list of do's and don'ts with the emphasis strongly upon the latter. Though very active in high school sports and student life, I did not dance, drink, smoke, go to movies, play cards on Saturday, or play *anything* on Sunday.

At eleven years of age I sensed the Lord calling me into the pastoral ministry. While always attracted to missions by the intrigue and mystique of pictures of savages and sunsets, the pastorate was far less appealing to a preadolescent boy with visions of grandeur. But when, at last, alone in my basement I surrendered all, peace came to my heart.

In order to fulfill this calling I attended Grand Rapids Baptist College and majored in Bible and also, out of sheer interest, history. Those were critical years in terms of my spiritual and intellectual development. Expecting quick, easy answers to the questions regarding the problem of evil (why does a loving, sovereign, God allow suffering?), the problem of free will and determination (if God is totally sovereign, how can man be free?) and the like, I was soon disappointed to find a paucity of easy solutions to these problems. Instead, my professors helped me to define the issues and work on the answers myself. They explained to me the necessity of developing a Christian world-and-life view and informed me that it was a lifelong process. They taught me *how* to think, not *what* to think. And they were patient with me. For this I will forever be grateful.

For several years I went through an intellectual rebellion, questioning everything. Writers like Voltaire and Kurt Vonnegut encouraged me to challenge all authority. Some fellow students resented my domination of discussion time, and a few professors seemed a little intimidated by my irreverent questions, but the sky did not fall and lightning did not strike. Through the years as I studied Augustine, Luther, Calvin, Whitefield, Wesley, Kierkegaard, Spurgeon, Augustus Strong, Carl Henry, Cornelius Van Til, and especially

Francis Schaeffer, gradually I began to fashion the foundation of my own world-and-life view, with Christ alone at the center.

Feeling the call to teach, I transferred from Grand Rapids Baptist Seminary to Michigan State University to study history. Though I had come to chafe at the legalism and strain at the ecclesiastical separation of my youth, I will always be thankful for what God engendered in my heart and mind through my early mentors: a deep love and devotion to Christ and an unswerving commitment to the authority of God's Word.

At Michigan State University, East Lansing, I pursued my masters and then my doctorate degree in modern European history, doing my dissertation on C. H. Spurgeon's social and political influence. My wife and I were very active at South Baptist Church, where our souls were fed and my own preaching style was deeply influenced by the pastor, Dr. Howard Sugden. He was expository in style and boundless in energy and humor. What a joy to know that Christians can laugh!

Upon graduation in 1973, the job market took me to South Carolina, where I became a Southern Baptist. They were broad enough to be unconcerned with my questions about eschatology, and they were not even familiar with the issues of separation and legalism that had caused me so much consternation.

Soon the denomination would begin to move itself to a more conservative position theologically, an unprecedented phenomenon historically. Although I have managed to keep myself uninvolved in the political maneuvering of the convention, I have been generally sympathetic with the theological concerns which have motivated the more conservative factions of the denominations.

MY THEOLOGICAL CONVICTIONS

Although I was raised in a Baptist home, the fact that I have remained one is due to a conscious choice arrived at after much thought and consideration. From my days as a student, searching for solid answers, I have been spurred on by 1 Peter 3:15, "Be ready always to give an answer to every man that asketh you a reason of the hope that is in you" (KJV).

A PEOPLE OF THE BOOK

One of the primary reasons I am a Baptist is that historically we have sought to be "people of the Book." That is, we recognize the Bible to be the final authority in all matters to which it speaks. It was because of the teaching of God's Word that our forefathers insisted on believer's baptism by immersion, and because of that conviction, were mercilessly persecuted during the time of the Reformation and subsequent years.

It is because we believe that congregational polity is biblically mandated that we practice it. It is because the Bible calls us to "make disciples of all nations" that we are driven to evangelism and missions. The Bible is to Baptists what a compass is to a mariner. Apart from its authoritative instruction, we are condemned to drift aimlessly on the ocean of life, driven about by every wind of doctrine that blows.

While one major religious organization claims that "the world sets our agenda," Baptists are convinced that those who are wed to the spirit of the age become widows in the next generation. Southern Baptists are so passionate about this that they have engendered a bloody civil war over issues such as inerrancy, infallibility, and the authority of Scripture.

I am an inerrantist. I believe that every word of the original manuscripts was God-breathed. Though the writers' personal idiosyncrasies were not overruled, the final result was exactly what Almighty God intended and, therefore, completely without error. To those who point out that we do not possess the original manuscripts, the response is, that is the reason for the whole discipline of textual criticism. Why bother to learn what is the purer text if the originals were not completely pure?

I need an inerrant Bible for epistemological reasons. The question of epistemology—how do we know what we know?—is the foundational issue of our generation. As rationalistic philosophy has become bankrupt, postmodern man is left with nothing but sheer relativism where truth is reduced to personal preference. Thus society is governed by the dictatorship of the majority and we are left without absolutes.

As a building is only as strong as the individual bricks and mortar that comprise it, so our doctrines are only as reliable as the individual words of Scripture from which they are derived. If the words themselves are unreliable, so too are the doctrinal truths they comprise. Baptists are people of the Book and when they cease to be that, they will cease to be Baptists. In fact, they will cease to be . . . period.

THE PRIESTHOOD OF BELIEVERS

While the Bible is the Word of God, and, as such, the final authority in all matters it addresses, Baptists have historically held that it is the right and responsibility of each individual to follow the leading of the Spirit in its interpretation and application. While pastors and teachers hold much respect among Baptists, the place of authority is found in God's Word alone. While theologians and the history of the church are influential, each individual is enjoined to wrestle with the Scriptures himself and seek the face of God concerning its meaning and application. Each soul is competent to read, hear from God, and apply the edicts of God's Word to his life and conduct.

POLITY

The issue of soul competency plays itself out in matters of church polity as well. As each individual is a priest in his own right, coming to God on his own without any mediator except Christ Jesus (1 Tim. 2:5), so each congregation is free to ferret out the solution to the problems it faces on its own. And while our polity is congregational, Southern Baptists have also been cooperative. We realize that the whole is greater than the sum of its parts, that we can accomplish more by cooperating with people of like doctrine and practice than we can do on our own.

Cooperation must not produce doctrinal compromise. Certainly, fellowship can be withdrawn by other congregations if a local assembly becomes antagonistic to things to which that fellowship of churches adheres. Nevertheless, the withdrawal of official fellowship is not a means of forcing any local congregation to do or to be anything other than what they believe God desires of them.

Confessions of faith have functioned this way in Baptist life. When people divert from these, it is certainly not a matter for official persecution. Baptists have suffered so much in that regard so that they will always oppose oppression in any form. But when individuals have departed from the "faith once delivered to the saints" (Jude 3 KJV), they have withdrawn fellowship, cooperation, and support. Doctrine matters to Baptists. The priesthood of the believers does not mean that "anything goes," theologically speaking.

Our local church here at Wedgwood cooperates with other Baptist churches in our county, state, nation, and world. Each one of these relationships is based on commonality of purpose, practice, and doctrinal convictions. They are voluntary, and any time we feel led, we can cease to cooperate with any of them and they with us. We work together, listen to one another, and pray for each other, but as a healthy extended family, no one tries to dictate to anyone what they must do.

MISSIONS AND EVANGELISM

Baptists today are, more than ever, driven by a desire to reach the world with the Good News of Jesus Christ. We are convinced that Jesus Christ is the only way to the Father (John 14:6) and that, apart from him, no one can be saved (Acts 4:12). Our energies are fired by the Great Commission (Matt. 28:19–20), and we are at our best when we are recruiting, training, strategizing, and reaching out to a lost and dying world. This compassion for the lost has historically been the glue that holds us together and the flame that fires our collective furnace. We are convinced that we have the answer to the world's problems in Jesus Christ, and we are duty-bound to get the message out to those who need it.

A BALANCE OF PASSION AND REASON

Baptists are passionate about their religious convictions. They hold their beliefs deeply. They are willing to fight and die for them, if necessary. Few, if any, have enjoyed the past two decades of conflict over authority and inerrancy. The conflict, however, shows that Baptists are passionate enough about their convictions to contend for them. Our passion is a sign of real life. The only place there is total peace and concord is in a cemetery!

In Christ's letter to the Ephesian church (Rev. 2:1–4), he commends them for their labor, discernment, persistence, and unending courage. What more could God want? "Yet I have this against you . . . You have left your first love"—your passion! Baptists love to sing "I Surrender All" and, in our better moments, we love to live it out.

One of our leading statesman, Vance Havner, was converted in a revival in the mountains of North Carolina. As he recalls it, "If I didn't have much theology in my head, at least I had a lot of doxology in my heart." He had passion.

But I am also a Baptist because they have balanced the leading of their heart, which can often be swayed by circumstance or culture or other unreliable influences, with the edicts of reason. Baptists seek for solid reasons for their convictions and their actions. Like the Tin Man in the *Wizard of Oz*, Baptists are convinced that "you gotta have heart." Hopefully, we are just as concerned about the Scarecrow's lament, "If I only had a brain." Paul's admonition in Colossians 3:23 "Whatsoever you do, do it heartily as to the Lord" is not contrary at all to Peter's reminder to "be ready always to give an answer to every man who asks for a reason (KJV)."

Our minds and our hearts both must be rooted in and subject to God's holy Word.

THE BLESSING OF OUR DIFFERENCES

I am a Baptist by conviction and by choice. But there is a higher, deeper conviction than that which claims my loyalty. By a miraculous working of God I have been born again into the family of faith, the church universal, the Redeemed from every kindred, tribe, nation, and generation.

God has a wonderful fascination with diversity. If you doubt that, consider the untold trillions of snowflakes, each with its unique design. And the body of Christ, though all redeemed by the blood of the Lamb, is wondrous in its incredible diversity.

In the inner cities of the U.S., African-Americans shout their praises to God as their preachers gasp their sermons to a responding congregation. In Austria, believers express their joy accompanied by magnificent pipe organs. I have worshiped in Africa where Christians dance their praises to the King. Saints in India pray with their palms together over their heads, pointing to the Father. Unbelievers point to the thousands of Christian denominations as a reason not to accept Christ. But should we not expect that a God so enamored with diversity would allow for diverse ways to worship and serve him?

For those who love mystery, liturgical churches which specialize in those things abound. For those to whom simple reason appeals most, God has provided churches where texts are analyzed, explained, outlined, projected on screens, and where the nuances of the original languages are scrutinized. Other people are doers, not thinkers. For these God has provided congregations that major on ministry: soup kitchens, counseling centers, free health clinics for the poor as well as clothes closets and twelve-step groups. Still others feel they haven't worshiped unless they have shouted, clapped, and danced their praise and the preacher is hoarse for days. Thank God he has provided for these as well in his body, the church.

Who would drive ten or twenty miles to a Baskin-Robbins ice cream parlor and only order vanilla? No! We love to choose from rocky road to peppermint pistachio to chocolate mint! We all love variety. Rather than complain about the differences in the body of Christ, let's celebrate them!

"THAT THEY MAY BE ONE"

While we celebrate our differences, Jesus, on his way to the cross, prayed earnestly that all his followers would be one, "that the world may believe that thou hast sent me" (John 17:21 KJV). Here is unsettling news. Southern Baptists, for all their resources and organizational power, will never reach the world for Christ. Neither will the Pentecostals or the Methodists, or any other particular corner of the kingdom. If any one of us could do the job, we would have to remove John 17 from the canon of Scripture. No, if and when the world is won to Christ, it will happen when believers of all denominations lay aside (not forget) their differences and bond together under the banner of all those who trust in Christ alone and seek to follow him.

As long as we emphasize our differences and use them as issues for censorship and division, a watching world will scoff at our claims for the King of Love. As long as we speak out to a secular media in condemnation of our brothers in Christ, the world will conclude that Christianity is just another man-made contrivance to inflict misery on others in order to advance personal agendas. I am a Southern Baptist by choice and conviction. I am committed to our doctrine and ministry. But I am also a member of the wider family of God, the body of Christ universal. All who have turned from their sin and trusted Christ as Savior and Lord are my brothers. And though we may disagree on certain particulars, we are family.

Can we not, here and now, purpose in our hearts never publicly to criticize a brother in Christ? Can we not commit ourselves to finding issues of commonality with those of like faith but different denominations? Can we not work together selflessly with all those who name the name of Jesus as Savior and Lord to reach an unbelieving world? The lateness of the hour demands it. The desperation of our generation compels it. The prayer of our Savior himself dictates it. So be it.

PART SIX

THOUGHTS FROM THE FAMILY ROOM

17

EVERYTHING A BAPTIST MOTHER COULD WANT

Donna Ascol

"Why are you a Baptist?" Though I have been in Baptist churches all of my life, until recently no one has ever asked me nor have I paused to ponder that question. My Baptist roots go deep. My maternal great-grandparents and grandparents were Baptist. My Baptist parents raised six children, all of whom have professed faith in Christ, have been baptized as believers, and are active in Baptist churches. I have a brother who is a Baptist student minister and cousins who are serving in Asia, Great Britain, and Africa with the Southern Baptist International Mission Board.

I married a Baptist pastor, who was raised in a Baptist home, and we are now raising our six children in the Baptist faith. It would be easy to plead tradition, convenience, or even laziness as a reason for remaining a Baptist. But the truth is, I just cannot help myself, I am a Baptist by conviction.

SCRIPTURE

This conviction is founded on the fact that Baptists have always been a people of the Book, a confessing people, a people who openly believe the Bible. As R. M. Dudley, a noted nineteenth-century Baptist pastor, editor, and professor stated, "The fundamental principle of the Baptists is their belief in the supreme authority and absolute sufficiency of the Holy Scriptures; and their separate existence is the practical and logical result of their attempt to apply this principle in all matters of religion. This is the bedrock on which the denomination rests."[1]

J. M. Frost, founding president of the Baptist Sunday School Board echoes that sentiment: "Baptists at different times in their history, and to meet impending claims and conflicts, have issued their confession of faith, and have always given this primal and decisive place to the Word of God as their one authority. This is the bedrock of their faith, the one rule of their practice."[2]

As a mother of six, my belief system and denominational standing do have an impact on future generations. This sense of responsibility increases for one, like myself, who is a home-schooling mom. My teaching design has the ring of eternity in it. I do not want my children simply to "fall" into the Baptist beliefs and confessions out of tradition or convenience. Rather, I want them to embrace Baptist principles out of commitment to truth. We have a rich denominational history and a promising denominational future, and I would love to bequeath this heritage and prospect to my children and grandchildren. I desire to teach them about great Baptist men and women of the faith who believed the Bible and were satisfied in the roles laid out for them.

They need to know about people such as Charles H. Spurgeon, William Carey, Adoniram and Ann Judson, Lottie Moon, John Broadus, and John Bunyan. I want my daughters enthusiastically to embrace their calling to be women wholly devoted to Jesus Christ like their heroic Baptist sisters who have gone before them. I want my son to be inspired and challenged by the testimonies of former Southern Baptist statesmen like James P. Boyce, P. H. Mell, John Dagg, and other founders of the SBC.

I am persuaded by J. P. Greene, who in 1923 ended three decades of service as the president of William Jewel College in Liberty, Missouri, when he issues this challenge to all Baptists: "We have an honorable and even glorious history, and our children should know it. We keep them in touch with our family history; why not also with our denominational history? . . . If they knew their own history, they would rejoice to belong to such a noble company."[3]

I want my children and their children to believe that the Bible is the unchanging Word of God. I yearn for them to be committed to spreading the saving message of the Book through the work of missions and evangelism, and to be submissive to the authority of the Bible both in doctrine and practice.

My earliest introduction to the Baptist life came through the study of God's Word in Sunday school. I grew up believing that the Sunday school hour was a necessary, integral, and nonnegotiable part of our Lord's Day observance. My parents faithfully accompanied their six children each week to the teaching hour prior to worship. It was during this time that many loving teachers opened God's Word to me. It was in Sunday school that I learned to love and revere the Scripture as God's holy and unchanging Word. I discovered the exciting and adventurous stories of the Old Testament. I was taught the importance of the observance of the Ten Commandments. I was captivated by the God-breathed words of the major and minor prophets, the poetry of the Psalms, and the wisdom of the Proverbs. I was inspired by the testimony of the apostles in the Book of Acts and in their letters.

As I have matured in my faith and, through the ministry of God's Word and Spirit, discovered more of his supremacy over all of life, I have come to a deeper appreciation of the role that Sunday school played in my early years. It was there that I was taught from both the Old and the New Testaments that God has a people whom he loves and calls his own. As I continued to study the biblical teachings on God's sovereignty in creation, providence, and redemption, I realized that these grand themes were first introduced to me by faithful Baptist Sunday school teachers.

More importantly, my Sunday school experiences and the many sermons I heard as a child were used of God to convince me that I was a sinner who needed Jesus Christ as my Savior. It was in Sunday school that my mind was engaged to know who God is, who I am before him, and what I must do. Coupled with that, it was my mother's Baptist experience that convinced her that her daughter needed to be converted. She was under no delusions (nor was I) that the fact that I was a child of believers in any way made me automatically a child of God. I am grateful that Baptists have historically placed a strong emphasis on teaching the Word of God through the means of Sunday morning Bible study. My life has been forever changed by the message of the gospel of Jesus Christ which was taught to me by my mother and my Sunday school teachers.

Currently, I have the privilege of teaching God's Word to a Sunday school class of teenagers at my church. It is a job that makes me tremble. To help these young people formulate their thoughts of God and to teach them about his purposes is a responsibility I find very sobering. I am grateful that I belong to a Baptist church that puts primary emphasis on the authority of the Scripture, thereby encouraging me to approach my task with great confidence. There is no hesitation on my part that what God's Word says is true and right and relevant to these young people. T. T. Eaton, a nineteenth-century Baptist pastor and editor of the *Western Recorder,* the Baptist paper in Kentucky, said it well: "What we must believe, what we must be, and what we must do, are set forth in the Bible with a clearness and a completeness found nowhere else. Not a doctrine, nor an aspiration, nor a duty is omitted."[4]

EVANGELISM AND MISSIONS

Because I am a Baptist and do believe that the Scripture is the supreme and infallible rule for my life, I can trust what it says about evangelism and missions. Baptists believe in missions. They have a long-standing and constantly developing system of sending the gospel into the entire world. From my first recollections of church life I have known that evangelism and missions are important to Baptists. I have been involved in various mission organizations such as Girls in Action, Acteens and Woman's Missionary Union.

Grace Baptist Church in Cape Coral, Florida, where I am a member, is a missionary church. Because my pastor has such an acute interest in evangelism and missions and desires to see God's Word spread, he has whetted our appetites to pray for the work of Christ around the world. As we have prayed, we have been led to support, teach, and encourage those who are called into missionary work. We recently sent one of our finest families to a country in central Asia where they are today trying to proclaim the gospel among an unreached people group. Our goal as a Baptist church is not only to pray but also to send our very best as our representatives into the uttermost parts of the world.

As a Baptist I have been taught and believe that every Christian ought to be actively involved in spreading the gospel. I agree with Curtis Lee Law's observation, stated in an article he wrote while pastoring the First Baptist Church of Baltimore, when he said, "The clearest vision that the world has of God is in the life of God's representatives. When the world shall see the Christ life in us, then will the Father be glorified."[5]

BELIEVER'S BAPTISM

One of the most distinguishing principles of our faith is the doctrine of believer's baptism. As a Baptist, I have never doubted the biblical basis for my baptism. I am convinced by Scripture that only those who are saved by God's grace are scriptural candidates for baptism. In Romans 6:4, Paul says,

"Therefore we were buried with Him through baptism into death, that just as Christ was raised from the dead by the glory of the Father, even so we also should walk in newness of life" (NKJV). Newness of life can only mean one thing—a life that has been changed. Baptism, in the New Testament, is an external sign of an internal work of grace already attained in the heart of the believer.

Consider the account of the Ethiopian eunuch in Acts 8. His baptism was warranted only after he had professed his belief in the Lord Jesus Christ: "Now as they went down the road, they came to some water. And the eunuch said, 'See, here is water. What hinders me from being baptized?' Then Philip said, 'If you believe with all your heart, you may.' And he answered and said, 'I believe that Jesus Christ is the Son of God.' So he commanded the chariot to stand still. And both Philip and the eunuch went down into the water, and he baptized him" (Acts 8:36–38 NKJV).

The same is true for the Philippian jailer and his household, who were baptized because they believed. This connection is sometimes missed if the account is not read in its entirety. Acts 16:30–33 (NKJV) says: "And he [the jailer] brought them out and said, 'Sirs, what must I do to be saved?' So they [Paul and Silas] said, 'Believe on the Lord Jesus Christ, and you will be saved, you and your household.' Then they spoke the word of the Lord to him and to all who were in his house. And he took them the same hour of the night and washed their stripes. And immediately he and all his family were baptized."

These four verses on their own might be used to support the baptism of unbelieving children who belong to believing parents. But when verse 34 is included in the account, it becomes clear that the ones who were baptized with the jailer also believed with him: "Now when he had brought them into his house, he set food before them; and he rejoiced having believed in God with all his household."

As J. G. Bow, author of *What Baptists Believe and Why They Believe It,* rightly puts it, "There is not the slightest evidence that anyone received the ordinance of baptism who did not profess faith in Christ; hence Baptists have ever held to believer's baptism."[6] Baptism is an act of obedience to the Scripture in response to the authoritative command of Christ. "Go therefore and make disciples of all the nations, baptizing them in the name of the Father and of the Son and of the Holy Spirit" (Matt. 28:19 NKJV).

I do not believe in baptismal regeneration nor do I believe that the baptism of an infant would bestow any earthly privilege or advantage. It is not essential for salvation. Rather, baptism is a testimony of God's grace in bringing the believer into union with Christ through repentance and faith. It symbolizes this union by depicting burial and resurrection to newness of life.[7] A great blessing effected by baptism of the believer consists of the visible covenanted union with a body of believers on earth.

So, why is all this important to me? Because historically Baptists have held that only those who have a credible profession of faith are candidates for baptism and, consequently, church membership. The new covenant spoken of in Hebrews (8:8–13, 9:15, 10:16–17, etc.) includes only those who know the Lord savingly. If I were not convinced of this, I could easily belong to a conservative Presbyterian or Reformed church. I agree with their regard for the sovereignty of God and their high view of worship, but I do not agree with their view of the covenant and how that applies to our children. Like my mother before me, I realize that my children need to be converted. I too am under no delusion that my child because of his or her standing in the Ascol home will be made a child of God. It is all of grace. I do not find presumptive regeneration, infant baptism, or confirmation in the New Testament.

What I do find is that there is only one entrance into the New Testament church and that is through believer's baptism. As Acts 2:41 says, "Then those who gladly received his word were baptized; and that day about three thousand souls were added to them" (NKJV).

Baptism is not the most important doctrine for Christians, including Baptists. It is important enough, however, to warrant a separate congregational identity. It is an ordinance of Christ, and a person should take seriously how baptism is to be administered. Differences among Christians on this issue are unfortunate and inevitable in a fallen world. As J. C. Ryle, a famous nineteenth-century Anglican bishop, laments, "The difference is a melancholy proof of the blindness and infirmity which remain even in the saints of God."[8] Nevertheless, maintaining a separate identity because of our insistence on believer's baptism is justifiable.

Consider the testimony of Ann Hasseltine Judson, wife of Adoniram Judson and missionary to Burma. As a newly appointed Congregational missionary, her study of the Scripture led her to forsake pedobaptism and embrace believer's baptism. In her journal, dated 1812, she wrote:

> *Sept. 1.* I have been examining the subject of baptism for some time past, and, contrary to my prejudices and my wishes, am compelled to believe, that believer's baptism alone is found in Scripture. If ever I sought to know the truth; if

> ever I looked up to the Father of lights; if ever I gave up myself to the inspired word, I have done so during this investigation. And the result is, that, laying aside my former prejudices and systems, and fairly appealing to the Scriptures, I feel convinced that nothing really can be said in favour of infant baptism or sprinkling. We expect soon to be baptized. O may our hearts be prepared for that holy ordinance! and as we are baptized into a profession of Christ, may we put on Christ, and walk worthy of the high vocation wherewith we are called. But in consequence of our performance of this duty, we must make some very painful sacrifices. We must be separated from our dear missionary associates, and labour alone in some isolated spot. We must expect to be treated with contempt, and cast off by many of our American friends—forfeit the character we have in our support, wherever we are stationed.[9]

The Judsons submitted to believer's baptism by immersion in Calcutta on September 6, 1812. William Ward, a colleague of William Carey, conducted the service. It was costly for the Judsons to become Baptists. They had to give up their association with their own mission support group and seek support elsewhere. It was a great step of faith that was born out of deep conviction.

REGENERATE CHURCH MEMBERSHIP

Of similar importance to me in my Baptist walk is the often neglected principle of a regenerate church membership. Baptists have historically believed that the membership of their churches should be made up only of regenerated, converted people. Unfortunately, the concept and practice of a regenerate church membership has been practically abandoned in many contemporary Baptist churches.

Membership today has been so substantially diluted in many Baptist churches that anyone who desires to join need only walk an aisle or express a desire to be accepted as a member. When the unregenerate are allowed to join the church, four things often occur; the unregenerate person is misguided spiritually, the church is seriously weakened, church discipline is overlooked, and the cause of Christ is undermined. It is hard to distinguish some Baptist churches from social clubs because they are filled with unconverted people. A study done by the North American Mission Board in 1996 found that the typical Southern Baptist Church had only 30 percent of its total membership who actually attended the worship service on Sunday morning. This is a significant and sad discovery. True converts desire to be under the preaching and teaching of God's Word.

Tom Ascol, my husband, has observed, "Those who do not demonstrate a real, saving relationship with Christ and who show no interest in growing spiritually have no business being received into a church's membership. This is not false idealism nor an argument for perfection in Christians. Rather, it is a simple recognition that where there is life, there will be at least some demonstration of it. . . . Spiritual fruit cannot be cultivated where there is no spiritual life. What does not exist cannot be 'formed' or shaped."[10] Belief in and application of the principle of a regenerate church membership will lead a church to exercise preventive or front-end discipline. This is essential before corrective discipline, as outlined in Matthew 18:15–20, 1 Corinthians 5, and other places in the New Testament, can ever be restored.

Edward Hiscox, author of *The New Directory for Baptist Churches,* describes what should be the distinctive characteristics of a Baptist church and its members this way: "They [Baptists] hold that a church is a company of disciples, baptized on a profession of their faith in Christ, united in covenant to maintain the ordinances of the Gospel, and the public worship of God; to live godly lives, and to spread abroad the knowledge of Christ as the Saviour of men."[11] Obviously, this would be difficult to accomplish in a church filled with unregenerate people. He further comments on the class of people that should be admitted as members: "Baptists say that godly persons, baptized on a profession of faith, are the only proper and suitable persons. That all others should be denied admission, and if already within the Church should be cast out."[12]

The newly revised *Baptist Faith and Message* speaks of the church as the body of Christ consisting of all of the redeemed of the ages, believers from every tribe, and tongue, and people and nation. While church membership should be very broad in its inclusion of every race and tribe of believers, it should be very narrow in its exclusion of all but professing believers. To do otherwise would be to diminish the separation between the world and the church.

J. G. Bow reiterates this point by saying, "The Churches of Christ are not reformatory schools, are not organizations into which natural men are to be taken and by the process of law, ceremony, or ordinance made children of God, but each ought to be a congregation of God's people, separated from the world. No unconverted man or woman can meet the duties and obligations of a church member, and should not assume such responsibilities."[13]

CONCLUSION

So why am I a Baptist? Pastor Dudley expresses well what is in my heart: "I am not a Baptist because Baptists practice restricted communion, or immersion, or refuse infant baptism. I am a Baptist because by the fundamental principle of Protestantism I am bound by the Word of God in all matters of faith and practice."[14] The emphasis on teaching, the love of missions and evangelism, the doctrine of believer's baptism and the historical commitment to a regenerate church membership all revert to a belief in the centrality of Scripture alone. I will say it again, Baptists are a people of the Book.

Article I of the *Baptist Faith and Message* concerning "The Scriptures" was recently and appropriately strengthened by the 2000 Southern Baptist Convention. It reaffirms our desire to live under the lordship of Jesus Christ by submitting to the authority of the Bible.

> The Holy Bible was written by men divinely inspired and is God's revelation of himself to man. It is a perfect treasure of divine instruction. It has God for its author, salvation for its end, and truth, without any mixture of error, for is matter. Therefore, all Scripture is totally true and trustworthy. It reveals the principles by which God judges us, and therefore is, and will remain to the end of the world, the true center of Christian union, and the supreme standard by which all human conduct, creeds and religious opinions should be tried. All Scripture is a testimony to Christ, who is himself the focus of divine revelation.[15]

God desires every area of my life to be governed by his Word. As I pursue this goal through the various callings that God has placed on me as a wife, mother, and teacher, I derive both strength and encouragement from fellowship with the people known as Baptists.

18

A BAPTIST'S INHERITANCE

Denise George

Not long ago I read an article about the child-rearing plans of billionaire computer genius Bill Gates, arguably the richest man in the world. Speaking of his wife Melinda and their daughter Jennifer, Gates said that Melinda had wanted to raise their daughter in the Catholic faith. But, Gates said, his wife "offered me a deal." If Gates would go to church he could bring up their daughter in whatever religion he chose. Gates said he was tempted by the suggestion because his religious background, Congregationalism, is preferable to Catholicism since it "has less theology and all."

Still, he hasn't yet taken up the offer. "Just in terms of allocation of time resources, religion is not very efficient," he said. "There's a lot more I could be doing on Sunday morning." One day, Jennifer Gates will inherit her father's money. She will probably become the wealthiest woman in the world. By the world's standards, Bill Gates will have left her a fortune.

By those standards, I have a modest background, but by a higher standard, I have been blessed beyond measure. I was born to Baptist grandparents. "Mama" and "Papa" educated me in the Baptist faith better than any seminary professor ever could. During the first years of my life, I soaked up like a sponge their teachings on Scripture. They prayed constantly—both with me and for me. I saw their faithfulness to missions and to reaching out to others who were hurting. I heard them tell everybody they met about Jesus, their Savior. They gave me the strong biblical foundation I stand on today. In short, they left me a great inheritance.

I appreciate my faithful, loving grandparents, George and Alice Williams, who first introduced me to Baptist beliefs, who took me to church and Vacation Bible School, and who taught me about Jesus. I was fortunate to be "born" into a Baptist home. Throughout these many years, I have decided to "stay" Baptist mainly because:

- I have studied and compared a variety of denominations, and I have found Baptists to be most consistent with Scripture.
- I appreciate the denominational governance—the autonomy of each Baptist congregation under the lordship of Christ.
- I love the way Baptists emphasize missions and practice Jesus' Great Commission.
- I am truly proud of my Baptist roots and all those saints who have helped place my feet on solid spiritual ground. I have also discovered several things about my Baptist heritage that cause me to rejoice in how rich an inheritance I have received.

BAPTISTS PRAY

Whenever I close my eyes, I can still see the slender form of my white-haired grandfather kneeling in prayer beside the family-room chair. It is one of my earliest and sweetest memories. So regularly did he pray for others that the chair's cloth arm was worn bare in the spot where he placed his hand.

My grandparents spent most of their prayer time praying for others. As a skinny, pigtailed girl, I remember my grandfather telling me that he and my grandmother "called my name every day in prayer." After I grew up and moved far away from their old white-gabled house in the South, I depended on their daily prayers. When I married, had children, moved around the world, and faced a legion of daily decisions and pressures, I was always aware of, and comforted by, their loving, prayerful petitions for me. I now look back and realize that those were the dearest, most caring words Papa and Mama could ever say to me. Until their deaths, in my mid-thirties, I always knew that no matter where I was, no matter what situation I faced, no matter how I hurt or grieved, somewhere on a little farm in Rossville, Georgia, my grandparents were praying for me. It brought me a comfort and strength like nothing else could.

My grandparents believed deeply in prayer. "'Nisey," they told me constantly, "prayer is powerful. Pray about everything." They taught me that prayer isn't simply something we do. Prayer is a relationship with God through Jesus Christ. They were serious about prayer. "The prayer of a righteous man is powerful and effective," Papa told me (James 5:16b RSV). He and I often searched the Scriptures together. "Devote yourselves to prayer, being watchful and thankful," Papa quoted the apostle Paul (Col. 4:2 RSV). "Pray continually," he taught me (1 Thess. 5:17 RSV). "Give thanks in all circumstances, for this is God's will for you in Christ Jesus," he said (1 Thes. 5:18 RSV). No God-given gift, from their garden's bounty to their grandchildren's good health, ever escaped their prayers of thanksgiving.

We Baptists believe that God hears our prayers. We believe God is omnipresent—that no inch of the universe is beyond his grasp. We believe God is omniscient—that God knows all things, past, present, and future. We believe in God's omnipotence—his mighty power. My grandparents taught me about God's omnipresence, omniscience, and omnipotence when they taught me, as a small child, to pray. I learned about God when I watched them live a life enveloped by prayer. And from their prayers and devotions, I came to love the God who cares for me, who hears my prayers, who is always a whisper away, and who is powerful enough to answer my prayers.

BAPTISTS BELIEVE IN THE CROSS

In the fifth grade, Mr. Pate (not his real name), my band teacher, caught me chewing bubble gum in first period homeroom. The punishment? Paddling. I had never been paddled before. So sad and timid, I didn't make waves in school. I didn't even make small splashes. I stood in front of Mr. Pate that terrible morning, my back straight, my chin up, my hand outstretched, and my pride waning. Tears welled in my eyes. To keep from crying, I stared hard at the new 1960 penny in my loafers. I wanted to run, scream, faint, anything but stand beneath Mr. Pate's wooden paddle with my trembling hand outstretched. My peers surrounded me as Mr. Pate questioned me: "Denise," he shouted. "Do you know what you've done wrong?"

My face flushed red. Timidity tied my tongue. One renegade tear toppled down my chin. I couldn't make a sound. "Yes! Mr. Pate!" I wanted to scream, but couldn't utter a sound. "I did wrong! I deserve this spanking! I knew the school's rule about chewing bubble gum when I popped two pink square blocks of it in my mouth. But everybody else was chewing it, and I wanted to fit in!"

Mr. Pate raised his paddle high in the air. I closed my eyes. That infamous wooden paddle had made even sophisticated sophomores scream for mercy. Just as the paddle started its downswing toward the surface of my skin, I heard someone speak up.

"I'll take her spanking," said a tall high school senior. "She's already been punished enough!" I couldn't believe my ears. This teenager whom I had never seen before looked at me and kindly smiled. Then he stepped up to Mr. Pate and outstretched his right hand. Surprised, Mr. Pate said: "OK. I'll paddle you instead. But," he added, "it's gonna hurt!"

With a profound force, Mr. Pate pounded the young man's open palm. Upon impact, a piece of the paddle broke off and bounced on the floor. The young man flinched, looked the teacher right in the eye, and again outstretched his flaming palm. Tears triumphed as I ran from the room. I would never again see this young man. I didn't even know his name.

That afternoon after school, I called Papa and told him about the high school senior who took my spanking. "That's amazing, 'Nisey!" he exclaimed. Then Papa used the incident as a teaching opportunity. "Run get your Bible," he told me.

When I returned, he told me to look up John 3:16. I read it to him from the old King James Version. "For God so loved the world, that he gave his only begotten Son, that whosoever believeth in him should not perish, but have everlasting life."

"We've read that verse a hundred times, Papa!" I told him. "What's that got to do with the paddling today at school?"

"Just think about it," he said. "You and I both are guilty of sin. We are the ones God has every right to punish." His voice grew excited. "You see, God's only Son, Jesus, stepped in front of that paddle—just like that high school senior did—and took our punishment for us! That's just what he did! Jesus took the paddling so you and I wouldn't have to! That's the whole meaning of the cross!"

Vicarious atonement! All at once, insight dawned, and I understood why Jesus died on that cross! He died for ME! The cross must become the center of my faith, Papa told me. I would one day learn from brilliant seminary professors all about original sin, expiation and propitiation, justification by faith alone, and penal substitution through God's own Son. But no seminary lecture could have ever brought me such deep theological understanding as Mr. Pate and his paddle.

BAPTISTS BELIEVE THE BIBLE

Mama and Papa both lived long enough to see the birth of my first child. My husband, Timothy, and I waited eleven long years for this little boy. When Christian Timothy was born, we entered into a whole new world! Neither Timothy nor I had ever changed a diaper! We knew nothing about taking care of a baby physically. But our Baptist grandparents had taught us much about taking care of a baby spiritually. They had passed on to us a great inheritance—deep love, respect, and reverence for the Bible, God's holy Word.

I remember the moment newborn Christian arrived in his new home. Timothy carried him into our bedroom and sat down in a comfortable chair. With noticeable new-daddy clumsiness, Timothy held our new son in his arms. He opened our family Bible to Psalm 1 and began to read God's Word to Christian.

"Blessed is the man that walketh not in the counsel of the ungodly," Timothy read, "nor standeth in the way of sinners, nor sitteth in the seat of the scornful. But his delight is in the law of the Lord; and in his law doth he meditate day and night (KJV)."

At three days old, Christian could hardly yet focus his eyes, but Timothy read nonetheless. After reading the psalm, Timothy and I placed our hands on our sleeping son, and together we prayed. As far as I am concerned, that moment together was the most important moment of Christian's life. For we had given him the very best we could give him. We had introduced him to God's Word, just as Mama and Papa had done many years before. The next evening, Christian again enveloped in his daddy's strong arms, Timothy read Psalm 2 and we prayed together as family.

Twenty-three months later, we welcomed our daughter, Alyce Elizabeth, into our family. Her first night home from the hospital, Timothy again turned to Psalm 1 and began reading. "Blessed is the man that walketh not in the counsel of the ungodly . . ." Then, as father, mother, son, and daughter—our completed family—we prayed.

I hope one day Christian and Alyce will study deeply the issues of scriptural inspiration and of the Bible's inerrant and authoritative nature. And as they study these concepts of faith, I hope they will look back and remember Mom and Dad and readings from the Psalms. I pray that I, too, can pass on that great biblical inheritance to my own children that my grandparents so faithfully passed on to me.

BAPTISTS CARE ABOUT HURTING PEOPLE

As a youngster I spent some wonderful summers with my grandparents on their small Georgia farm. On hot afternoons I would lie down in front of the big noisy fan in their family room and take in all the delicious smells of the kitchen. Chicken fried in big iron skillets. Biscuits and pound cakes baked in the oven. Homegrown ears of silver white corn boiled on the stove. My missions-minded grandmother spent most of her life in her kitchen.

She took seriously Jesus' command to feed the hungry "least of these." She spent long hot summer days at her stove, her frail arms stirring homemade soup and ladling it into big Mason jars to be delivered by my grandfather to the community's needy families. By evening time, Mama had fed the poor and hungry and sick of the whole neighborhood. I watched her missionary heart reach out to others, teaching them about Jesus, handing out Bibles, giving warm blankets to street people. She daily put into action Jesus' commission to reach out to the world in his saving name.

One hot afternoon, as I sprawled out in front of the fan, I heard a knock at the back door. Mama opened the screen door to a ragged little girl, dirty and barefoot. When Mama smiled at her, the girl held out two worn dishtowels with trembling hands. "Mrs. Williams," she whispered, "I'm selling these dishtowels. Would you like to buy one?"

I expected Mama's immediate answer. "Yes, I certainly would," she told the girl. "I'll buy them both." When Mama paid her for the towels, I saw her put extra coins in the girl's hand. "And this money is just for you," I heard her say.

My grandparents taught me ecclesiology—they simply took me to church with them. They taught me about ethics and concupiscence—they simply told me what the Bible said about right and wrong, and how we humans often preferred wrong over right. They taught me about Christology and conversion—they introduced me to Jesus. They taught me the truths of *creatio ex nihilo* when they told me that, from nothing, God created the world and everything in it.

When Mama held my hand and we walked and prayed in her flower gardens, she taught me about the cosmological argument. She said: "'Nisey, God created these roses, and he makes them grow and bloom." Mama didn't need to explain to me the Chalcedonian formula. She simply told me: "Jesus is all human, and, at the same time, Jesus is all God." It was enough. I understood it. I believed it.

And Mama taught me to live the faith. I simply watched her day after day in her kitchen canning vegetable soup and loading it into Papa's Chevrolet. She showed me that as Baptists, we take seriously Jesus' command to "go and make disciples of all nations, baptizing them in the name of the Father and of the Son and of the Holy Spirit, and teaching them . . ." (Matt. 28:19–20b RSV). She showed me that we obey his commission when we reach out to others next door with our heart and our homemade soup.

Today I am grateful to the Cooperative Program of the Southern Baptist Convention for the ways it sends missionaries all over the world to reach out to the lost, the hungry, and the hurting in Christ's name. Through my prayers and gifts, I intend always to help support this wonderful program. On a much larger scale, they do just what my grandmother did during the long years of her life.

I think a lot about young Jennifer Gates. I pray that the Lord would bless her with more than just money, which is temporary and fleeting. Mama and Papa were not billionaires. They didn't have even a fraction of Bill Gates's money. In fact, they often counted out pennies to make a purchase. But how much richer is the inheritance they left me—my Baptist roots—an inheritance far more valuable than mere money.

PART SEVEN

THOUGHTS FROM THE PROFESSOR'S LECTERN

19

A MERE CHRISTIAN, AND A BAPTIST TOO

Douglas Blount

Asked about his religious commitments, a fellow graduate student—who subsequently became, and remains, a dear friend—answered, "I am what C. S. Lewis called a 'mere Christian.'" Motivated both by a desire to lay aside any encumbrance to unity among God's children and by an awareness of his own fallibility in doctrinal matters, my friend had decided not to affiliate himself with any particular Christian denomination, group, or sect. He attempted to hold only those beliefs found in the earliest Christian creeds, beliefs "common to nearly all Christians at all times."[1]

While I appreciated both his concern for unity and his theological humility, I nonetheless thought my friend's reluctance to identify with a particular community ill-advised. After all, in the preface to *Mere Christianity,* Lewis himself writes: "I hope no reader will suppose that 'mere' Christianity is here put forward as an alternative to the creeds of the existing communions—as if a man could adopt it in preference to Congregationalism or Greek Orthodoxy or anything else. It is more like a hall out of which doors open into several rooms. If I can bring anyone into that hall I shall have done what

I attempted. But it is in the rooms, not in the hall, that there are fires and chairs and meals. The hall is a place to wait in, a place from which to try the various doors, not a place to live in. For that purpose the worst of the rooms (whichever that may be) is, I think, preferable."[2]

Of course, it seems obviously important that one not confuse one's own denominational context with *the* church, as if no one outside it belongs to Christ. But it also seems important—though perhaps less obviously so—that those who remain in the merely Christian hall cut themselves off from the very fellowship which my friend desired to promote. For fellowship comes within community, and Christian communities are located within Lewis's rooms, not his hall. Nowhere else can one find the warmth, rest, and nourishment which come within those rooms, within those "existing communions."

Now I find myself within a particular corner of the room called "Baptist," a corner reserved for Southern Baptists, among whom I count myself. And I have been asked to discuss why I am in that corner. Presumably, in so doing, I am to give reasons for my Baptist commitments, reasons which explain my having such commitments. But, of course, explanations work at many different levels.

On one level, for instance, my Baptist commitments can be explained quite accurately by an appeal to God's sovereignty: *in His providential wisdom, it pleased God to arrange the world so that I am a Southern Baptist.* While such an explanation is true, it seems nonetheless unhelpful for at least two reasons. First, except for saying something about my view of God's relation to the world and events in it, an explanation given in terms of divine sovereignty is not very informative; second, and perhaps more to the point, such an explanation makes for an unsatisfactorily short discussion.

On another level, one might explain my Baptist commitments in terms of certain sociological facts: *I was raised in a Baptist home, attended Baptist churches from an early age, associated primarily with other Baptists as a youth, and so on.*[3] Given my lack of sociological training, however, I am ill-equipped to offer such an explanation. What, then, shall I do? Well, if I am to explain my Baptist commitments in an informative way without engaging in unwarranted speculation, it will be by identifying those features of Baptist thought which I find most attractive. In what follows, I seek to do just that. Before doing so, however, I acknowledge a few of the debts I have incurred while sojourning in the Baptist room.

PARENTAL INFLUENCE

Chief among mortals to whom I owe my faith are my parents. Without their commitment to raising their children in the church, only God knows where I now would be. I remember very distinctly responding to the love of one who gave his Son for my wickedness. At seven years old, I was no theologian, but I understood that I was wicked (though, of course, not *how* wicked) and that God had allowed Jesus to die in my place. I placed my trust in God because I could imagine no other response to such love. And, of course, whatever understanding of such things I had at that time came primarily from my parents.

Several years later, our family moved from Louisville, Kentucky, to Dallas, Texas. This proved to be particularly hard on my brother, in his early teens at the time. (I was young enough to remain unaffected by the change.) Well, as we looked for a home among the Baptist churches in the area, neighbors invited us to visit First Baptist Church, Dallas. Now, while my parents were pleased to visit FBC, they had no interest in joining so large a church. But there we found a youth program in which my brother and I felt almost immediately at home. And so, much to our surprise, we became members of First Baptist Church, Dallas, within months of moving to Texas.

This was extremely significant for my spiritual development. At the church's summer youth camp, I developed a strong interest in apologetics—the practice of defending the faith in order to encourage believers in their faith and remove stumbling blocks to faith for unbelievers. Our camp pastor that year was Josh McDowell. He devoted one of the evening sessions to evidence for Christ's resurrection. That session introduced me to apologetics, and I soon read whatever I could by Lewis, McDowell, and Francis Schaeffer. At youth camp, I also answered a call to vocational ministry. In my case, the call to ministry came not by way of mystical experience, but rather by way of a settled conviction—presumably brought about by the Holy Spirit—that my professional life was to be spent serving the church.

Eventually, the interest in apologetics combined with the call to vocational ministry and experiences in college to produce a commitment to training ministers not only to think Christianly themselves but also to help those to whom they minister do so as well. As a freshman in college, I saw a number of friends lose their faith. Some of these literally abandoned the faith; others simply ceased taking the faith seriously, refusing to allow it any practical significance in their lives. Invariably, it seemed, these friends had been raised in the church and taught *what* to think about the faith, but they had not been taught *how* to think about it. Consequently, they were particularly vulnerable to intellectual challenges to Christianity encountered in the classroom.

Such vulnerability seemed—and continues to seem—to me wholly unnecessary. If I was not as vulnerable to such challenges as some of my friends, the credit for that fact belongs primarily to my youth minister at First Baptist Church—Robert Jeffress, now pastor of First Baptist Church, Wichita Falls, Texas—who worked hard to ground the church's youth in the faith. Seeing friends lose their faith made a deep impression on me and led to the professional commitment mentioned above.

HISTORY AND PHILOSOPHY

Given my interest in apologetics, history was an obvious choice for undergraduate study. Along the way, however, I began taking courses in philosophy, a discipline for which I developed more than a passing interest. While some see philosophy as antithetical to Christian faith, this seems to me clearly mistaken. After all, a significant period of Western intellectual history was dominated by Christian philosophers such as Augustine and Anselm. Of course, these philosophers were also theologians, a fact which belies modern attempts to draw a precise line of demarcation between philosophy and theology.

Still, since the beginning of the Enlightenment, philosophy as a discipline *has* grown increasingly hostile to Christianity. Here one only need look at the procession from Locke to Hume to Kant to Hegel to Nietzsche. And, of course, bad philosophy begets bad theology. It is no accident that the German theologians of the mid-nineteenth and early twentieth centuries worked in a climate heavily influenced by Kant and Hegel. But it does not follow from this that Christians ought to avoid serious philosophical reflection. Our response to faith*less* thinking should be faith*ful* thinking, not no thinking.

Although many facets of Baptist thought present themselves as candidates for discussion, I shall emphasize the two characteristics of Southern Baptists which seem to me most important—our commitments to missions and to the authority (and, by implication, the inerrancy) of the Bible. One of the first actions of the newly constituted Southern Baptist Convention in 1845 was to form two mission agencies—one for domestic missions (known now as the North American Mission Board), the other for foreign missions (known now as the International Mission Board).[4] And while much else has changed since 1845, the Baptist commitment to missions—to proclaiming the gospel of

Christ to all people—remains undiminished. Indeed, one might say that missions is the SBC's *raison d'être,* our reason for being. It unites us.

But, contrary to what some have said, it cannot be the *only* thing that unites us. For, of course, common mission implies common message. We cannot be united in proclaiming the gospel of Christ if we are not united in our understanding of what that gospel *is.* If we seek to fulfill the Great Commission, it is because we hold in common certain beliefs (that Jesus speaks with divine authority, that the Bible truly reports his words, that he commanded his followers to make known his words and works to all people, and so on). In other words, our common missionary endeavors arise out of common doctrinal commitments.

Biblical Authority

Among those common doctrinal commitments is belief in the ultimate authority of the Bible. Of course, like the Baptist commitment to missions, the Baptist commitment to biblical authority predates the SBC. Consider, for instance, this excerpt from the Philadelphia Confession of Faith of 1742: "The supreme judge by which all controversies of religion are to be determined, and all decrees of councils, opinions of ancient writers, doctrines of men, and private spirits, are to be examined, and in whose sentence we are to rest, can be no other but the Holy Scripture delivered by the Spirit, into which Scripture so delivered our faith is finally resolved."[5]

That the Bible stands as the ultimate authority follows from the fact that it "has God for its author."[6] Thus, Scripture carries with it the very authority of God himself. That it does so also underlies the Baptist aversion to creeds. For the refusal to place conciliar decrees, ancient opinions, human doctrines, or private judgments above—or even on par with—Scripture results from a commitment to its divine authorship and consequent authority; such decrees, opinions, doctrines, etc. are to *be judged by*—rather than *to judge*—the Bible. As T. T. Eaton states, "'Thus saith the Lord' is an end of all controversy."[7]

Notice that Baptists' anticreedalism arises not out of an extreme optimism about the individual's ability to arrive at truth apart from the community. Rather, it stems from their insistence that the Bible—our community's book—is God-breathed (cf. 2 Tim. 3:16). Thus, one cannot use the popular slogan, "No creed but the Bible," to advance the unbiblical suggestion that, at least when it comes to theology, every man *is* an island. Unfortunately, some have attempted to advance just such a suggestion, arguing for an understanding of the priesthood of all believers according to which each believer is his own priest and thus free to believe whatever he wants to believe.

If such were the meaning of the doctrine of the priesthood of all believers, then one could hardly imagine a more unfortunately named doctrine. For, if one considers, say, Old Testament priests, one sees that they *always* function within community. And, of course, a priest's community always placed significant constraints on what beliefs and practices were open to him. To be sure, what beliefs and practices the community left open to him was no matter of its own arbitrary whims.

Rather, the people of God—whether in the Old Testament or the New—have always sought to regulate themselves according to God's revelation of himself. Still, one who thinks that priesthood involves the freedom to believe (and do) just whatever one wants to believe (and do) knows nothing of the Old Testament understanding of priesthood; in short, a "lone ranger" view of priesthood is a false concept. Being a priest has much more to do with responsibility than with freedom. Views to the contrary seem more in keeping with the rugged individualism of which we Americans are so fond than with biblical notions of priesthood.

Discussing Martin Luther's understanding of the priesthood of all believers, Timothy George writes, "But for Luther the priesthood of all believers did *not* mean, 'I am my own priest.' It meant rather: in the community of saints, God has so tempered the body that we are all priests to each other. We stand before God and intercede for one another, we proclaim God's Word to one another and celebrate His presence among us in worship, praise, and fellowship. Moreover, our priestly ministry does not terminate upon ourselves. It propels us into the world in service and witness."[8]

Likewise, for Calvin, "The priesthood of believers is not a prerogative on which we can rest; it is a commission which sends us forth into the world to exercise a priestly ministry not for ourselves, but for others."[9] So, then, the freedom involved in the priesthood of all believers is the freedom both to serve and to submit to one another.

BIBLICAL INERRANCY

Above I indicated that I believe biblical inerrancy follows from a commitment to biblical authority. By "biblical inerrancy," I mean the view that whatever Scripture affirms is true.[10] Of course, committing oneself to the view that whatever Scripture affirms is true does not amount to committing oneself to any particular view of what it affirms. Inerrantists often disagree among themselves on how particular biblical passages ought to be understood, but this does not undermine their claims to be inerrantists. Now, unless my experience is misleading, many of the objections raised against biblical inerrancy involve confusing the question of whether the text speaks truly with the question of what it says.

As for me, I have difficulty seeing how a person can affirm biblical authority on the one hand and deny biblical inerrancy on the other. Does commitment to ultimate biblical authority not involve commitment to believing whatever the Bible affirms *precisely because* the Bible affirms it? After all, if a person needs further corroboration of the Bible's claims before he accepts them, how can he claim to be treating the Bible authoritatively? Is he not then treating the Bible as *an* authority (i.e., as one source among many) rather than as *the* authority? In a strictly technical sense, I suppose that a person *might* be able to commit himself to believing whatever the Bible says without accepting biblical inerrancy. That is, I suppose that a person *might* be able to act *as if* he believed the Bible to be inerrant without actually believing it to be so. And, in that case, perhaps he would be treating the Bible as *the* authority. But what could motivate a person to take such a position? What would be the advantage of being such an *ersatz* inerrantist?

Of course, the question might be turned on its head: Why be an inerrantist? Here my response is twofold: First, that the Bible has God for its author provides a very strong *prima facie* reason to believe it to be "totally true and trustworthy."[11] Of course, *prima facie* reasons can be overthrown, but I know nothing which overthrows this one. And since this *prima facie* reason remains intact, I find it ultimately compelling. Second, I believe that biblical inerrancy has been the historically dominant position of both Christians in general and Baptists in particular.[12] Now, if within the church there has been a strong consensus about an issue for most of its long history, one needs a very compelling reason to take a contrary view of that issue. In this case, I know no such reason.

Having been asked to explain my Baptist commitments, I have indicated something of what lies behind them. But the reasons given above may be peculiar to me; I do not assume that others share them. Still, they are enough to keep me comfortably ensconced in the Southern Baptist corner.

20

DISTINCTIVELY AND UNASHAMEDLY BAPTIST

Stan Norman

I am a Baptist. I was born into a Baptist family and was raised in Baptist churches. Denominationally, I am a Southern Baptist. I am proud of my Baptist heritage and of my denominational affiliation. I love Baptists and have given my life to assist them in their pursuit of God's will and the extension of his kingdom. Baptist life is all I have ever known.

For many sincere, committed Baptists, these considerations are sufficient reasons to "be a Baptist." And, for most of my early life, these provided adequate justification for me to remain a Baptist. As I grew older, however, I began to reflect critically upon my confessional and denominational heritage. Further, I felt that I needed more rationale for my faith than just the that's-the-way-it's-always-been argument. I was an adult and a student at Southwestern Baptist Theological Seminary before I began seriously to wonder, *Why am I a Baptist?* Other than my upbringing, what reasons did I have for being a Baptist? Furthermore, what does it really mean to be a Baptist? As I reflected on these questions, others also began to surface. For example, are Baptists really that different from other Christians? If so, how?

Over the next few years, these and other questions continued to haunt me. I was, in a sense, suffering from a theological-denominational identity crisis. In addition to this, my life's situation further aggravated my internal conflict. I was serving as a pastor of a Southern Baptist church. I was receiving ministerial training at a Baptist seminary. Yet, being a pastor of a Baptist church and a student at a Baptist school did not provide the answers I longed to have. To make matters worse, my own denomination was engulfed in a struggle that could be described in part as a quest for its own Baptist identity. All realms of my professional, educational, and denominational life seemed consumed with the issue of Baptist identity. I finally determined to embark upon a pilgrimage to discover exactly what makes a Baptist a Baptist.

As I researched and studied Baptist history and theology, I made several important discoveries that strengthened and informed my Baptist faith. I believe that these convictions give Baptists their distinctive theological identity and provide strong, compelling reasons for being a Baptist. I am a Baptist because of what Baptists believe about the Bible, what Baptists believe about the church, what Baptists believe about their Christian mission, and how Baptists express their convictions.

BAPTISTS AND THEIR BIBLE

The first and most important reason why I am a Baptist is found in the Baptist view of the Bible. Along with other Christian denominations, most Baptists appeal to the Bible as their ultimate, or sole, source for theology. Baptists believe that they distinguish themselves from other Christians, however, by claiming a complete dependence upon Scripture as their foundation for belief and practice. Baptists contend that other Christian groups incorporate extrabiblical sources for religious authority, among which are tradition and experience. Baptists contend that they alone consistently regard the Bible as their religious authority.[1]

Biblical authority is of paramount importance for the development of the distinctive theological identity of Baptists. Other forms of religious authority are perceived by Baptists as intrusions into the unique relationship between God and the individual person. Baptists resolutely oppose any authoritative imposition between God and man. Such intrusions interfere with the faith relationship between the Creator and his creation. Because of this aversion, Baptists oppose certain uses of creedal statements. Instead of appealing to creeds as the authoritative basis for theological development, Baptists claim the Scriptures as their rule for all matters of conviction and conduct.

Baptists have always rejected certain forms of creedalism. For example, they reject any creedalism where the government attempts to regulate or coerce religion or faith. Baptists also repudiate any creedalism that elevates manmade interpretations equal to or above biblical authority. They interpret these uses of creeds as attempts to replace God's authority with human authority.

Opposition to these uses of creeds, however, is not the same as a voluntary, conscientious adherence to specific, select doctrines. Baptists have supported the usage of certain statements to express their doctrinal identity and have even used the term *creed* to describe the practice. This form of creedalism does not undermine the superlative position the Bible enjoys in Baptist life. In fact, this expression of creedalism is found in some writings on Baptist distinctives.[2]

Two perspectives on the role of the Scripture are found in Baptist theology. One school of thought contends that the entire Bible is that which gives Baptists their unique theological identity.[3] Another group of Baptists argues that the New Testament is that which is of final religious authority for Baptists.[4]

In light of this, should Baptists affirm the entire Bible or only the New Testament as their final authority? It seems to me that asking this question in isolation from other considerations is rather superficial. The answer must be determined in part by the particular theological issues under consideration. All Baptists in one form or another recognize the inspiration and authority of both Old and New Testaments.

For example, doctrines such as the nature and personhood of God, the doctrine of creation, or the doctrine of sin and the fall of humanity require the authoritative and inspired voice of the Old Testament for theological construction. No Baptist, past or present, would ever discount the value and place of the Old Testament as revelation from God, its vital place in the biblical canon, and its necessity for theological construction. The Old Testament must be used for the doctrinal development of many beliefs that are crucial to the Christian faith.

If, however, the doctrine under consideration is the nature and purpose of the church, then the New Testament certainly provides fuller and clearer revelation on the matter. Baptists do recognize the progressive nature of revelation. Progressive revelation is the notion that later revelation builds upon and expands previous revelation. The New Testament provides revelation on the distinctive traits of Baptists that are not fully developed or revealed in the Old

Testament. In this sense, the New Testament supplies and fulfills what is lacking or unclear in the Old Testament. A regenerate church membership, the ordinances, church polity, and similar doctrines are best constructed and interpreted from the New Testament. As Baptists, we construct our doctrine of the church from the New Testament.

Early Baptists objected strongly to giving equal weight to both Old and New Testaments in the construction of the doctrine of the church. Many of their Christian contemporaries developed their understanding of the nature and purpose of the church primarily from Old Testament texts. Baptists pointed out that the theological rationale for state-established churches and infant baptism was developed in part by subordinating New Testament teachings on the subject to Old Testament texts. The doctrine of a New Testament church for these non-Baptist denominations was therefore built primarily upon Old Testament passages. Baptists rejected outright this method of theological formulation. This helps explain in part why some Baptists were so adamant in using only the New Testament to develop the doctrine of the church.

We would do well to remember and receive the lessons of these early Baptists. I would concur with the notion that the Baptist understanding of the church comes from the New Testament. Most of the distinctive theological identity of Baptists is enmeshed in their doctrine of the church. This affirmation does not, however, exclude or diminish the value of the Old Testament for other doctrinal developments or considerations. With these qualifications in mind, it seems appropriate to say that Baptists find their distinctive theological identity primarily in the New Testament.

BAPTISTS AND THEIR CHURCHES

The second reason why I am a Baptist is because of our ecclesiology. Baptists have always exemplified great concern for the church. Whenever Baptists discuss their unique theological identity, the doctrine of the church will usually surface. One could argue that Baptists best express their theology within the nature and ministries of a Baptist church. In a sense, the distinctive theological identity of Baptists "lives" in the Baptist church. The Baptist church is the most visible expression of those elements that distinguish Baptists from other Christian denominations.

Baptists argue that their unique ecclesiology is most visible in their beliefs of a regenerate church membership, baptism, and congregational polity. These convictions are not in and of themselves peculiar to Baptists. Baptists do claim, however, a distinctive expression of these doctrines in two ways.

First, Baptist churches are distinctive because their ecclesiology is always shaped and directed by the New Testament. Baptists desire to construct a "primitive" church as closely as possible upon the teachings found in the New Testament. Second, Baptists recognize that these doctrinal tenets are found selectively or partially in other Christian denominations. Baptists argue, however, that the combination of these items as an expression of New Testament authority is found only among Baptists.

The doctrine of a regenerate church membership is at the heart of the Baptist conception of a New Testament church. Baptists believe that each congregation most resembles the New Testament model when it is comprised and governed by those who claim Jesus Christ as Lord and Savior and covenant together to practice their faith in voluntary assembly. Baptists contend that a visible, local church should have as members only those persons who have experienced God's grace through faith, who have been baptized, and who freely associate and participate with the local church. Only those who have been regenerated by the Holy Spirit through a personal faith in Christ and who have professed their faith in believer's baptism are scripturally qualified for church membership.

This idea is different from the doctrine of a state church. In this paradigm, all who live within a certain geographical area or those born into certain denominational traditions are members of the church. Conversion is not essential for church membership in this model. For Baptists, this perspective undermines the very heart of the gospel. They argue that only born-again, baptized believers should be members of a church.

The Baptist understanding of a regenerate church membership is not a claim that every Baptist is converted or that every Baptist church has a pure, regenerate membership. Many unconverted people, some honestly misled about their faith and others more deceptively intentioned, are counted among the members of Baptist churches. Further, this emphasis upon a regenerate church membership is not a judgment that all other non-Baptist Christians are unconverted. Baptists do not claim that they are the only Christians in the world. However, the general consensus is that Baptist principles, when consistently applied, will theoretically exclude from church membership all but the converted.

Baptists assert that other denominations affirm theological tenets that allow persons who are not born-again membership in their churches. These churches, by having doctrines that permit the unregenerate into church membership, cannot be considered "pure, spiritual" churches; that is, true

New Testament churches. Baptists contend that their distinctive doctrines logically and inevitably lead a church to be a pure, spiritual body of believers in Christ.

Another evidence found in Baptist thought that demonstrates this concern for the church is the doctrine of believer's baptism. Baptists maintain that the New Testament teaches immersion as the proper mode of baptism. Baptists consistently affirm the importance of the meaning contained in immersion. Also, since the New Testament pattern for baptism is immersion, Baptists believe that the Bible's authority mandates the mode as immersion.

Baptists are also concerned with the meaning of believer's baptism. believer's baptism is the baptism of conscious believers who are capable of exercising their own will. Baptists contend that this meaning of baptism is what distinguishes Baptists from other Christians, specifically those who practice infant baptism. Although insisting that baptism is unnecessary for salvation, Baptists contend that it is important and necessary for church membership.[5]

Congregational church government is another evidence of the Baptist concern for the church. Baptists readily admit that congregational polity is not their sole theological property. They do claim, however, to make a unique contribution to the doctrine by joining believer's baptism together with soul competency to form a distinctive church polity. This arrangement of doctrines permits Baptists to claim that their view of church government is unique to them.

Baptists best express their distinctive commitment to biblical authority in the way they "do church." The doctrines of a regenerate church, the ordinances, and church polity are attempts to have a church established on the authority of God as expressed in the Bible, not on the authority of men as expressed in human traditions. Baptist distinctives developed in part as a reaction against Christian denominations that Baptists felt were not seeking pure churches composed only of those who have testified to a regenerating work of God.

Baptists have always been concerned that the church should reflect God's intentions as closely as possible. Thus, the Baptist understanding of the church is the attempt of Baptists to reflect their obedience and submission to biblical authority. To put it another way, a Baptist church visibly manifests the Reformation premise of *sola scriptura.*

BAPTISTS AND THEIR MISSION

Another reason that I am a Baptist is because of the manner in which Baptists perceive their mission. Baptists may be best known for two doctrinal corollaries that have been a part of their distinctive theological identity since their inception. These are soul competency and religious liberty. Although these two concepts are distinct, consideration of one of these traits in Baptist thought naturally leads to discussion of the other.

The function of these two tenets is to promote and protect the mission of the church in its proclamation of the gospel and its various ministries. This is not to say that Baptists need religious liberty in order to exist or to carry out their mission. History has shown us that Baptists can flourish in the most oppressive and religiously intolerant contexts. Baptists do argue, however, that religious freedom and soul competency provide a far more suitable environment for the free preaching the gospel, an opportunity for genuine conversion experiences, and the building of churches composed of regenerate members.

Individual, or "soul," competency implies an unhindered access to receive or to reject a personal, individual relationship with God. Each person is responsible to address his or her spiritual standing before God. The social order is obligated to provide an unhindered or unobtrusive environment to allow persons the freedom to deal directly with God. Baptists hold adamantly to the notion that an individual has the ability and responsibility to approach God directly without any human intermediary.[6] Soul competency has penetrated deeply into the distinctive theological identity of Baptists, particularly in American Baptist life.

In a sense, soul competency offers the potential of a direct, immediate communion of the person with God. Every person has within himself a "secret place" in which God speaks to him or her, and he or she in turn can potentially address God. Baptists argue that this concept is vital because the spiritual nature of the Christian faith mandates that each person deal personally with God. This process is uniquely individual. No other entity or person can participate in this personal encounter between God and the individual.

The essence of an individual's spiritual vitality, therefore, allows for no intrusions. The response of the individual and the proclamation of the gospel by the church are both predicated upon the freedom and competency of the individual. Baptists oppose any attempts by any individual or group to impede or hinder the soul's right to commune with God.

Religious liberty was a revolutionary idea during the first centuries of Baptist life. Not only did Baptists include their sentiments on this subject in separate treatises and confessions of faith, but they also treated it extensively in their distinctive writings. The reason for their insistence on religious freedom is attributed to their understanding of the gospel as requiring a voluntary, intentional response without external coercion. Baptists contend that the essence of faith is a free and voluntary response to God.

As Baptists understand it, religious liberty is the right of each person to be free and uncoerced in his pursuit, or his lack of pursuit, of a personal relationship with God. The theological traits that distinguished Baptists from other Christian denominations compel them to appeal uncompromisingly for the right of a free church in a free state. According to Baptists, no person should be constrained to become a church member who did not voluntarily surrender to Christ as Lord and who did not willingly receive baptism as a personal confession to this submission. Faith freely expressed and baptism personally affirmed are the necessary prerequisites for church membership. This understanding of the church and of Christian living is best realized within the context of religious freedom.[7]

In order to have a New Testament church that reflects an unequivocal commitment to the Bible, Baptists contend for a free church in a free society. Religious freedom helps ensure the authenticity of the conversion experience and protects the voluntary nature of a free church. Soul competency stipulates the prerogative and responsibility of every person to give an account of his or her own life to God. The genuineness of this accounting must occur in a context that removes spiritual coercion and religious manipulation. The Baptist emphasis upon a regenerate church membership necessitates an environment in which men and women can be confronted freely with the claims of the gospel of Christ and can then embrace or reject those claims responsibly and volitionally.

In this sense, religious liberty and soul competency are theological by-products of a regenerate church membership. Both religious freedom and soul competency promote the purity of a church that is built upon the absolute authority of the Bible for faith and practice.[8]

BAPTISTS AND THEIR CONVICTIONS

A fourth reason that I am a Baptist is because of the rich tradition Baptists have in engaging and expressing unashamedly their convictions to non-Baptists. I call this propensity of Baptists to express their distinctive convictions "polemical intention." Polemical intention is the notion that Baptists deliberately develop the distinctive theological traits that distinguish them from other Christians. The polemic is the purposeful critique of other denominations in light of their differences with Baptists. This concept is an indispensable part of the Baptist identity.

Polemical intention is theologically concerned and directed toward various issues. The polemic typically critiques the authoritative basis of the doctrines of non-Baptist Christians. The intent of the polemic is to discover and identify the theological deficiencies of these other groups in comparison with the Baptist position on the issue. The goal of this effort is to highlight the supremacy and uniqueness of the distinctives of Baptists.

The polemic can have various expressions. Particular doctrines such as infant baptism, state-established churches, grace conveyed through religious rituals by specially ordained priests, religious traditions, and noncongregational church government have felt the brunt of the Baptist polemic. Baptists have criticized specific denominations, including Roman Catholics, Episcopalians, Congregationalists, Methodists, Presbyterians, Lutherans, and Campbellites. Certain religious movements have also been castigated, including the National and World Council of Churches. Baptists have on occasion even reproved themselves.

DISTINCTIVELY AND UNASHAMEDLY A BAPTIST

Our world today still needs Baptists. The concerns posed by our modern milieu provide challenges and opportunities for the theological distinctives of Baptists. On the one hand, we must guard our distinctive theological identity from cultural accommodation. To concede our distinctive Baptist identity to the "spirit of the age" would change the essence of our Baptist confessional tradition. We would no longer be Baptists. On the other hand, we as Baptists must be astutely aware of cultural concerns. If we are not, we run the risk of preserving our Baptist distinctives in ways that are unintelligible or meaningless to our contemporary context. We Baptists would be "distinctively irrelevant."

As our Baptist forebears have taught us, our Baptist distinctives are both biblical and relevant. Our unique Baptist convictions embody the great truths of the Bible that define our Christian identity and kingdom mission. Our Baptist distinctives are dynamic enough that they can speak meaningfully to any contemporary context and do so in a way that engages the issues of the age. In light of these considerations, I am now and will always be a Baptist.

21

BLOOD IS THICKER THAN WATER

Donald S. Whitney

Perhaps a better title for this chapter would be, "Why I Am *Still* a Baptist." Writing on "Why I Am a Baptist" might lead some to presume that I came to Baptistland from neutral ground. Anyone who imagines such a scenario may envision me in a pristine postconversion condition at which point I evaluated the various doctrinal and ecclesiological positions from an objective ivory tower, unencumbered by any traditions, experiences, or prejudices from my past. Then, disinterested and totally unbiased, I chose to reside in the Baptist realm of Christ's kingdom because my exhaustive research identified the Baptist position as the one most faithful to Scripture. Unfortunately, this is not the case. I didn't become a Baptist this way, and I find it hard to believe that anyone would follow such a path before settling on their church or denominational home.

The reality is that I was born into a Baptist home where I was taken to a Southern Baptist church at least Sunday morning, Sunday night, and Wednesday night beginning nine months before I was born. My dad was a Baptist deacon and Sunday school teacher prior to becoming a father. My mother taught children in Sunday school and Vacation Bible School, read parts in Training Union, and attended the Woman's Missionary Union years before I entered the world and was put on the Cradle Roll. I suppose I considered myself a Baptist even before I even called myself a Christian.

I was nine years old when, by the grace of God, I was brought under conviction of my sin and need for Christ by the Holy Spirit through the preaching of God's Word. After repenting and trusting in the person and work of Jesus Christ to make me right with God, I was immersed upon my public profession of my faith in Christ. All this happened in Calvary Baptist Church of Osceola, Arkansas, where I was received into membership after my baptism. That's how I came to be a Baptist.

GROWTH AS A BAPTIST

That small-town Baptist church of a hundred or so attendees was my church home throughout my childhood and adolescence. Not infrequently I was the only young person present on a Wednesday night (especially on business meeting nights) or for a Sunday night Training Union class. But by the time I went to college and could go to any church I wanted, I was a Baptist by choice. During my first week on campus I began attending both the Baptist Student Union and the largest Southern Baptist church in town.

Thus I remained in the bosom of Baptist life throughout college. However, I was also involved with the campus Fellowship of Christian Athletes at least as much as with the BSU. The FCA brought me into frequent fellowship with other evangelicals on campus and was the means of occasionally introducing me to non-Baptist churches. By this means my firsthand awareness of the non-Baptist Christian world began to expand.

After graduation I attended law school at the University of Arkansas and immediately joined a large SBC church near campus. During this year I sensed God's call to preach, a call that was confirmed by that Baptist church when it licensed me to the gospel ministry. The next fall I enrolled in Southwestern Baptist Theological Seminary in Fort Worth, Texas, choosing it because of the influence of several alumni whom I respected. I never considered attending any other Southern Baptist seminary, much less a seminary that wasn't Baptist. There I heard not only a Baptist perspective on theology and the church, but heard it contrasted with non-Baptist views. Moreover, from Tom Nettles and Leon McBeth, I learned church history—and particularly Baptist history—for the first time. I left Southwestern more of a Baptist than ever.

As I entered the pastorate, the preaching and teaching responsibilities caused me to investigate firsthand the Baptist doctrines and distinctives I had always believed. Then in February 1981, I was preaching through John in the morning and Ephesians in the evening. I came to Ephesians 1:4, "He chose us in him before the creation of the world," and I was forced to come to grips with the doctrine of election. The more I studied the Scriptures, the more the knot in my stomach tightened. Everything I found seemed to contradict what little I had been taught on the subject. My seminary professors had differed on the doctrine, but I found it so perplexing and inflammatory that I had deliberately avoided thinking about it while in school. But I no longer had the luxury of taking no position.

Previously I had believed that election was either true or false; now I knew that was a false dichotomy. My studies revealed that *every* Bible teacher believed in election, it's just that they differed in their beliefs. I had imagined that *election* was a theologian's term, but suddenly I realized that it was one of God's words. Words like *election* and *chose* are words that God put in the Bible, and they mean something.

Oddly, I remember that twenty-nine was the number of sources in my library that I investigated on the subject, including commentaries, dictionaries, and books on theology. Most of these were not from Baptists, however. What finally gripped me hardest was a section in *Abstract of Systematic Theology* by James P. Boyce, the founding president and theology professor of The Southern Baptist Theological Seminary.

It was on this weekday in February that I think I understood grace for the first time; or at least my understanding of it made a quantum leap upward. Though I would never have put it so crassly, I think my belief was, "Yes, God saved me by grace, but at least I had enough sense to know what to do when I heard the gospel." On this day I realized that I contributed nothing to my salvation but my sin. God chose to save me without any obligation to do so, and without any worthiness on my part. Election meant that God selected me for his family, and he did so while passing over others who were no more unworthy of salvation than I. Even the repentance and faith that I expressed that night as a nine-year-old were gifts of grace. I put my head on my desk and sobbed for a long time.

Shortly afterward the Baptist pastor who had given me the Boyce book supplied me with others that began teaching me theology consistent with Boyce's perspective. While the Baptist pot into which I had been stirred all my life had been overwhelmingly flavored with various competing theological flavorings, I became increasingly aware of how much of the original stock had been saturated with a robust, God-centered theology. This theology was held almost unanimously by early SBC leaders, like Boyce, as well as John Broadus and Basil Manly (from whom the familiar "Broadman" name was developed). All this is to say that through these means my Baptist roots had been deepened like a three-hundred-year-old oak tree.

SHOULD I REMAIN A BAPTIST?

Despite all this, shortly afterwards questions begin to arise about my commitments to Baptist beliefs and ways. One reason was that within two years of my seminary graduation I found myself pastoring in a suburb of Chicago in what Southern Baptists call "pioneer missions" territory (due to the small percentage of Southern Baptists in the area). When I arrived, there were 650,000 people in DuPage County, 300,000 of which identified themselves as Catholic and 250,000 as Lutheran. For the first time in my life I was living in a place where Southern Baptists weren't the dominant denomination. In addition, there were Baptist groups there that I never knew existed, such as the nearest Baptist church to ours, which was in the North American Baptist denomination.

Beyond that, however, living in a community adjacent to Wheaton, I found myself surrounded by evangelical churches and organizations of all types. Within ten miles of our church were the headquarters of more than fifty evangelical ministries such as TEAM, Christianity Today, Tyndale, Greater Europe Mission, InterVarsity Press, and Slavic Gospel Association, not to mention Wheaton College. Ecclesiologically I couldn't have been in a more diverse place in all America.

Never had I heard more from a non-Baptist position. Never had I been so challenged by church members and visitors about my Baptist beliefs. On the one hand, this caused me to grow stronger as I had to think through reasons for my beliefs and practices. I discovered that many of my theological positions and church customs were at that point little more than previously unchallenged assumptions. "Show me from the New Testament," a new convert from Catholicism once asked sincerely in regard to church membership, "that I'm to officially join anything." I blinked, having never before been asked about the validity of formally placing one's name on a church roll. Eventually I did show him the New Testament basis for church membership, but his question demonstrates how some of the most basic tenets of my Baptist perspective were unexpectedly and frequently challenged.

In addition to moving out of the Baptist South, the other reason I began to reconsider my Baptist heritage was my continuing maturity in theology. Most of my newfound theological and pastoral heroes were pedobaptists. Few of my Southern Baptist forebears (John L. Dagg and James P. Boyce being notable exceptions) were published, and if they were published, their works weren't widely known. Pedobaptists, including Presbyterians, Anglicans, and Congregationalists, were publishing multivolume works decades before Baptists organized their first churches. And for decades thereafter, Baptists typically struggled more with being persecuted than getting published.

As a result, by the time I started reading books by and about theologically minded ministers, the great body of this literature was predominantly pedobaptistic. The English Puritans, writing from about 1550 to 1700, were (and are) special favorites. Then there were Thomas Boston, Matthew Henry, Jonathan Edwards, and many others up through a twentieth-century hero, Martyn Lloyd-Jones. There were the significant exceptions of John Bunyan, Charles Spurgeon, and Arthur Pink, but my library of ministerial mentors became increasingly sprinkled with pedobaptists. After a while it became easy to think, *Most of those whose books and lives I love to read are not Baptists. They were right on so many crucial issues about God and the gospel, so maybe they are right on the issues where they differ from Baptists. And if they are, how can I remain a Baptist?*

The only other religious bodies I remotely considered were conservative, confessionally oriented Presbyterians. Their overall appeal, and one that I have seen become irresistible for many former Baptists, was what I have come to call a "Presbyterian ethos." The cherishing of a theological heritage, the concern for defining and defending the truth, the seriousness about the things of God, the love of learning, the blending of head and heart in ministry, and a cultural sophistication that characterizes so many of these brothers were powerfully attractive to me.

Such attractions were first getting my attention about the time I was pastoring in Arkansas and was asked to preach the doctrinal sermon at the annual associational meeting. As one pastor realized I was reading from the New American Standard Bible, he slammed his KJV shut and shouted, "I ain't gonna listen to *this* sermon!" and walked out. Imagine a young minister looking over the denominational fence after an experience like that. It was humiliating to hear Presbyterians described as "Baptists who can read," and to remain a Baptist. I hungered for theological fellowship among fellow ministers, and instead found that more were interested in methods or activities than doctrine and preaching.

So I observed not only many things in certain forms of Presbyterianism that *drew* me, but I began to see more and more in Baptist life that *repelled* me. While attending associational, state convention, or national convention meetings, I would see and hear things that sometimes tempted me to think, *These are not my people.*

One repellant was all the fighting in the SBC. Very few, I trust, were actually enjoying it, and many—even among my fellow conservatives who were invariably on the "winning" side—were weary of the battles and their aftermath. But as I looked at the denominational landscape, ecclesiological conflict was flaring up everywhere. So to leave Baptist life for another denomination would merely be exchanging one war for another. Besides, there's a time to "contend for the faith" (Jude 3).

I was also sickened by the atheological bent common among Baptists. Church growth pragmatism was everywhere. While pastoring in Chicagoland I was on the steering committee of a ministerial fraternal that monthly hosted some of the best-known theologians, Bible teachers, and preachers in evangelicalism—at no charge. And yet, despite frequent appeals by various methods to dozens of my Southern Baptist brothers over the years, rarely did more than one of them attend any meeting. But as David Wells made plain in *No Place for Truth: Whatever Happened to Evangelical Theology?* this was not a problem unique to Southern Baptists. Pragmatism was creeping into even the most confessionally rigorous groups. Confessional standards, as useful as they are, will not by themselves stop erosion.

So while the grass sometimes looked greener across the denominational fence, the longer I looked across it, the more I saw just about the same weed problems on the other side as on mine.

STILL A BAPTIST

The study and conversations I have had throughout the years have given me many more positive reasons to remain a Baptist than just this negative one: "If I become something other than a Baptist, I'll find most of the same troubles there too, so I might as well remain Baptist." I wanted better reasons than that for remaining Baptist. Many of my Baptist colleagues had experienced some of the same struggles as I. A pastor friend with a Ph.D. in New Testament from Southwestern made the full transition to the Presbyterian ministry and then returned to us. His insights, and the observations of others who left the ranks of pedobaptists, were enlightening.

As I kept reading the books and lives of my spiritual heroes, the minority of them who did have Baptist convictions were often powerful and persuasive. Chief among them was C. H. Spurgeon, who was immersed after his conversion despite being raised in the home of a pedobaptist minister. While ecumenical in spirit, Spurgeon was unapologetically Baptist in an ecclesiastical culture that was overwhelmingly pedobaptist. And since he is widely recognized as perhaps the greatest preacher since New Testament times, reading Spurgeon always makes me glad to say, "I am a Baptist."

However, more than anything else, the concentrated theological exchange with brothers who were in the process of becoming pedobaptists has most convinced me of the Baptist position. In the last five years of the twentieth century I was a participant in or observer of a handful of these dialogues, including one with a minister who had a Ph.D. and another with a pastor who was also founder of a college. Their challenges forced me to look at texts and to think theologically in ways I had not previously considered. But even as we parted ways and they had their children sprinkled, I was more certain than ever that the historic Baptist interpretation of Scripture was correct.

When one considers the significance of baptism and considers the gut-wrenching importance to Christian parents of the spiritual condition of their children, it is inconceivable to me how someone can believe that the New Testament would not explicitly speak (which pedobaptists admit) of infant baptism. I cannot imagine, believing as I do in the perspicuity and sufficiency of Scripture, that a new believer who had no previous church background and knew nothing of the debates about baptism, would read the Bible and conclude that infants should be sprinkled.

Furthermore, I am totally unpersuaded by pedobaptist arguments for the inclusion of unconverted people (namely sprinkled infants) into the membership of the church. Unlike the old covenant, I see no room in the new covenant for any but those who know the Lord. "This is the covenant I will make with the house of Israel after that time, says the Lord" in Hebrews 8:10–11, where he says this about "all" those who will be in that new covenant:

> I will put my laws into their minds,
> And I will write them on their hearts.
> And I will be their God,

> And they shall be my people.
> And they shall not teach everyone his fellow citizen,
> And everyone his brother, saying, "Know the Lord,"
> For all will know me,
> From the least to the greatest of them.

There is a truckload more to the debate over the immersion of believers versus the sprinkling of infants, but that is beyond the scope of this chapter and has been dealt with elsewhere. Let me add one other word on it here and note my concern about it among Baptists. One result of admitting the unregenerate to the church rolls is that over time the practice tends to dilute the message and liberalize the witness of the church. This is one of the greatest dangers to Baptists today. In our well-motivated zeal to evangelize, we have too often compromised, in practice, our zeal for a regenerate church membership. The annual statistics reported by the Southern Baptist Convention indicate that two-thirds of SBC church members are not in church on a given Lord's Day. In light of 1 John 3:14 ("We know that we have passed from death to life, because we love our brothers"), we have a biblical basis for questioning the spiritual condition of the majority of our members.

While there will always be "tares among the wheat" since God alone can see into the heart, surely we need to do a better job of discerning whether those who desire baptism and church membership have truly been born again from above. If we do not, we may soon find that the pool from which leaders and teachers are chosen is filled with unbelievers. Maybe this is why so many churches have such ungodly conflicts and why hundreds of SBC ministers are forcibly terminated each month. We want as much healthy growth as God will give our churches, but not cancerous growth.

Space does not permit me to comment on how other historic Baptist distinctives have become more precious than ever through the years. But I would affirm those which were noted as foundational Baptist doctrines in William Cathcart's monumental *Baptist Encyclopedia:*

> The Baptists of this country hold that the Word of God is the only authority in religion, that its teachings are to be sacredly observed, and that to religious doctrines and observances there can be no additions except from it; they hold that a man should repent and be saved through faith in the meritorious Redeemer before he is baptized; that immersion alone is Scripture baptism;

> that only by it can the candidate represent his death to the world, burial with Christ, and resurrection to newness of life; that baptism is a prerequisite to the Lord's Supper; they hold the doctrines of the Trinity, of eternal and personal election, total depravity, regeneration by the Holy Spirit, justification by the imputed righteousness of Christ, progressive sanctification, final perseverance a special providence, immediate and eternal glory for the righteous after death, and instant and unending misery for the ungodly. They hold the doctrinal articles of the Presbyterian Church, and they only differ from that honored Calvinistical community in the mode and subjects of baptism, and in their congregational church government. They hold that all regenerated believers are saved, whether they are immersed or sprinkled, or lack both ceremonies; and they insist on the immersion of believers because Christ was immersed, and because he enjoins immersion upon all believers.[1]

To these I would add the doctrines of religious liberty, the separation of church and state, the priesthood of all believers, the autonomy of the local church, the discipline of the local church, and the priority of missions and evangelism.

I also want to add a word about Baptist spirituality. From my earliest Sunday school days I remember my teachers always expecting the class to read the Bible daily. Stewardship of money was emphasized even to the children. Scripture memorization, worship, service, and evangelism were, too. While some of the personal spiritual disciplines found in the Bible are acknowledged too little in Baptist life (and in evangelicalism as a whole) today, the most important ones—intake of God's Word and prayer—are given the high priority they deserve. A good balance with the corporate spiritual disciplines is common among us as well. And as I have matured I have discovered a healthy, proportional spirituality characterizing Baptists throughout their history. Baptists don't have to turn to Catholic spirituality, as a growing number presently seem to find necessary, to learn Christlikeness. The true gospel, combined with true theology and ecclesiology, produces the best disciples.

Many other groups unite with us on nearly all the above doctrines and practices. But in my heart and mind I am convinced that overall the best fruit of the Reformation and of evangelicalism is found upon the Baptist branch of Christ's vine.

BLOOD IS THICKER THAN WATER

Having said that, I want to confess with all genuine Christians, regardless of label, that the blood of Jesus is thicker than the water of baptism. Baptists are one with all true believers in Christ. We amen the words of the psalmist, "I am a friend to all who fear you" (Ps. 119:63).

In harmony with that, I adopt these words from R. M. Dudley's chapter in a Broadman Press classic from 1900, *Baptist Why and Why Not* as my own Baptist resolve: "If I am a Baptist and I am proud of it, I want that it shall affect me not in the way of making me narrow and bigoted and intolerant, but humble, patient, and loving toward those who differ from me, and hearty, generous, energetic, and persevering in the use of my time, talents, and means for the furtherance of the good cause. Let us show our devotion to our principles, not by boastfulness and arrogance, but by a watchful attention to the needs of the cause we love. Thus shall we best show to men our fidelity and zeal; and thus best help the truth in its onward march to complete and final victory."[2]

PART EIGHT

THOUGHTS FROM EVANGELICAL LEADERS

22

A BAPTIST BECAUSE OF THE BIBLE

Wayne Grudem

I am a Baptist because of the Bible. Let me explain.

CHILDHOOD IN WISCONSIN

There was no Baptist church in Jim Falls, the northern Wisconsin town of 286 people that was my home for the first thirteen years of my life. Most of the other boys with whom I played baseball and rode bikes and built snow forts went to the Catholic church. They couldn't eat meat on Fridays, they attended mass every Sunday, and, when they were old enough, they all memorized sections of the Latin Mass, which they carried around on pieces of card stock while they were learning to be altar boys. I sometimes felt left out, but it was good practice in learning to stand alone for what I believed.

Our family didn't go to the large Catholic church in town, or the only other church, a smaller Methodist church. Every Sunday we drove twenty-six miles to attend the First Baptist Church of Eau Claire, Wisconsin. But why a Baptist church? I think ultimately it was because of the Bible.

Neither of my parents had grown up Baptist. My father's family went to Minneapolis Gospel Tabernacle, an Assemblies of God church at 13th and Lake Street in Minneapolis. My mother's family went to First Covenant Church, an Evangelical Covenant church in downtown Minneapolis. But when they had moved to Jim Falls, Wisconsin (where my father became part owner of a creamery), what they brought from their previous church backgrounds that went deeper than particular denominational traditions was a strong confidence in the Bible as the absolutely reliable Word of God. Therefore, they chose to drive an unheard-of distance to go to church every Sunday.

And so one could say I am a Baptist because I grew up in a Baptist church. But considering that I was born to two non-Baptist parents in a town with no Baptist church, it is remarkable that it turned out that way. The Bible is the fundamental reason for it all, because my parents searched until they found a church where the Bible was faithfully preached, and that Bible-believing church was a Baptist church.

I was baptized at age twelve in that church, after making a public profession of faith before the congregation. Our pastor had explained to me the meaning of baptism, and why we baptized by immersion, pointing to passages that clearly spoke of people going "down into the water" and coming "up out of the water" (Mark 1:10; Acts 8:38–39). He also explained how baptism was a symbol of death to our old manner of life and rising to walk "in newness of life" as it says in Romans 6:4: "We were buried therefore with him by baptism into death, so that as Christ was raised from the dead by the glory of the father, we too might walk in newness of life."

It all seemed quite clear and straightforward to me at age twelve—this was what the Bible said about baptism, and this was what we should do in obedience to Christ. It still seems quite clear and straightforward to me at age fifty-two.

We moved to Eau Claire when I was thirteen, and that allowed more involvement with church youth group and other activities. My favorite was the class in Christian doctrine taught by my pastor to junior high students on Thursday afternoons. We worked through a little book by E. Y. Mullins called *Baptist Beliefs*.[1] I was absolutely fascinated to find that we could learn summaries of the teachings of the Bible on various doctrines. I devoured every lesson, learning words such as *omniscience, omnipotence,* and *omnipresence* with great eagerness. Looking back at that book now, I am surprised to find that I differ with a number of points that I had underlined in pencil at age fourteen, but one fundamental truth was reinforced in that class—our pastor wanted to be sure that our doctrine derived from Scripture, and he had a deep confidence that the Bible could always be trusted.

It became more clear that our family's commitment was to the Bible and its teaching, and not to any single church or denomination, when First Baptist Church of Eau Claire called another pastor a couple of years later. The new pastor had been tainted by the liberalism that was sweeping through the American Baptist Convention, and I remember one Sunday sermon when he said you didn't have to believe in the virgin birth of Christ. That Sunday afternoon I remember my father, quite upset, talking at length with the new pastor by phone. That was only one sample of a "Baptist" church that was becoming less truly Baptist, because it was becoming less truly biblical.

Our family eventually left and went instead to Salem Baptist Church in Eau Claire, a Baptist General Conference church with a Bible-believing pastor (where I would be ordained to the Christian ministry many years later).

COLLEGE YEARS: A CRUCIAL DECISION

I think that the most decisive event in my theological thinking occurred one afternoon in the summer of 1966. I had gone off to Quebec City to study French for the summer at the University of Laval, and I suddenly found myself, at age eighteen, in the middle of a population that was more than 99 percent Roman Catholic. I was suddenly aware that at the end of the summer, after returning home briefly, I would leave to start my freshman year at Harvard (where I had been accepted). I had a real sense that I was "leaving home" that summer and needed to decide what I was going to believe.

How could I know that what my parents had taught me was true? How could I know that what I had learned in those two Baptist churches was true? How could I know that anything was true?

Sitting alone in my dormitory room in that predominantly Roman Catholic university on a hot summer afternoon, I decided that I really wasn't sure whether anything that my parents or my church had taught me was true. Maybe they had made some mistakes, and how was I to know?

As I thought about this, in the space of a few minutes I decided that I knew one thing for sure: *the Bible was true.* It was God's Word, and I could trust it. I decided at that moment that I would begin with that one conviction and go forward from there. I would test everything by measuring it against what the Bible said. If the Bible supported what my parents and my church had taught me, then I would agree with parents and church. If the

Bible did not support what I had been taught, then I would change my beliefs to bring them into line with the Bible.

Looking back on that afternoon, I am confident that God guided that decision. But what factors did he use to persuade me to believe the Bible above everything else? From a human standpoint, I had been strongly influenced by the confidence that my parents had in the Bible (they have read aloud a chapter from the Bible every night of their fifty-three years of marriage and continue to do so still today). I had also been influenced by the confidence of my two previous Baptist pastors (A. Kenneth Ham and Neal Floberg), whose trust was clearly in the Bible more than in any system of doctrine or denominational tradition. And I know I was also influenced by my grandmother, Hildur Sheady, who encouraged me to start memorizing passages from Scripture as soon as I was able to read.

But I think that an even deeper reason for that decision was the self-attesting power of Scripture itself: I had been reading from the Bible every day since age five or six, and the Holy Spirit had implanted in my heart, through the words of Scripture, a deeply settled conviction that these were indeed the words of God speaking to me.

I looked for a Baptist church in Quebec City that summer. Through the yellow pages I found a tiny Baptist church that had no building but met in the YMCA, a mission effort sponsored by something called Baptist Mid-Missions, whose pastor, John Garrisi, wonderfully encouraged me that summer.

I went off to Harvard that fall, and the first Sunday I attended a Baptist church just across the street from the university campus. It troubled me that during the Scripture reading the pastor read from Matthew's Gospel, but when he came to verses about God's judgment against sin he skipped over them and went to a later part of the passage that talked about God's love. So the next day I showed up in his office and asked why he had skipped those verses. When it was apparent that his answer wasn't convincing me, he asked, "Are you a freshman?" I said, "Yes." He said, "Well, you've got a lot to learn." I never went back to that church.

There probably were some Baptist churches in the Boston area that believed the Bible at that time. But as I looked for a church that had strong Bible teaching, I eventually ended up at Park Street Church in Boston where Harold John Ockenga preached forty-five-minute expository sermons without notes every Sunday morning and evening. I, along with many other university students from the Boston area, drank it all in week after week and grew in my Christian faith. Park Street Church was a conservative Congregational church, not a Baptist church, but my baptistic convictions remained unchanged during those years.

WESTMINSTER SEMINARY AND JOHN MURRAY

The real challenge (from a Baptist standpoint) came during my years at Westminster Seminary in Philadelphia. There were no Baptists on the faculty, nor could there be, for all regular faculty members had to subscribe to the Westminster Confession of Faith. I had gone to Westminster because I had read several writings of its previous faculty members (such as J. Gresham Machen, John Murray, and E. J. Young), and I knew that the seminary believed wholeheartedly in the full authority and inerrancy of Scripture. I agreed with many of the doctrinal positions taught there at the seminary. But I just found the Presbyterian arguments for infant baptism to be unpersuasive.

I remember at one point during my seminary career that I decided to think through this question in more detail. In particular, I decided that I would try to read the best argument for infant baptism that I could find, to see if it might persuade me. I purchased *Christian Baptism* by John Murray,[2] in part because I had long admired so many of Murray's other writings. But the book was disappointing.

I still have the copy of Murray's book that I read in 1971 or 1972, and I find my marginal comments to be interesting even today. As a seminary student, I read Murray's explanation for "they both went down into the water" and "they came up out of the water" (referring to Philip and the Ethiopian eunuch). When I found that Murray was happy with the thought that they "stood on the brink" or "stepped into the edge," and that Philip baptized the eunuch by "scooping up the water and pouring it or sprinkling it on him" (p. 27), I wrote in the margin, "Come on! They at least went *into* it. And why? Certainly not to scoop up a little water with the hands!"

Later in the book, Murray wrote that baptism and circumcision "are signs and seals of the covenant of grace, not of certain external blessings accruing from or following upon the covenant of grace. And this is so even though many who bear the sign and seal do not possess and may never possess the blessings of the covenant itself" (p. 55). I wrote in the margin, "!??!" I failed to understand how something could be a sign and seal of something that was not signed and sealed.

When Murray wrote, "Baptism is not administered by revelation of God's secret will" (p. 56), I wrote in the margin, "But *profession of faith* is the *external* indication that God has given so that 'fallible men' may have indication *not* of God's secret will, but of the *fact* of conversion—in order to determine who should be allowed in the church."

Murray said, "With respect to infants, the sign is properly dispensed in many cases where the recipients do not possess and may never possess the inward grace signified. It may be said that such are only in external covenant relationship. But it may not be said that baptism is simply the sign and seal of such external relationship" (p. 56). I wrote in the margin, "Double-talk!"

Murray quoted with approval the *Directory for the Public Worship of God* prepared by the Westminster Assembly, saying that "children, by baptism, are solemnly received into the bosom of the visible church . . . and united with believers. . . . They are Christians, and federally holy before baptism, and therefore they are baptized" (p. 59). I wrote, "Justified? Then saved!" I knew that that could not be true. But then why call them "Christians" and "federally holy"?

Regarding Acts 2:38–39, Murray quotes verse 39 as saying, "For the promise is to you and to your children" (p. 70). I wrote, "Why don't you finish the verse?" I knew that the verse continued, "and to all that are far off, every one whom the Lord our God calls to him," and that two verses later the text explains who exactly was baptized: "so *those who received his Word* were baptized" (Acts 2:41). This could not be infants.

Murray said, "Summarily stated, baptism represents the inclusion of the person baptized in the body of Christ and in the fellowship of the saints" (p. 79). I wrote, "But not for infants, or else it is a false sign for many." When Murray wrote, "Only those united to Christ, and who are members of his body have a right to present their children for baptism" (p. 80), I wrote, "But under the old covenant, *all* (male) Israelites were circumcised, not just those who professed faith." A further marginal note indicates that I realized even then that the requirement for entrance into the old covenant community of God's people was a physical, external requirement (you either had to be born as an Israelite, or just come and live among them), but in the new covenant the requirement for entrance into the spiritual community of God's people, the body of Christ, is an internal, spiritual requirement, namely, saving faith.

Where Murray wrote about baptism, "as seal it authenticates, confirms, guarantees the reality and security of this covenant grace" (p. 87), I underlined the word *guarantees* and drew an arrow to the margin where I wrote, "to the unregenerate? A pretty poor guarantee."

I had already heard several arguments for infant baptism in classes and from other students, and I had thought that Murray's book might provide some better arguments than those. (I guess some students were persuaded by them, but I just could not see it there in the text of the Bible.) After reading Murray's book, I concluded that there *were* no other major arguments. This was it. But the reasoning did not seem at all persuasive to me. So after reading this book I decided that my baptistic convictions were secure. John Murray was one of the ablest theologians and exegetes of the twentieth century. But at the end of this book I had a distinct sense that he was trying to defend something that simply could not be defended adequately from Scripture.

I loved Westminster Seminary and treasure the memory of my years there as some of the very best years of my life. In countless ways my understanding of Scripture and my theological convictions were deepened and strengthened during my years there. Lifelong friendships with other students and faculty members were begun and continue to this very day. In addition to that, I have a lifelong appreciation for the unity in Christ that I share with Presbyterians and every other non-Baptist evangelical who believes the Bible. I am thankful for many opportunities for fellowship with them and joint participation in many kinds of interdenominational ministry activities. Yet with regard to the doctrine of baptism, I went into Westminster Seminary a Baptist and came out a Baptist (as did many other students), and I remain one to this day.

OTHER REASONS

There are other reasons for my baptistic convictions than I have mentioned in this article. I have detailed these in the chapter on "Baptism" in my *Systematic Theology*,[3] so I need not discuss them in detail here. It seems to me clear that the New Testament authors consider baptism to be *an outward symbol of beginning the Christian life* (Gal. 3:27; Rom. 6:3–4; Col. 2:12; as well as several narrative passages such as Acts 2:41; 8:12; 11:44–48; 16:14–15; 16:32–33). Therefore, it seems right to conclude that the *symbol of beginning the Christian life* should only be given to *those who show evidence of having begun the Christian life.* Nowhere in the New Testament is baptism understood as a symbol of *probable future regeneration,* yet it seems to me that at root that is what the pedobaptist argument boils down to. And that seems to me to be far different from the New Testament picture of baptism. Paul did not say, "For as many of you as were baptized into Christ *will probably someday put on Christ,*" but, "For as many of you as were baptized into Christ *have put on Christ*" (Gal. 3:27 NKJV).

I have not spoken of other Baptist distinctives in this essay—distinctives such as the idea that church membership is voluntary, and that membership in the church is for believers only, and that a high value should be placed on the priesthood of all believers and their ability to understand Scripture for themselves, and that the primary authority for church government should rest within the local congregation itself. Other denominations and groups of churches also share some or all of these distinctives, and I am thankful for them wherever they are found. But on this decisive point, the doctrine of believer's baptism, this story explains why I am a Baptist. I am a Baptist because I believe the Bible, and because I am convinced that believer's baptism is what the Bible teaches.

23

FIFTY YEARS A BAPTIST

Carl F. H. Henry

Editors' Note: This article was originally published in the January 1958 issue of Foundations: A Baptist Journal of History and Theology, *as "Twenty Years a Baptist." It is reprinted here with the author's permission. American evangelicalism's preeminent theologian is just as Baptist today as he was when this article was first written.*

On an anniversary one may be indulged for reminiscing. To ponder one's spiritual ancestry, and perchance to conjecture one's personal and total denominational future, becomes both sobering and challenging.

THE BAPTIST DISTINCTIVES

To "become" a Baptist is more exacting than to become a Roman Catholic, or even a Protestant of traditions into which one is "born." The Baptist emphasis on regenerate church membership and believer's baptism implies a salient experience of spiritual decision and personal resolution.

Twenty-five years ago I was converted to Christianity from virtual paganism. Religion had been mainly a matter of private indifference to my Roman Catholic mother and to my Lutheran father. In early teens I was both baptized and confirmed in the Episcopal Church where I attended Sunday school and became exposed to the vocabulary of the Book of Common Prayer. In my twenties an assorted volley of religious encounters impinged upon me: a Seventh-Day Adventist plied me with catastrophic forebodings from the book of Daniel; an elderly Methodist woman emphasized my need to be "born again"; a Presbyterian minister deplored my newspaper coverage for the New York press in contrast to his coverage of Long Island for God; a university graduate in the Oxford Group pushed me to personal decision for Christ.

This ecumenical potpourri lacked any Baptist ingredient, to be sure. Yet by the grace of God on June 10, 1933, I gained firm assurance of spiritual regeneration and of divine forgiveness for sin on the merits of the saving work of Jesus Christ. That very day, had the risen Redeemer commanded, I would have gone to China or to any of the uttermost parts.

Student days in the interdenominational climate of Wheaton College propelled me toward baptistic views as I studied Scripture, interacted with campus associates, and reflected on contemporary religious life. In 1937, consequently, I was immersed on profession of faith and became a member of Babylon Baptist Church on Long Island, after the local pastor somewhat carefully reviewed the implications of this step. In 1940, while completing theological studies at Northern Baptist Seminary in Chicago, I was ordained to the Baptist ministry at a student pastorate, Humboldt Park Baptist Church. My persuasion of Baptist distinctive had deepened and strengthened through these years. Indeed, I came to wonder at and regret the limited insight of their heritage possessed by many Baptists.

What historical distinctives have shaped the uniqueness of the Baptist witness? The order in which they impressed me in collegiate days was as follows: (1) the final authority of Scripture above all creeds and speculation; (2) the priesthood of all believers; (3) believer's baptism by immersion; (4) the autonomy of the local church; and (5) the separation of church and state. While I might not use this precise order on tenets now, I would surely insist on the inclusion of each one. Obviously, not all Baptist distinctives are exclusively baptistic. The priesthood of believers is a Reformation doctrine also; the final authority of Scripture is affirmed by many creedal communions; the Greek Orthodox Church practices immersion, although of infants. But the total combination of these tenets and their special emphasis is unique to Baptists. Stressing personal conviction and religious experience alongside its unchanging biblical inheritance, the Baptist witness flourishes best where these Baptist distinctives are actively nourished.

Baptists historically are a people of resolution, a people enjoining spiritual rebirth, a people circumscribing their primary resources within the New Testament revelation. With the passage of time it becomes increasingly easy, and perilous, to neglect by mere assumption this respect for the authority of Scripture. Reliance upon Scripture to reveal the saviourhood and lordship of Jesus Christ, and his plan and purpose for mankind, is more than the first tenet of authentic Baptist belief; it is the foundation stone for the other principles which, if unsettled, jeopardize the total Baptist spiritual structure. Baptist distinctives of rebirth, of resolution, of resource are fixed in the confidence that the New Testament revelation is the climax of divine disclosure.

THE BAPTIST DISTRACTIONS

All Protestant groups today, including the Baptist denominations, face a common problem. Can individuality of missionary enterprise be maintained in the totality of Christian onslaught against paganism? Can Baptists vindicate their uniqueness without discrediting the legitimate Christian status of other denominational groups? Must they grant the validity of all other denominations in order to share passionately in the ecumenical conflict with non-Christian religions? Can Baptist distinctive be preserved and promulgated without endangering the larger unity of Christian witness? Will the broader perspective reduce the Baptist focus?

Anyone profoundly loyal to Baptist convictions but who also grieves over the spirit of fragmentation that has ailed Protestantism since the Reformation (which the Baptists claim to antedate) must reach some decision. A continuing deferment of solution to these problems from one generation to the next can only lessen confidence and respect for parental status and authority.

As I see it, Baptists are not so much interested in promoting the Baptist denomination as such in the world as in advancing the one church that Christ heads through the Baptist witness. But we should not feel that to realize this purpose requires surrender either of Baptist distinctives or of denominational fervor. While the Baptist tradition is for us the preferred medium to communicate the life of Christ in his church, we do not on that accord deny that some measure of genuine Christian status attached to other traditions, even as we are quick to admit that something less than full Christian status often intrudes into our own!

We decry homicidal competition in Christian enterprise. But we do not consider a one-denominational monopoly that virtually cancels Protestant free enterprise the means to an ideal religious climate. We believe that denominationalism can serve as a unitive rather than a divisive factor. In other words, I do not think that Baptist and ecumenical interests necessarily conflict.

Unfortunately, our Baptist leaders in American are not significantly influential as a theological force in other traditions. A lamentable contribution to this fact is the virtual disappearance within our Baptist denominations of a great theological scholarship and literature. Baptist ecumenical participation has not sharpened the doctrinal edge of the Baptist witness. Actually, this dullness of theological precision and accord prevails at the strategic and opportune time when concern for theological considerations is gathering fresh ecumenical force.

The joint interest in specific Baptist distinctives and in universal Christian priorities is best guarded and prospered by unwavering dedication to the requirements of the scriptural revelation. Authentic Christianity and convincing denominationalism will survive only in this biblical frame of delineation. Can we really understand the tradition through which the gospel was first mediated to us unless we understand it in terms of the claim of Scripture upon us in the face of competitive and contrary climes? Whatever reinforces the New Testament consciousness is good, therefore, both for ecumenical Christianity and the Baptist witness.

Distraction from the primary authority of Scripture as the revealed source of doctrine and ethics plagues Baptist sturdiness in other telling ways: when biblical polemics no longer, or only flickeringly, vitalize and confirm Baptist conviction, the vision and expansion and responsibility of distinctly Baptist trusts modulate and even deviate into increasingly non-Baptist concerns. Baptist interest in ecumenical Christianity, because uncorrelated with the priorities of biblical theology and action, has engendered division within the Baptist denominational life of the North, and has chilled ecumenical interest in the Baptist denominational life of the South. While assertedly advancing ecumenical Christianity, Baptist participation has frequently divided and subdivided Baptists themselves.

The theological tensions that gripped denominational life during my seminary days were often cushioned in the interest of convention harmony. But many young Baptist ministers were never able to correlate the divergent emphases on (1) the advancement of a pure Baptist witness, (2) an inclusive budget (not supporting exclusively evangelicals), and (3) sympathy for an ecumenical theology. My own Baptist ordination is a reminder of this state of affairs. At that time geographic propinquity of Northern Baptist Theological Seminary and the University of Chicago Divinity School had made the

Chicago Baptist Association a storm center of theological debate and a house of compromise.

In preparation for this sacred rite I spent hours in prayerful meditation on the person and work of our Lord, and on the great biblical verities of the gospel, his commission. My dedication was *einmalig,* as once-for-all as the unchanging truth I was called to proclaim. Yet the night my ordination was approved, the committee accepted a second candidate whose theological views were, in my opinion, far removed from biblical Christianity and from historic Baptist theology.

The convention leadership seldom, if ever, confronted these theological tensions with courage and candor. Many pastors and church-goers recognized this course of moderation as being impossible between two positions that had gone beyond the point of arbitration. Those who refused to label modernism as heresy and by an emphasis on evangelism rather than on theology sought to advance the Baptist enterprise were increasingly suspected of minimizing the doctrinal aspect of Christianity, and therefore of imperiling whatever other Baptist distinctives remained.

In 1946 this smoldering resentment burst into open conflagration in the fundamentalist-modernist test of strength at the Grand Rapids convention. The plotted political maneuvering, both of the Roger Williams Fellowship and of the Fundamentalist Fellowship, as well as of forces seeking to moderate between them, was a disheartening spectacle and debacle to younger ministers who had come in search of Christian unity in uniqueness. Under conviction to oppose recognition of modernism as authentic Christianity, I permitted my name on the fundamentalist ballot. The fundamentalist ticket was defeated 2,483 to 605, with 236 split ballots. Thereafter no substantial Christian minority was either so repeatedly ignored or so tirelessly pressured for conformity. This harassment led finally to a costly outcome, namely, withdrawal of about 300 churches under the banner of the Conservative Baptist Association, and increasing support of the Conservative Baptist Foreign Mission Society, which had been formed in 1943.

While the theological issue is frequently represented as the only issue at stake in Grand Rapids, that was not the case. The test of strength did not show that there were 2,483 liberal delegates. Membership in Northern Baptist churches at that time was about 85 percent evangelical; so it is likely that most delegates who voted antifundamentalist were actually disposed to various shades of conservative theology. Many resented the pugnacious features of fundamentalism, and feared the consequences of convention control by a power bloc.

Even if lacking in courage to register their theological convictions, many evangelicals who voted against the fundamentalists were motivated by a sense of Baptist concern. These delegates may not have realized to what extent the official life of the Convention was already at that time being maneuvered by leaders who ignored baptistic answerability to the local churches. But while denominational executives were often culpable of a questionable political shrewdness, the fundamentalist revolt was infected with an equally serious characteristic, that of a vitriolic spirit.

To many, the fundamentalist secession held promise of a new era of denominational peace. But the cost of this withdrawal to contemporary Baptist history is larger than is usually acknowledged or recognized. At the time, denominational harmony was promoted. On the other hand, doctrinal sensitivity became blunted, and Baptist enthusiasm and fellowship in the comprehensive sense were impeded and stifled.

On the basis of complaints against theological modernism, Southern Baptists scooped up more and more northern territory. Swedish Baptists, at one time supporting their own missionaries under a united program, inaugurated their separate endeavor under the Baptist General Conference. Conservative Baptists launched their competitive missionary venture under the keyword *confidence,* exploring, as it were, a weakening faith in the work of the regular convention. Although a concerted Baptist impact remained a strategic concern (the Northern Baptist Convention became in name the American Baptist Convention; the German Baptist Convention became the North American Baptist Convention; and one wit proposed that Southern Baptists launch a pioneer invasion of the interstellar spaces), the doctrinal misgivings that haunted both ministry and laity remained unresolved.

Even some conservative seminaries were disinclined to sharpen theological principles. Collapse of the old liberalism had not felt the evangelical theological thrust sufficiently to experience repentance from heresy. For the sake of organizational peace, theological positions were evaluated in terms of "gain" or "loss" in denominational equanimity rather than in terms of "revealed truth" or "false doctrine."

The Green Lake theological conference revealed a gratifying unity in some positive beliefs of American Baptists. There was little disposition, however, to press a question earlier Baptists would certainly have urged: what ought Baptists to believe in view of an authoritative New Testament revelation? Unless there stands behind the interest in what Baptists do believe this concern for what they ought to believe, Baptist theology is of questionable strength in the life of the Baptist community.

Symptoms of theological anemia in Baptist life in the North are serious and apparent: the absence of great Baptist preaching in most of the great cities; absence of an ideologically vigorous Baptist student work in the university centers; absence of a great theological literature shaped by seminary faculties.

Perhaps the most alarming of all symptoms, however, is failure to establish in the North a Baptist university, or even a Baptist college, whose evangelical intrusion into thought and life would outstrip or even match that of interdenominational schools that for more than a generation have siphoned their students largely from Baptist ranks. I do not now propose establishing some new venture; present institutions hold unrealized potential that awaits release through proper vision, and some of them now display large areas of vitality and virtue. Baptist collegiate work, however, by its failure to inspire theological trust and moral enthusiasm, has permitted interdenominational institutions to corner evangelical confidence.

Baptists have properly accepted liberal arts education as a genuine Christian responsibility; yet they have been too often inundated by secular preoccupations to preserve and actualize the goal of Christian education. They have disproportionately favored the rightful claims of academic beliefs. They have avoided the dangers of legalistic morality, while failing to demonstrate patterns of Christian student behavior suggestive of the biblical virtues. These ambiguities explain student preference for interdenominational schools over denominational ones.

A personal experience comes to mind at this point. A dozen years ago the presidential committee of a Baptist college extended me an informal invitation to the school presidency. I was to meet with the committee, which would take proper formal action and make official announcement at the commencement season. My preliminary associations revealed a wholesome past dedication of school personnel to Christian faith and practice. Why, therefore, could and should this treasured heritage not be published, both to declare convictions and to provide a norm of self-examination and rededication for both faculty and students? Faculty subscription to a doctrinal statement and student acceptance of a minimal code of conduct represent to me a valid and functional way of safeguarding our Baptist schools from some of the theological and moral sloughs into which they have mired. In the absence of such protective factors, I feel to this day that my name was rightly withdrawn from consideration.

Whether we speak of Baptist ecumenical interest or of Baptist educational concern, I am convinced that any activity not conformed to the Bible as the inspired rule of faith and practice becomes a mere distraction. Only through acknowledgment of this scriptural foundation, and justification of Baptist positions in the light of this criterion, can Baptists everywhere be impelled to the conviction that the same concern controls their unity in Christ. This matchless distinctive of Bible-relatedness can quicken both total Christian and individual loyalties. It will armor Baptist engagement in the Christian enterprise from easy capitulation to alien encroachments.

THE BAPTIST DIRECTIVES

Since Baptist thought and life in America moves in several spheres, each more or less competitive with the other, it is truly by way of hope, rather than of authority, that we may speak of Baptist directives. By this term I mean those guiding principles whose cheerful observance will best yield a sense of mutuality and of common Baptist concern. Despite others' disillusionment and faithlessness in the live possibility of such achievement, many reasons fire my own personal burden for a shared and unifying Baptist propellant.

Our home has long harbored American Baptist and German Baptist interests; my sympathetic awareness and support of the evangelical thrust of the Conservative Baptist Foreign Mission Society has not been lacking, although regretting excessive charges of liberalism sometimes leveled against American Baptist enterprise; my District of Columbia church membership affiliates me technically with both American and Southern Baptist Conventions. While I have often marveled at the vigorous Sunday school, Training Union, and missionary organizations of Southern Baptists, at the same time I have not always been able to reconcile their strong claims of theological fidelity with the disposition in some quarters to infiltrate biblical theology with biblical criticism.

One of the inescapably urgent needs in contemporary Baptist life is revival of an unbroken virility in biblical and theological scholarship and literature. Southern Baptists often close their theological history with E. Y. Mullins or W. T. Conner; Northern Baptists with A. H. Strong. Unquestionably, the great evangelical realities may and do indeed survive through several or even many generations by reference and application to past doctrinal classics. No amount of academic inbreeding, however, will unconditionally guarantee a throbbing theological loyalty apart from a constant reaffirmation of the great essentials by respected contemporary thinkers and participants in denominational and Christian enterprise.

Neither ecumenical spirit nor erasure of doctrinal distinctives is as likely to merge diverse elements of present Baptist thought and life as is mutually refurbished regard for authoritative biblical imperatives and mutually reinstated fidelity to the theology of revelation. Arbitrarily to equate denominational, and in this case Baptist, affiliation with membership in the body of Christ is obviously theologically naive and increasingly theologically unrealistic. Our century is surrounded and crowded, rather, by the insistent problem: in thought and in practice does the quantitative and qualitative value ascribed to the Word, incarnate and written, produce both a Christian and a Baptist? The turmoil over Baptist distinctives, within Baptist distractions, yields ambiguous Baptist directives.

While this reflection on an anniversary occasion may not provide comprehensive solutions for denominational problems, it nonetheless reinforces my conviction that Baptist distinctives are valid, and that the Baptist mission in the closing decades of the twentieth century is valid, and that the Baptist mission in the closing decades of the twentieth century is extraordinarily urgent.

24

SO WHAT'S A NICE SOUTHERN BAPTIST LIKE ME DOING IN A PLACE LIKE THIS?

C. Ben Mitchell

Even though I've been a Baptist for over a quarter century, I wasn't born a Baptist. I was converted in a Baptist church when I was eighteen years old, under the ministry of a faithful expositor of the Word. By a serendipitous providence, the first time I ever heard the gospel was in a Southern Baptist church pastored by Dr. Robert L. Mounts, presently director of the department of family life for the Florida Baptist Convention.

Under Bob's tutelage I became a Baptist by personal conviction. It was in a theology class he taught at that church where I first learned the names and read the works of our great Baptist forebears such as William Carey, Charles Haddon Spurgeon, Andrew Fuller, John Gill, Isaac Backus, John Leland, James Petigru Boyce, P. H. Mell, A. H. Strong, and E. Y. Mullins. In that same theology class, however, I also learned about and read Augustine, Luther, Calvin, Pelagius, Wesley, Whitefield, Edwards, Hodge, Murray, and

Boice. The doctrine of baptism was thoroughly defended in their works, first from a Baptist perspective, then from a pedobaptist perspective. The doctrines were set side by side for examination, evaluation, critique, and comparison with Scripture.

At the end of that process, and after having been taught by some of the best Baptist and non-Baptist theologians alike, I came to understand that believers alone are the proper subjects of baptism and that the only proper mode is immersion. That fact did not mean my appreciation for my pedobaptist brethren and teachers was diminished, but that I knew I could not personally affirm their convictions on baptism.

Similarly, I became a Southern Baptist through being encouraged (even coerced) in those theology classes to examine alternatives from a scriptural, doctrinal, ecclesiological, and historical perspective. Ecclesiology was taught to be important. In those classes I learned about Landmarkism, independent fundamentalism, Methodism, Lutheranism, Presbyterianism, Catholicism, and the range of Christianity in its denominational expressions.

When I compared what I believed with the doctrinal and ecclesial affirmations of those denominations, I found greatest harmony with Southern Baptists. I wasn't a Sunbeam. I wasn't a BYU member. I wasn't a Mission Friend. Those are all wonderful groups, but I became a Southern Baptist through theological instruction, not through childhood training.

For me, then, becoming a Baptist in general, and a Southern Baptist in particular, was a process brought about by the providence of God, the faithfulness of a local church pastor, the potency of biblical revelation, and the inner witness of the Holy Spirit. Subsequently I have come to embrace what I hope is an even fuller, more comprehensive expression of Baptist faith.

I'M A BAPTIST BECAUSE OF THE SCRIPTURE PRINCIPLE

From their earliest days Baptists have been committed to the reliability and trustworthiness of the Bible. The Short Confession of Faith of 1610, a proto-Baptist confession, affirms in its first article, "We believe *through the power and instruction of the Holy Scriptures* that there is only one God" (emphasis added). By 1612, Thomas Helwys and his brethren would maintain that "the scriptures of the Old and New Testament are written for our instruction" and are "to be used with all reverence, as containing the Holy Word of God, which only is our direction in all things whatsoever." Moreover, Helwys's *Declaration of Faith,* as the confession was called, was suffused with textual references, showing its dependence on that Word. Later, to show their unity with other evangelical Christians, our Baptist forebears declared that "Holy Scripture is the only, sufficient, certain, and infallible rule of all saving knowledge, faith, and obedience" (Second London Confession of 1677).

Since I wasn't reared with a Bible in my hands, I came to believe that the Scriptures of the Old and New Testament were true through examining the Scriptures' own truth claims and by the illuminating power of the Holy Spirit. I learned within the text of the Bible itself that Christ died for our sins according to the Scriptures and was buried and raised again on the third day according to the Scriptures (1 Cor. 15:3–4). After hearing the gospel of the risen Lord Jesus and experiencing the transforming power of the Spirit, I understood precisely what the apostle meant when he told the Thessalonians, "Our gospel came to you not simply with words, but also with power, with the Holy Spirit and with deep conviction" (1 Thess. 1:5).

For me as an ethicist, the Scripture principle has everyday importance. Our views on social justice, racism, cloning, euthanasia, abortion, homosexuality, and other issues must not be based on the changing opinions of the secular academy, but on the unchanging verities of the inerrant Word. It is from the Scriptures alone that we discover that human beings are made in the image and likeness of God. It is in the Scriptures alone that we are told to love our neighbor as we love ourselves. It is in the Word of God alone that we learn that God's gracious design is for one man to be joined to one woman in a one-flesh relationship for life. Baptists have been and are committed to the Scripture principle.

I'M A BAPTIST BECAUSE OF THE LIBERTY PRINCIPLE

Again, from our earliest days Baptists have affirmed that the conscience is free to obey God. Article XVII on religious liberty in the *Baptist Faith and Message* did not rise *ex nihilo.* That "God alone is Lord of the conscience, and He has left it free from the doctrines and commandments of men which are contrary to His Word or not contained in it" is a conviction that predates Baptists. Nevertheless, it is a conviction that defines Baptists. While we agreed with our Presbyterian and Congregationalist brethren on the infallibility of Scripture, we did, after all, trace our heritage partly through the Anabaptists, brothers and sisters who bled and died for liberty of conscience to worship God according to the Bible.

Later, Roger Williams and Obadiah Holmes championed this God-ordained liberty, arguing that John Cotton and the Massachusetts Bay Colony were not lords of their consciences. Williams suffered exile and Holmes was whipped severely for religious freedom. To this day Baptists defend and proclaim this liberty.

On 2 June 2000, Baptists and other evangelicals joined the cause of religious liberty in *The Chicago Declaration on Religious Freedom: Sharing Jesus Christ in a Pluralistic Society,* affirming that "the freedom to worship God without government coercion and to exercise liberty of religious conscience is fundamental to any serious notion of human rights and the dignity of humankind." Furthermore, the declaration is explicit that religious liberty is not for Baptists alone: "We pledge to defend the rights of others to hold their own religious convictions, to challenge our beliefs, and to attract converts to their religious faiths." Religious liberty is not granted by any denomination, government, group, or sect, but by the God who made us in his image. As a Baptist, I was pleased to have a part in drafting and signing that declaration.

I'M A BAPTIST BECAUSE OF THE REGENERATE CHURCH PRINCIPLE

One of the indelible marks of Baptists is their commitment to a church comprised of believers only. Membership in the body of Christ is not enjoyed by birth or by infant baptism, but by conversion alone. According to our Baptist brethren in 1644, God's people are those who have been made "a spiritual house, an holy priesthood, to offer up spiritual sacrifice acceptable to God through [Christ]; neither doth the Father accept, or Christ offer to the Father any other worship or worshippers" (London Confession of 1644, Article 17).

Perhaps the *Principles of Faith of the Sandy Creek Association,* an early and highly influential association in the American South, put it more clearly: "IX. That true believers are the only fit subjects of baptism, and that immersion is the only mode. X. That the church has no right to admit any but regular baptized church members to communion at the Lord's table." In those two crisp articles, a regenerate church membership is clearly articulated.

Further, because Baptists believe the Scripture requires a regenerate church, Baptists have practiced discipline. In both its formative expression (e.g., training in discipleship) and its corrective expression, discipline distinguished Baptists from many religious sects. Baptists affirm a believers' church.

I'M A BAPTIST BECAUSE OF THE EVANGELISM PRINCIPLE

Because of the Scripture principle and because of the regenerate church principle, Baptists take seriously the mandate of our Lord Jesus to spread the gospel to the ends of the earth (Matt. 28:18–20). In fact, Baptist history may be written as the history of gospel expansion. Everywhere Baptists have gone they have shared their faith, planted churches, and sent missionaries. William Carey, Adoniram Judson, Lottie Moon, and Annie Armstrong are more than revered names in Baptist life; they were men and women of unusual courage and models of selfless devotion to the gospel of Christ.

Baptists hold that evangelism is not only a privilege but also a duty of followers of Christ. As the *Baptist Faith and Message* puts it, "The new birth of man's spirit by the Holy Spirit means the birth of love for others. Missionary effort all rests thus upon a spiritual necessity of the regenerate life, and is expressly and repeatedly commanded in the teachings of Christ" (Article XI).

It is no accident that Southern Baptists have thriving North American and International mission boards. Students of Southern Baptist history will know that the evangelistic and missionary mandate of our Lord Jesus was at the core of our birth pangs as a denomination. As a beneficiary of those Baptists of the past, I am personally grateful for their insistence on and unswerving commitment to obeying the command of the Lord Jesus to be witnesses and to following the example of the believers in the Book of Acts who sent out missionaries beyond their own borders.

I'M A BAPTIST BECAUSE OF THE ASSOCIATIONAL PRINCIPLE

From the beginning, Baptist churches related to one another in associations of churches that were unified in matters of faith and practice. While Baptists were separatists with respect to the established church, they were by no means isolationists. For instance, in 1777 the Kehukee, North Carolina, Baptist Association maintained as an essential part of their credo that "for the mutual comfort, union and satisfaction of the several churches of the aforesaid faith and order, we ought to meet in an Association way, wherein each church ought to represent their case by their delegates and attend as often as is necessary to advise the several churches in conference." By 1925, Southern Baptists described their associational principle in terms of cooperation, arguing that "members of New Testament churches should co-operate with one another in carrying forward the missionary, educational, and benevolent ministries for the extension of Christ's kingdom."

As both a former pastor and in service to a denominational agency presently, I also believe in the associational principle. One of the hallmarks of Southern Baptists is their conviction that churches of like precious faith can do more together than they can do separately. Moreover, there is a prescriptive element to Baptist associationalism. We believe we *should* join with others who share our deeply held commitments and that we *should* inform one another when we deviate from those commitments.

I'M A BAPTIST BECAUSE OF THE COMMITMENT TO THEOLOGICAL EDUCATION

While there has been an unmistakably anti-intellectual element in Baptist life historically, more recently Baptists have been champions of theological education. Not only do some of the great universities, like Brown, and the University of Chicago, owe their genesis to Baptists, but at least since 1856, Baptists in the South have had theological education on their minds.

James Petigru Boyce's clarion call to form a seminary for the training of Southern Baptist ministers was issued in his speech at Furman University, "Three Changes in Theological Institutions." Though Baptist universities like Furman had been working for some time to educate Christians, there was not among Baptists in the South an institution whose sole purpose was to educate ministers for the churches. Boyce's call was a revolutionary summons for (1) a seminary for every called minister regardless of previous training, (2) a curriculum of the highest scholarly standards, and (3) a confessional standard to be heartily embraced and formally signed by every faculty member.

When he learned of Boyce's address, Francis Wayland, a leader in Baptist education himself, wrote to Boyce: "I wish you every success. I hope you will be well sustained, and that Baptists, as they have done before, may show other Christians how the church of Christ is to be built up by following more closely in the steps of the Master" (letter of 16 January 1857).

I owe an inestimable debt to Southern Baptist theological education. I am the product of Southwestern Baptist Theological Seminary, where I was privileged to sit under some of God's choice servants such as Curtis Vaughan, James Leo Garrett, L. Russ Bush, and one of the editors of this volume, Tom J. Nettles. I was also honored to serve as a faculty member at The Southern Baptist Theological Seminary, the incarnation of Boyce's vision for ministerial training. I can say with utmost confidence that Baptist theological education is alive and well for the foreseeable future.

In light of what I've said above, one might ask, "So what's a nice Southern Baptist like you doing in a place like this?" Having declared how and why I came to be a Baptist, the next logical question would be, "So why aren't you teaching in a Southern Baptist institution or pastoring a Southern Baptist congregation?" The answer to that question is at least twofold. First, I'm not *presently* teaching at a Southern Baptist institution. While I am delighted to be where I am for the moment, I do not know what the future holds. Perhaps in the future the Father's good pleasure will lead me again to a denominational institution. Moreover, I have been serving Southern Baptists through the Ethics and Religious Liberty Commission since 1988, first as a trustee and, since 1992, as a staff member. Second, and more importantly, while I am unashamedly and unreservedly a Southern Baptist, I am first and foremost an evangelical Christian.

American evangelicalism may have a relatively recent history, but it is nevertheless a vital movement. Southern Baptists, especially, owe a huge debt to their non-Southern Baptist evangelical brothers and sisters. After all, evangelicals supplied the intellectual rigor, theological scholarship, and collegial encouragement that in many ways made the conservative resurgence in Southern Baptist life possible.

While personally a member of a Southern Baptist church for decades, Carl F. H. Henry is best known not as a Southern Baptist, but as an evangelical scholar and founding editor of *Christianity Today* magazine. His monumental six-volume work, *God, Revelation and Authority*, gave Southern Baptists and other evangelicals the historical and theological backbone upon which to construct, among other things, the *Chicago Statement on Biblical Inerrancy*, the watershed document of evangelicalism in the last quarter century.

Furthermore, leaders like Henry, Kenneth Kantzer, Harold Ockenga, E. J. Carnell, Charles Fuller, Gleason Archer, Everett Harrison, Francis Schaeffer, and others set the tone for evangelical cultural engagement in the face of social, moral, and religious decline.[1]

This world and life emphasis was, arguably, the donation of evangelicals to Baptists who, for the most part, focused their attention on evangelism and mission. For many Baptists, with the exception of some New England Baptists like John Leland, for instance, cultural engagement had to take its place behind doctrinal and ecclesiological survival. Today, however, Baptists, especially Southern Baptists, are at the forefront of evangelism, social ministry, and cultural engagement, active with other evangelicals as cobelligerents in the world, though we're not as active as we ought to be.

In my own view, Southern Baptists are uniquely indebted to their non-Southern Baptist evangelical kin. We have a huge membership, plentiful resources, and growing respect. Southern Baptists need to come alongside their evangelical brethren, many of whom struggle daily for financial and other resources, to assist them as together we bring the glorious gospel of the risen Christ, and its social and ethical implications, to new generations. If I'm right that evangelicals "carried the water" for Southern Baptists early in the resurgence, then Southern Baptists should work harder out of respect and gratitude to build intentional partnerships with our evangelical comrades.

Hopefully, the future is bright for Southern Baptists. We face a number of important challenges in the twenty-first century. Our size, which is in so many ways a blessing, can become a liability if we fail to equip, mobilize, and get our arms around this gentle giant known as the Southern Baptist Convention. Frankly, we don't have a history of playing well with others. In the face of the cultural pressures that we feel, there is a tendency for us to move toward isolationism and separatism. Instead, we must build new bridges with evangelicals and other non-Baptists who share our basic world-view. At the same time, we must affirm wholeheartedly that which makes us Baptists. The way ahead is not easy, but by God's grace, it will be exciting and fruitful.

25

GRACE—NOT RACE—COUNTS HERE

Roger Nicole

I was born in the vicinity of Berlin, Germany, in the middle of World War I. My father was a Swiss minister who was functioning as the chaplain of French Protestant prisoners of war in Germany. He was ordained in the Free Church of Geneva, a body that had separated from the state Reformed Church in order to avoid compromising situations resulting from the union of church and state and to conform more clearly to an evangelical stance.

This church practiced infant baptism, but permitted members who held to believer's baptism to postpone the service until they could profess personal faith. Thus, my brother, my sister, and I were sprinkled in infancy. We were nurtured in a Christian atmosphere with love for the Lord and deep respect for the Scripture. On December 3, 1923, I attended a revival service and experienced conversion at the same time as my sister, who was four years older than I. At the age of thirteen I sensed God's call to the ministry and oriented my life and studies in that direction. I was a faithful member of the League for the Reading of Scripture. In my years as a teenager I began to be concerned with complex theological issues such as inspiration, predestination, prophecy, and baptism. On baptism, I could not see in the Bible a clear evidence of the baptism of infants. I did not understand the relevance of my father's statement in response to my query that circumcision was administered to infants.

Having completed my A.B. in classical languages, I went to Paris to continue study in that area. I took the full course offered at the Institut Biblique of Nogent/Marne, an interdenominational Bible school founded and directed by Dr. Ruben Saillens, a very strongly convinced Baptist, a disciple of Charles H. Spurgeon. Dr. Saillens was the most eloquent and effective pulpiteer in the francophone world. He also was the most spiritual man that I have ever known. I still cherish in my memory the echo of his voice, "Nicole, why don't you get baptized? Here what counts is grace, not race." Meanwhile, my elder brother and sister had received believer's baptism by immersion in a very live Baptist church in the north of Paris, and my parents did not appear offended in this development.

GORDON DIVINITY SCHOOL

In 1938 I came to the U.S.A. to pursue my theological studies at Gordon Divinity School in Boston, where I had a good contact with some Baptist professors and students. I was increasingly persuaded of the scriptural soundness of believer's baptism. Although I was not a Baptist, I was called in 1939 to be the pastor of two French Baptist churches in Worcester and vicinity. I was hesitant to proceed to my own baptism because I did not understand on what basis Presbyterian and Reformed people baptized infants while denying strongly the concept of baptismal regeneration.

In my theological studies, I became better acquainted with the biblical notion of the covenant. In this framework I could see the argument drawn from the age of circumcision in the Old Testament to the appropriateness of infant baptism in the New Testament. Yet I perceived that Old Testament circumcision had a twofold reference: (1) as a spiritual sign of a relation to God's covenant with His people and (2) as a national sign betokening a membership in the Jewish nation on which God bestowed a special blessing in the Old Testament (Rom. 9:4–5).

Since the second reference was superseded in the New Testament, leaving room only for a spiritual relationship with God, it was apparent to me that a possible shift would occur as to the proper subjects of the covenant sign and seal. The study of the New Testament elicited for me the following:

1. Discipleship was prerequisite for baptism (Matt. 28:19).
2. True repentance was prerequisite for baptism (Acts 2:37–38).

3. Saving faith was prerequisite for baptism (Acts 8:12; 18:8).

4. Regeneration was prerequisite for baptism, which actually portrayed symbolically the change brought about by the new birth (Acts 10:47; Rom. 6:2–5; Gal. 3:26–27).

I then applied to be baptized and become a member of my church in Worcester. This occurred in April 1943, a few weeks before my graduation with the doctorate in theology.

I was happy to find that the Baptist position provided room by virtue of a ceremony of infant dedication for the main truth reflected in infant baptism on the basis of God's covenant. There is a special blessing of God upon the family of believers. There are duties of believing parents and of their church of which they must be reminded and called upon to make a solemn commitment.

There is a parallelism here in the observance of the Lord's Supper. In the Old Testament, the Passover was celebrated as a family unit, and this included the children from infancy (Exod. 12:3, 26–27, 44–49). Yet in Protestant churches, participation in the Lord's Supper is generally limited to believers who are able to examine themselves (1 Cor. 11:28) and to discern the significance of the elements (1 Cor. 11:29). The Baptist theology of baptism remedies this inconsistency. Those who are baptized may partake of the Lord's Supper. Participation in both ordinances is the privilege of the new covenant people.

AUTHORITY OF THE BIBLE

In studying the history of Baptist movements, I was pleased to find strong commitment to the truthfulness of Scripture. All of the Baptists were at the start firm believers in the infallible authority of Scripture. Only in the late nineteenth century did serious doubts begin to surface. The inerrancy of the Bible was a fundamental element of my faith, so that I found myself in great harmony with the Baptist movement in its origins. As I am now a member of a Southern Baptist church in Florida, the recent return of Southern Baptists to this historical conviction pleases me personally and honors him who is the truth.

I also learned that Baptist theology reflected what I believed the Bible to teach about the doctrine of salvation. I noticed that the early Baptists in Anglo-Saxon lands were able to avoid some of the vagaries of the continental Anabaptists. Furthermore, in England where a distinction between General and Particular Baptist prevailed for some time, the former group tended toward rapid theological decline, while the latter group carried the lion's share of consistent Baptist work. It is to the Particular Baptists that the overwhelming majority of Baptists in the United States were historically related.

The confessional history from New England, to Philadelphia, to Charleston demonstrates this.

When the movement of Free Will Baptists occurred, the majority of Baptists in the North reacted by subscribing to the New Hampshire Confession of Faith, emphasizing the sovereignty of God. In the South, the Baptist movement was perhaps even more committed to its confessional heritage, as was James Petigru Boyce, founder and first president of The Southern Baptist Theological Seminary.

With this confessional heritage, I still affirm my belief in the radical and pervasive depravity of unregenerate humanity. This depravity prevents human beings from exercising true repentance or faith unless they are regenerated by the power of the Holy Spirit, in connection with the ministry of the Word of God, which the Baptist confessions describe as "effectual calling." Because this calling includes the renewal of the human will, it does not violate human will. But as the *Baptist Faith and Message* says, it is "consistent with the free agency of man." This work of the Spirit conforms to the eternal plan of the Father, whereby he has from all eternity chosen out of the mass of perdition an innumerable number of individual sinners to be the objects of his saving grace without regard to any preferential feature in themselves.

I am convinced that the Father's supreme intention in giving his Son and Christ's supreme intention in offering himself as a substitutionary sacrifice was to bring about a full salvation for his people, not just to remove an obstacle to the salvation of every sinner. I am convinced that those in whom God has begun his good work of regeneration, which is then further developed in sanctification and ultimately in glorification, will by virtue of his perseverance ultimately be brought to perfection in heaven (Phil. 1:6; Rom. 8:38–39). I am so pleased that Southern Baptists have consistently affirmed this truth, even though apart from the other aspects of God's grace its foundation may be endangered.

The presence of this view of salvation as a dominant stream in Baptist theology held great importance for me. Having a right doctrine of baptism, the church, and the Lord's Supper would hardly be any real advantage without a correspondingly true understanding of the grace of God in the gospel. This view of the gospel, however, is much more consistent with a Baptist ecclesiology than in any other context. In accordance with that conviction, therefore, it is important for me to affirm that in this great theological stream I am joyfully a Baptist.

PART NINE

CONCLUDING THOUGHTS

26

BAPTIST AFTER ALL: RESURGENT CONSERVATIVES FACE THE FUTURE

Russell D. Moore

There's a moment in every day when I cannot help but think of Woolmarket Baptist Church. Sometimes it's when I am preaching from my New American Standard Bible and unconsciously translate into the King James because it just seems right to end the passage with "and great was the fall thereof." Sometimes it's when I am baptizing a new believer and I can hear in my own voice the words of my faithful boyhood pastor, M. L. Faler: "Because you have confessed Jesus as your Savior and upon your profession of faith in him, I baptize you, my sister . . ." Sometimes it's simply when I realize that no matter how much I resonate with the theology of hymn writer Isaac Watts, a part of me will always prefer Fanny Crosby.

My home church on the outskirts of Biloxi, Mississippi, was typical of many Southern Baptist congregations in the 1970s and 1980s. We weren't "Sword of the Lord" fundamentalists like our friends who had to wear long pants even to swim. We were Billy Graham conservatives—solidly orthodox, fervently missionary, no axes to grind. Ours was a community steeped in revivalism, with a steady diet of dispensational end-times speculation here and there. Experiencing tremendous growth in the mid-1980s, we built a "family life center" gymnasium, even though the rapture of the church would probably take us all before the note was paid off. The apocalyptic literature so many of us were reading was sometimes more science fiction than biblical exegesis, but it propelled us to vigorous evangelism, meticulous Bible study, and expectant hope.

Our congregation was not a utopia. The only thing that made some of us question the pretribulational rapture was occasional business meetings that looked suspiciously similar to what we had been told about the battle of Armageddon. But I barely remember those business meetings. What I do remember vividly is that I never sat through a worship service that did not culminate in an appeal to sinners to be reconciled to God through the blood of his Son. I remember that our pastors held doggedly to the authority and inerrancy of the Bible, and they even believed it enough to preach the text. It is from these people that I learned what it means to be Baptist.

I remember the day, however, when as a college student I began to question whether my home congregation was even Baptist at all. A bright, articulate Baptist minister told me that the doctrinal convictions I had been taught were not distinctively Baptist, but instead were "evangelical," maybe even "fundamentalist." Real Baptists, he insisted, did not believe in an "old Princeton" concept like biblical inerrancy. Baptists, he said, held to the *Baptist* distinctives of soul competency, the priesthood of the believer, believer's baptism, separation of church and state, and religious liberty. Baptists were not "creedalists," like my home church seemed to have been.

For a while I wondered if he might be right. Perhaps I had spent my childhood in a backward congregation of fundamentalists, exiled from our freedom-loving "authentic Baptist" counterparts. I was forced to explore the issue. I began a long process of biblical and historical analysis that led me right back to what I had learned at Vacation Bible School opening assembly. The Scriptures claim to be the unerring Word of God. They speak with the very authority of the Creator who breathed them out. Furthermore, I was elated to find that my confirmed evangelical views were not out of step with my Baptist identity. There was an entire confessional heritage that was both authentically Baptist and doctrinally conservative.

This moderate clergyman's view of Baptist identity is hardly unique. Since the inerrancy controversy of the 1970s and 1980s, moderate Baptists have claimed the mantle of the "authentic Baptists." For instance, Russell Dilday, former president of Southwestern Baptist Theological Seminary, writes that conservative Baptists are simply "pseudo-Baptists, rogues inside the family who either never knew or have forgotten what our true identity is."[1]

I find such arguments unconvincing, both theologically and historically. Still, the question is not altogether an unfair one. Are we just parachurch evangelicals who happen to have Baptist backgrounds? Will we pass on to our children a generic evangelical conservatism instead of a distinctively Baptist identity? The question for a new generation of conservative Southern Baptists might be more than just "Why are we Baptists?" Now that the battle for the Bible has been won, perhaps we should ask, "Are we Baptists at all?"

On this side of the resurgence, conservatives must be careful that we do not unconsciously believe the caricatures we have read about ourselves in the state Baptist newspapers. The Baptist distinctives are not ideological weapons to be used against us. They are our heritage. Indeed, they can only survive in the context of the biblical authority and confessional conviction for which we have fought. The stakes are simply too high. If there are to be any Baptists at the turn of the *next* century, we cannot concede Baptist identity to the ever-diminishing left flank of the denomination.

BELIEVER'S BAPTISM BY IMMERSION

Early last century, orthodox Baptists were aghast at the liberal theological stances of modernist Harry Emerson Fosdick of New York's Riverside Church. Their denunciation of Fosdick, however, was not limited to his rejection of such fundamentals as the virgin birth, substitutionary atonement, and the second coming, but extended to his downgrade of baptism as well. In a scathing commentary, fundamentalist John Roach Straton quoted Fosdick as asking: "Why should baptism divide? If I had my way baptism would be altogether an individual affair. Any one who wanted to be immersed I would gladly immerse. Any one who wanted to be sprinkled I would gladly sprinkle. If anybody was a Quaker and had conscientious scruples against any ritual, I would gladly, without baptism, welcome him on confession of his faith. Why not?"[2]

Straton argued that Fosdick's jettisoning of his Baptist heritage on immersion was not incidental to his rejection of the cardinal tenets of the faith, but was instead a natural outgrowth of it. Straton recognized that believer's baptism is a conservative issue because baptism cannot be severed from its kerygmatic content.

Conservative Southern Baptists should not be intimidated into thinking that others are the conservators of believer's baptism. This is hardly the case. Freed from the constraints of biblical inerrancy and denominational ties, some moderate Baptists are calling for a new, sacerdotal understanding of baptism that is a marked departure from the Baptist distinctives they once championed. Feminist theologian Molly T. Marshall, for example, calls for a Baptist "liturgical renewal in our theology of the sacraments" that sees in baptism itself the mysterious and grace-bearing presence of God.[3]

Similarly, some Baptist moderates have broadened the Baptist tent wide enough to welcome sprinkling and even infant baptism. The moderate newspaper *Baptists Today,* for instance, published a special feature on the centrality of believer's baptism that advocated acceptance of those christened as infants into the membership of Baptist churches. "For the sake of ecumenical cooperation, we must convince Baptists to accept those believers who have been baptized as infants, and we must convince other denominations to baptize only believers in Jesus Christ," the author asserts. "Even as we don't require baptism of those adults, teenagers, and children who were baptized apart from conviction but later came to believe, so we should not require the baptism of those who believe though they were baptized as infants."[4]

Mike Clingenpeel, the moderate editor of the *Religious Herald,* writes that his refusal to limit baptism to immersion comes from his commitment to "soul competency."[5] This is quite an evolution from the days when the *Religious Herald* published books indicting sprinkling and pouring as "barbarisms" and "substitutes for baptism" that must be "ruled out" by Baptists.[6]

Will Campbell, the poet laureate of the Baptist left, is even more remarkable as he describes his baptism of his infant grandson.

> My daughter Bonnie asked me if I would baptize her three-year-old son, Harlan, on Christmas. And my daddy was here. At that point, he had been a Baptist deacon for 60 years. And I was afraid. In Baptist circles infant baptism is quite a scandal—particularly if not by immersion.
>
> So I asked in deference to him, "Daddy, do you believe in infant baptism?" And he said, "Believe in it, son? I've actually seen it." That was his way of saying, "Don't be silly! Baptize

> your grandson!" So we did, at the breakfast table. Harlan got to giggling while we were doing this. And when we got finished, he said (he called me Papa), "'Papa, what'd you put on my head?" I said, "Water." And he said, "Why?"
>
> Bonnie was squirming. She didn't want her three-year-old son traumatized by her daddy's horse-and-buggy theology. But it was a fair question, so I was glad to answer it. I talked about guilt and forgiveness. He said, "What is guilt?" I said, "You know that big lump you get in your throat when you and your mama quarrel?"
>
> Well, when I got through with the little homily, he jumped down from the table, wiped the last of the runny egg with his biscuit and started off toward the door to the television room. Then he came back and grabbed me around the knees, looked up and, in the throes of a deep-down belly laugh said, "Well, well, Papa. Thank you then."[7]

How can Campbell, who has long claimed the "authentic Baptist" label in his criticism of SBC conservatives, sprinkle water on the head of a three-year-old who doesn't even understand guilt, and call it baptism? Campbell's comments on his own baptism are instructive here. He recounts that there was "nothing really unusual about it": "Joe, my brother, joined the church, so I was going to join too. He originally tried to talk me out of it. And the white britches that were ordered from Sears and Roebuck for me to be baptized in didn't come in on time. I said, 'I hate Sears and Roebuck.' Joe said I wasn't supposed to get mad. He told me that he would be the propitiation for my sins. That's what baptism is all about."[8]

As with Fosdick, Campbell's baptismal views fit naturally with his understanding of the gospel. "Jesus didn't talk about the 'Plan of Salvation' or the Trinity or any of these things, that I can find," Campbell concludes. "He talked about the backward notion of community: things like a cup of cold water."[9]

Nonetheless, conservative Baptists are not immune from a downgrade on this front themselves. Out of tactical necessity, the postwar evangelical movement's parachurch ministries often downplayed ecclesiological particularities as they sought a new day of united evangelical action. The new evangelicals did not wish to duplicate fundamentalism's debilitating infighting over denominational distinctives, eschatological positions, and certain questions of personal morality. As such, baptism was, and is, sometimes seen by some as an uncomfortable obstacle to be overcome.

This approach has sometimes spilled over into Baptist life, with results the postwar evangelical leaders never intended. Some evangelical Baptist theologians have followed brilliant defenses of believer's immersion as *the* New Testament meaning of baptism with an inexplicable conclusion that churches should not require such baptism for church members. Some baptistic evangelical pastors will debate the issue vigorously with their pedobaptist counterparts, but gladly accept as church members those sprinkled as infants. More commonly, many conservative Baptist pastors are finding it harder and harder to explain to angry church members why Methodist Aunt Gladys should have to be "rebaptized" to join the church.

Inerrantists must ask themselves, however, whether the Bible has spoken to this issue. When the resurrected Lord Jesus commanded his disciples to baptize the nations, did he have anything specific in mind? If by baptism he meant the immersion of believers in water, then how can we do otherwise, regardless of the discomfort it may cause our evangelical pedobaptist friends?

Another pitfall for Baptist conservatives on the baptism issue is pedobaptism itself. For some Southern Baptist churches, baptism has become a kind of Bar Mitzvah expected of all children nearing adolescence. Well-meaning Vacation Bible School workers ask children if they love Jesus and want to go to heaven, then promptly lead them to the baptistry. Little thought is given to the fact that the answers to these questions do not necessarily indicate a regenerate heart. Indeed, the child who responds that he hates Jesus and wants to go to hell most likely would be referred to a therapist.

Paige Patterson, an architect of the SBC conservative resurgence, has expressed grave concerns about the Southern Baptist drift toward "a shallow form of easy-believism in evangelism, which was augmented by a trend of baptizing more and more children at increasingly tender ages so that the very denomination that had built its reputation opposing infant baptism became to an embarrassing degree practitioners of a sort of 'late stage' pedobaptism."[10] The result, Patterson argues, are Baptist churches filled with unregenerate members, making them "superlative fishing waters for the various cults."[11] Who can argue with Patterson's observation here? Conservatives face another threat to a Baptist view of baptism in the trivialization of the ordinance. W. A. Criswell's instructions to pastors on "how to baptize beautifully" seems almost antebellum to some contemporary Baptists: "We do not throw our beloved dead into the grave. We carefully and tenderly lower them into the grave. Since baptism is a burial, we also should baptize our candidates that way. We should not throw them into the water, dash them into the water, or splash the water all over everywhere as we lower the candidate into the watery grave. Contrariwise, we shall lovingly and tenderly lower them down into the water, then raise them up in triumphant exaltation."[12]

Such gravity is quite a contrast to the friend who recently told me he jokingly wore a life jacket into the waters to baptize his daughter, since he had slipped in the baptistry the week before. Baptism is sidelined when its gospel meaning is forgotten, even if it is not denied. If baptism is nothing more than our version of "first communion" or a way to "nail down" assurance of salvation or a hoop to jump through on the way to service on the flower committee, then it is nothing at all.

Inerrantists, however, should be ashamed to have this problem. After all, the centuries-long debate over baptism was fought on the grounds that Baptists believed an outside authority, the Bible, compelled them to immerse believers. If contemporary conservatives are to contend for the faith once for all delivered to the saints, they must contend for every aspect of that faith, including the command of the Lord Jesus to baptize his sheep. If this part of our Baptist heritage will survive the relativistic morass of the coming century, it will be because conservative evangelicals recognize that biblical authority applies not only to the crusade tent, but to the baptistry as well.

REGENERATE CHURCH MEMBERSHIP

An even more endangered Baptist distinctive is the understanding of the church as a body of regenerate believers. In opposition to their pedobaptist opponents, Baptists have always held that the world, not the church, is to be composed of wheat and tares. The church is made up of those whose hearts have been transformed by the work of the Spirit and whose confession reflects a common experience of grace. The new generation of conservatives cannot take this issue for granted. After all, they are the ones who have fought so hard for the assertion that regeneration is a life-changing work of the Spirit, not simply an awakening to an already-existent reality. In years past, this manifested itself not only in a refusal to baptize infants, but also in a concerted effort to obey the biblical command to discipline church members who fell into scandalous sin.[13]

Much has been written regarding the appalling lack of church discipline in contemporary congregational life. This applies not only to the refusal of high-profile moderate congregations to confront sexually predatory national politicians on their membership rolls. Sadly, it applies to some of our most conservative Baptist congregations as well. Many churches simply have never seen church discipline in action, unless it was the sad spectacle of the local "fighting fundamentalist" independent church arbitrarily ousting a deacon for listening to a Willie Nelson album.

If the next generation of Baptist conservatives is to reclaim the distinctive of regenerate church membership, we must recognize that our chaotic church life is not only in direct violation of Scripture; it is inherently antievangelistic. It proclaims to the watching world that we do not really believe what we so fervently preach.

"Religion is frequently not so much the product of a dogmatic belief as it is the provider of a convenient language that allows communities to express moral beliefs that they would hold on entirely secular grounds," contends philosopher Francis Fukuyama.[14] When a self-proclaimed believers' church winks and nods at the adulterer in the choir, we are conceding to Fukuyama that he and a long line of cultured despisers are right. We do not really believe in the God of our evangelistic tracts. Our young couples vote Republican, our children watch "VeggieTales," and our teenagers sign their True Love Waits cards. What more could we possibly want?

If a Baptist church holds to regenerate church membership, this means it is affirming that it believes the names on its membership roster to be the names of Christians. In our door-to-door evangelism, we do not nod silently when the homeowner tells us he is going to heaven because he has lived a good life. Why then would we allow those with just as little evidence of regeneration to plummet toward hell, reassuring themselves all the way that they are members of our churches? Do we love the names on our church rolls any less than the names on our visitor cards?

If we believe in an inerrant Bible, we will recognize that "truth without mixture of error" includes Matthew 18 and 1 Corinthians 5. If we really believe in the justice of God, we will not allow the slumlord or the abortionist to claim the name of Christ's church while grinding underneath his feet the helpless and the poor. If we really believe the exalted Jesus Christ rules from heaven over his church, then we will listen to the way he commands that it be governed.

Such an understanding will propel Baptists to champion once again the centrality of the church in the plan of salvation. The New Testament nowhere presents the church as merely a vehicle for individual believers to "grow" and "be fed" through instruction and fellowship. Nor does it portray the church as merely a cooperative effort for the global missions task. In the new covenant, the people of God and the gathered church are synonymous. Jesus did not die for a collection of isolated individuals, but for his church (Acts 20:28).

When the New Testament addresses those who have walked away from life in the local congregation, it does not speak to them as "inactive members" in need of better "follow-up" after a particularly offensive business meeting. It speaks of them as unbelievers on the brink of the wrath of God (Heb. 10:19–39; 1 John 2:19). Evangelistic conservatives will love these people enough to say more than just "we miss you at church."

SEPARATION OF CHURCH AND STATE

Too often Baptist conservatives consider themselves especially vulnerable on the Baptist distinctive of church/state separation. Some Baptist conservatives have even avoided the concession that there *is* a separation between church and state, for fear it would mean removing crèches from the public square or forbidding prayers at high school graduation exercises. More and more Baptist evangelicals, however, are recognizing that church/state separation, when it is defined by the biblical canon, is part of our conservative heritage.

Some warn that a renewed Baptist confessionalism will lead to scary schemes to take over the structures of government. The SBC's Ethics and Religious Liberty Commission, however, led by conservative Richard Land, has staunchly opposed direct government aid to Christian schools, teacher-led school prayer, and other encroachments on the separation of church and state. Conservatives maintain that biblical church/state separation does not mean that Baptists cannot fight for the lives of the unborn. It does not mean that we cannot prophetically denounce debauchery in the Oval Office. It does not mean we must gag our mouths in the public square.

Historic evangelical Baptists believe the state to be ordained of God, but we also affirm that the church is ruled by the crucified one, whom God has set on the throne of David. We must reclaim the understanding that the church is the initial manifestation of the kingdom of God, a kingdom in miniature situated now among the other kingdoms of this world.

Every Baptist congregation should remind the watching powers of this age that the church is an alternative community, ruled by a just and righteous King (Ps. 72). The activities of every Baptist congregation should be a perpetual visual reminder that the tranquility of injustice soon will be disturbed, as the kingdom represented in their midst crushes the kingdoms of this world

(Dan. 2:44) and the entire cosmos trembles before the indisputable sovereignty of the church's risen head.

The resurgence of Baptist confessionalism should prove to revitalize, not sidetrack, our commitment to church/state separation. After all, conservatives are the ones who refused to follow social gospel pioneer Walter Rauschenbusch in decimating the distinction between the church and the world. Every time an SBC missionary baptizes a Chinese convert in defiance of the totalitarian regime, he is proclaiming the very same message that Thomas Helwys, John Bunyan, and John Leland once preached so long ago.

If Southern Baptist conservatives embrace this biblical vision of the church, we will not fear anyone's skewed understanding of the relationship between the church and the political order, but neither will we seek the ultimate answer to the "culture wars" in the election of any candidate to political office. Instead, we will engage the culture politically and theologically, but we will also demonstrate kingdom-righteousness within the walls of our churches. We will submit to the governing authorities even as we wait for the one who will come, not to praise Caesar but to bury him.

RELIGIOUS LIBERTY

The next generation of Baptist conservatives may have fewer moderates labeling them as threats to religious liberty, but they will have the secular culture even more eager to do so. After all, the world sees self-styled evangelicals bombing abortion clinics, theonomists calling for the United States of America to be governed by the Mosaic civil code, and even a few Christian neoconfederates arguing that slavery wasn't so unbiblical after all. Of course, these groups do not represent Baptist confessionalism, but secular onlookers often have neither the theological understanding nor the inclination to make such distinctions. To them, Christian orthodoxy means political oppression.

By presenting a clearly biblical and distinctively Baptist view of religious liberty, however, Baptist conservatives can offer a better way. It is their birthright. After all, the historic Baptist commitment to religious freedom cannot be disjointed from a biblical foundation that affirms the necessity of the new birth. Inerrantists know that no Supreme Court majority can ever regenerate a single human heart. In this we agree with George W. Truett: "Persecution may make men hypocrites, but it can never make them Christians."[15] Conservatives therefore should seek religious liberty precisely because we believe in evangelism.

This is already beginning to occur as Southern Baptist conservatives find themselves ringing the bell of religious liberty with increasing frequency. Condemned by the secular media and the religious establishment, Southern Baptists have been forced to issue statements claiming the right to share their faith with unbelievers. Against an often-bullying bureaucracy, Southern Baptist conservatives have been compelled to argue that school children have the religious freedom to gather together voluntarily for prayer.

Against some ironic suggestions from Baptist moderates that the courts could overrule conservative restrictions on the pastorate to men, Baptist conservatives may increasingly be forced to contend for the liberty of churches to call their pastors in line with their biblical convictions.[16] With hearts broken by the crucifixion of fellow Christians in the Sudan, Southern Baptist conservatives have been a growing prophetic voice for religious freedom around the world. As Southern Baptists realize that true biblical conservatism often puts them at odds even with Bible-belt culture, religious freedom will be increasingly an explicitly conservative cause.

SOUL COMPETENCY?

Perhaps no claim to "authentic Baptist" credentials has been more controversial than the discussion of "soul competency." Again, the debate has often been caricatured into a struggle between moderates supporting the concept and conservatives opposing it. In the heat of the controversy, however, conservatives often pointed to soul competency as the basis for appealing to grassroots Baptists for change in the denomination. Likewise, a growing number of communitarian moderates have criticized "soul competency" as an outdated vestige of Enlightenment individualism.[17]

Conservatives have been right to be suspicious of "soul competency" rhetoric when it is used to suggest that confessionalism is not authentically Baptist, especially as the full implications of such "soul freedom" become clearer.[18] Southern Baptist conservatives can reclaim the mantle of "soul competency," however, by understanding the gospel context in which it was first arti culated. We recognize that no one's proxy faith can save a neighbor at the coming judgment. He will stand before the tribunal of God with a mediator in the Lord Jesus, or he will stand alone.

In short, the sound of soul competency is not the voice of a dean celebrating the latest lesbian at his divinity school; it is the voice of R. G. Lee thundering "Payday Someday!" Indeed, soul competency is perhaps the most sobering aspect of our Baptist heritage because it means no individual can claim innocence before the judge of all humanity. It should propel us to the streets and to the mission fields, urgently pleading with perilously competent souls to find salvation in Christ.

THE FUTURE OF BAPTIST CONFESSIONALISM

The American movement of secular political conservatives found cohesion after World War II in a united front against the global communist threat. Libertarians, paleoconservatives, neoconservatives, and religious activists largely put aside their internal conflicts to stand together against totalitarianism.[19] As the Cold War thawed, however, these conservatives found that without a common enemy, the old tensions could threaten to crack the movement apart.[20]

Baptist confessionalism is not a political movement. Still, if we bear the responsibility for carrying Baptist identity into a new century, we must recognize that we may face a similar quandary. During the inerrancy controversy, conservatives could see easily how necessary it was for us to coalesce in common commitment to biblical authority and confessional fidelity. As the Baptist left isolates itself further from denominational life, conservatives must avoid organizing ourselves into narrowly defined special interest groups of competing theological emphases.

There *will* be complete doctrinal unanimity among Baptist conservatives, but it will not be achieved until the millennial reign of Christ. Until then, we may never even agree on whether there will *be* such a millennial reign. On the foundational doctrines we must stand united and constantly work for even greater doctrinal consensus. But, contrary to the spin control of our critics, confessionalism does not mean lockstep groupthink. My coeditor and I understand differently what the Bible teaches about the relationship between Israel and the church, about the appropriate method of public invitation, and about various other second-order issues. We differ on these things, however, in the unity of a common submission to a larger framework of biblical truth.

The resurgent conservatism of the last twenty years does not instantly eradicate in-house debates on such questions as whether the earth is only six thousand years old or whether faith precedes regeneration or whether the Lord's Supper can be taken with leavened bread. It does, however, ensure that we treat even these less-than-primary questions with gravity, in submission to a commonly accepted authority and a commonly held body of doctrinal convictions. In this, we have the opportunity to demonstrate that the essential Baptist distinctives are not isolated abstractions, but are parts of a recovered theological whole. Only then can the distinctives of Bapt ist identity be guarded for generations yet unborn.

It would be wrong to say, however, that the Baptist distinctives are forever secure now that the denominational leadership is solidly conservative. There are pitfalls along the way, to be sure. Incipient threats to Baptist identity may be found even in the polar opposite wings of the Baptist conservative movement.

The "seeker-sensitive" movement is an all-too-easy target. Despite some of the silliness on the extremes, the evangelistic impulse here has equipped multitudes for planting churches, evangelizing the lost, and establishing Baptist witness in places previously thought impervious to the gospel. Some nontraditional churches have been much more intentional about meaningful church membership and other Baptist imperatives than some of their critics.

The temptation for a new generation, however, could be to see Baptist identity as a nuisance in the quest for converts. The effort to minimize an offensive "denominational brand name" will be counterproductive if we produce a generation of "anonymous Baptists," those whom we believe cannot handle the truth about Christ's design for his church. It will be tragic indeed if a future Broadman & Holman catalog includes a book titled *Why I Am a Community Church (SBC) Member.*

But it will be equally tragic if the volume is entitled *Why I Want to Be a Presbyterian, but the Bible Won't Let Me.* A growing number of inerrantists are coming to see that being Baptist means theological substance, not just freedom and not just programs. The temptation here may be to a gnostic-like pride that verges on a loathing of one's Baptist heritage. As some of the essays in this volume will testify, it is quite easy to talk oneself into infant baptism when the lure of another, seemingly more intellectually robust, confessional tradition is in view. Even some who choose to remain Baptist sometimes sound as though they consider themselves to be burdened and embarrassed by the "typical" Baptist congregations, often the very churches that led these individuals to Christ. Such is not fertile soil for the Baptist witness.

WHY AM I A BAPTIST?

Some are perplexed by Baptists like me. James Dunn, for example, surveys the landscape of Baptist conservatism and exclaims, "Oh for the days of Baptist Training Union when we knew who we were!"[21] But I was there for Training Union. An "authentic Baptist" grandmother made sure of it. It was there, from Baptist ladies like Mrs. Hattie V. Felsher, that I learned to be a biblical inerrantist. In fact, if it hadn't been for them, I would probably be

Baptist in the same way Woody Allen is Jewish. I still would know all the hymns by heart. I still would know the difference between an RA and an Acteen. But I would be a nominal Baptist, not an authentic one.

In the aftermath of the Baptist battles, I have come to realize what my home church seemed to know all along. The responsibility for conserving the Baptist heritage rests upon those who believe the very Bible in which our forebears found these Baptist distinctives in the first place. Woolmarket Baptist Church might have been mistaken in expecting the Antichrist in the 1980s, but they were right to teach me to cherish biblical authority, believer's baptism, the regenerate church, religious liberty, church/state separation, and even soul competency. They were authentic Baptists, after all.

ENDNOTES

PREFACE

1. Cecil Staton, Jr., *Why I Am a Baptist: Reflections on Being Baptist in the 21st Century* (Macon, Ga.: Smyth and Helwys, 1999).
2. Louie D. Newton, ed., *Why I Am a Baptist* (New York: Thomas Nelson, 1957); Joe T. Odle, ed., *Why I Am a Baptist* (Nashville: Broadman, 1972).
3. Robert C. Ballance, Jr., "Baptist Born, Baptist Bred," in *Why I Am a Baptist: Reflections on Being Baptist in the 21st Century,* 7.

1. BEING A BAPTIST: WE MUST NOT SELL IT CHEAP

1. R. G. Lee, "Why I Am a Baptist" in Joe Odle, ed. *Why I Am a Baptist* (Nashville: Broadman, 1972), 21–22.
2. C. A. Jenkens, *Baptist Doctrines* (St. Louis: Chancy R. Barnes, 1882), iv.
3. J. M Frost, *Baptist: Why and Why Not* (Nashville: Sunday School Board of the Southern Baptist Convention, 1900), 9, 12.
4. Ibid., 11.
5. O. C. S. Wallace, *What Baptists Believe* (Nashville: Sunday School Board of the Southern Baptist Convention, 1913; reprinted by Calvary Baptist Church, Piqua, Ohio, 2000), 4.
6. Louie D. Newton, *Why I Am a Baptist* (New York: Thomas Nelson & Sons, 1957), 47–71.
7. Ibid., 97–106.
8. Ibid., 290–91.

9. Ibid., 284–285.
10. Ibid., 300–301.
11. Ibid., 229
12. Ibid., 304.
13. Odle, 9–10.
14. Ibid., 57.
15. Ibid., 73, 54.
16. Ibid., 88.
17. Ibid., 93.
18. J. B. Gambrell, *Ten Years in Texas* (Dallas: Baptist Standard, 1910), 129.
19. B. H. Carroll, *An Interpretation of the English Bible: Colossians, Ephesians, and Hebrews* (Grand Rapids: Baker Book House, 1973; reprint of Broadman Press, 1948 edition), 146, 148.
20. *The Christian Index*, 20 October 1887.
21. From "The Cotton Grove Resolutions," Robert A. Baker, *A Baptist Sourcebook* (Nashville: Broadman, 1966), 142.
22. Hercules Collins, *An Orthodox Catechism* (London: 1680), preface.
23. Oliver Hart, *The Character of a Truly Great Man Delineated and His Death Deplored as a Public Loss* (Charlestown, S.C.: Printed by David Bruce, 1777), 24.
24. Abraham Booth, *An Apology for the Baptists* (London: Printed for W. Button, 1812), 144–45.
25. Ibid., 147.
26. Roger Williams, *The Complete Writings of Roger Williams*, 7 vols. (New York: Russell & Russell, 1963), 3:13.
27. J. B. Cranfill, *From Memory* (Nashville: Broadman, 1937), 118, 149.
28. Helmut Thielicke, *Encounter with Spurgeon*, trans. John W. Doberstein (Cambridge: James Clarke & Co., 1978), 1.
29. Ibid., 47.
30. Greg Warner, "Baptist Identity Dismantled, Reforming, Bill Leonard Says," Associated Baptist Press, 5 May 2000.
31. Gary E. Parker, *Principles Worth Protecting* (Macon: Smyth & Helwys, 1993), 50.
32. Charles Spurgeon, *Sword and Trowel*, February 1888.
33. The Baptist Union statement may be found in William L. Lumpkin, *Baptist Confessions of Faith* (Valley Forge: Judson Press, 1969), 345–46.
34. *Annual of the Northern Baptist Convention, 1922* (Philadelphia: American Baptist Publication Society, 1922), 133.

35. *Annual of the Northern Baptist Convention, 1925* (Philadelphia: American Baptist Publication Society, 1925), 85–86.

2. IN DISREGARD OF CARNAL EASE

1. Alvah Hovey, *A Memoir of the Life and Times of the Rev. Isaac Backus* (Harrisonsburg, Va.: Gano Books, 1991 reprint of Alvah Hovey, *A Memoir of the Life and Times of the Rev. Isaac Backus, A.M.* Boston: Gould and Lincoln, 1859), 28–29.
2. Ibid., 36.
3. Ibid., 37, 38.
4. Ibid., 37–40.
5. Isaac Backus, *A History of New England with Particular Reference to the Baptists.* (New York: Arno Press, 1969, reprint of Newton, Mass.: Backus Historical Society, 1871), 2:109, fn 1.
6. Ibid., 111, fn 1.
7. Ibid., 116.
8. Ibid.
9. Ibid., 117.
10. Ibid., 118.
11. Ibid.
12. Hovey, *Memoir,* 334–39.

3. PAINFULLY MORTIFIED, BUT JOYFUL IN THE TRUTH

1. James D. Knowles, *Memoir of Mrs. Ann H. Judson* (Boston: Lincoln & Edmands, 1829), 9–10.
2. Ibid., 13.
3. Ibid., 15.
4. Ibid., 17–18.
5. Ibid., 30.
6. Ibid., 18.
7. Ibid., 19.
8. Ibid., 23.
9. Ibid., 24.
10. Francis Wayland, *A Memoir of the Life and Labors of the Rev. Adoniram Judson, D.D.* 2 vols. (Boston: Phillips, Sampson, and Company, 1853), 1:34–35.

11. Knowles, *Memoir,* 63–64.
12. Ibid., 61–62.
13. Wayland, *Memoir,* 1:105–106.
14. Knowles, *Memoir,* 62–63.

4. A BAPTIST: PRINCIPLE, NOT SENTIMENT

1. Henry Thompson Louthan, ed., *The American Baptist Pulpit at the Beginning of the Twentieth Century* (Williamsburg, Va.: Published by the editor, 1903), 731.
2. John A. Broadus, *Memoir of James Petigru Boyce* (New York: A. C. Armstrong & Son, 1893), 317.
3. George Braxton Taylor, *Virginia Baptist Ministers,* Fourth Series (Lynchburg, Va.: J. P. Bell, 1913), 400.
4. This same appeal to the Bible saturated Kerfoot's article in *Baptist Why and Why Not* (Nashville: Sunday School Board, 1900), 353–60. Entitled "Why the Baptist Doctrine," the chapter pointed with great clarity to the authority of Scripture as the decisive issue. "Baptists, however, are sure," Kerfoot wrote with confidence, "that the Word of God is the only infallible and all-sufficient rule of faith and practice, and that nothing should be taught for doctrine which is not contained therein." Moreover, Kerfoot continued, a Baptist believes "all that is taught therein must be believed; and that all that is commanded there ought to be obeyed as commanded." Later, Kerfoot says that the Baptist "feels bound by the Baptist doctrine, which as he understands it, is the Bible doctrine." Again, "His Bible, as he understands it, compels him to do so. This is not bigotry or intolerance on his part; it is simply his sense of what God requires at his hands." And finally, "Why then the Baptist doctrine? Simply this: We think the Bible teaches it, and demands of us that we hold it. The principle may not be sacrificed to sentiment."

5. WHAT IS A BAPTIST?

1. E. Y. Mullins, "Baptists and the Bible," *Encyclopedia of Southern Baptists,* vol. 1 (Nashville: Broadman Press, 1958), 143.
2. P. E. Burroughs, *The Baptist People from the First to the Twentieth Century* (Nashville: Sunday School Board of the Southern Baptist Convention, 1934), 65.
3. Mullins, "Baptists and the Bible," 143.

4. This article reprinted by permission from the October 2000 issue of *SBC Life,* the journal of the Southern Baptist Convention Executive Committee.

7. SHOOT-OUT AT THE AMEN CORRAL: BEING BAPTIST THROUGH CONTROVERSY

1. Robert A. Baker, *The Baptist March in History* (Nashville: Convention Press, 1958), 31.

8. WHERE I BURIED OLD ERROLL HULSE: A JOURNEY IN BELIEVER'S BAPTISM

1. Erroll Hulse, *The Testimony of Baptism* (Haywards Heath, Sussex: Carey Publications, 1982).
2. *New Geneva Study Bible* (Nashville: Thomas Nelson Publishers), 38.
3. John Calvin, *Institutes of the Christian Religion,* vol. 2, ed. John T. McNeill, trans. Ford Lewis Battles (Philadelphia: Westminster Press, 1960), 1303–59.
4. It is needful that I make clear that the convoluted reasoning and vilification of Calvin in this section contrasts sharply with the rest of his writing in the *Institutes,* which is excellent and edifying.
5. Karl Barth, *Die Taufe,* 39–40, cited in Paul K. Jewett, *Infant Baptism and the Covenant of Grace* (Grand Rapids: Eerdmans, 1978), 111.
6. Murray Adamthwaite, "Baptism Is Immersion!" *Reformation Today* 109 (May-June 1989), 30–40.
7. Joel Beeke, *The Quest for Full Assurance* (Edinburgh: Banner of Truth, 1999), 293ff.
8. H. F. Stander and J. P. Louw, *Baptism in the Early Church* (Garfontein, South Africa: Didaskalia Publishers, 1988).
9. Most Presbyterian denominations accept Roman Catholic infant baptism. This demonstrates that they are not consistent in their claim to base their practice on the Abrahamic Covenant. If that were so, they would reject the sacralism of the Roman Catholic and Anglican churches.
10. Adoniram Judson's book on this subject, *Christian Baptism,* has been recently republished by Audubon Press.

11. FROM A WELSH REVIVAL TO A BAPTIST PULPIT

1. Louis Berkhof, *Systematic Theology* (Carlisle, Penn.: Banner of Truth, 1949), 632.

12. WHEN OUR SENSES GET IN THE WAY: FROM CATHOLIC SACRAMENTS TO BAPTIST CONVENTION

1. David Bryant, *In the Gap: What It Means to Be a World Christian* (Madison, Wis.: InterVarsity Missions, 1979).

13. ALL THINGS CONSIDERED . . . A BAPTIST

1. Mark Dever, ed., *Polity: Biblical Arguments on How to Conduct Church Life* (Washington, D.C.: Center for Church Reform, 2001).

15. MISERY LOVES COMPANY? A PRESBYTERIAN PASTOR COMES HOME

1. This has been recently published as *A String of Pearls Unstrung: A Journal on Baptism* (Cape Coral, Fla.: Founders Press, 1998).

17. EVERYTHING A BAPTIST MOTHER COULD WANT

1. R. M. Dudley, "The Distinctive Baptist Way: Our Reasons for the Separate Existence of the Baptists," *Baptist Why and Why Not,* 26.
2. J. M. Frost, "The Confession of Faith," *Baptist Why and Why Not,* 196.
3. J. P. Greene, "Why Education by Baptist Schools," *Baptist Why and Why Not,* 78.
4. T. T. Eaton, "Why the Bible and Not Other Standards," *Baptist Why and Why Not,* 34.
5. Curtis Lee Laws, "Why Missionary and Not 'Omissionary,'" in *Baptist Why and Why Not,* 75.
6. J. G. Bow, *What Baptists Believe and Why They Believe It* (Nashville: Sunday School Board of the Southern Baptist Convention, n.d.), 36.
7. Paul Clarke and others, *Our Baptist Heritage* (Leeds, England: Reformation Today Trust, 1993), 18.
8. J. C. Ryle, *Expository Thoughts on Mark* (Edinburgh: Banner of Truth, 1985, 204.

9. Sharon James, *My Heart in His Hands* (Durham, England: Evangelical Press, 1998), 55.
10. Tom Ascol, "Bill Clinton and the Discipline of Our Churches," *The Founders Journal,* 34 (Fall 1998), 3.
11. Edward T. Hiscox, *The New Directory for Baptist Churches* (Grand Rapids: Kregel Publications, 1970 [formerly published by Judson Press, 1894]), 15.
12. Ibid., 17.
13. Bow, 23.
14. Dudley, "The Distinctive Baptist Way," 30.
15. Report of the Baptist Faith and Message Study Committee to the Southern Baptist Convention, 14 June 2000.

19. A MERE CHRISTIAN, AND A BAPTIST TOO

1. C. S. Lewis, *Mere Christianity* (New York: Macmillan, 1952), 6.
2. Ibid., 11–12.
3. Notice that the two sorts of explanation given here—the first theological, the second sociological—can be seen as complementary rather than competing accounts. For, of course, the sociological explanation can be seen as fleshing out some of the means God used to bring it about that I am Baptist.
4. Cf. H. Leon McBeth, *The Baptist Heritage: Four Centuries of Baptist Witness* (Nashville: Broadman Press, 1987), 412–32.
5. *Baptist Confessions, Covenants, and Catechisms,* ed. Timothy and Denise George (Nashville: Broadman and Holman, 1996), 59.
6. The quotation is from article I of the *Baptist Faith and Message* (2000). That biblical authority finds its grounding in the Bible's divine authorship is certainly no new idea for Baptists: "The authority of the Holy Scripture, for which it ought to be believed, dependeth . . . wholly upon God (who is Truth itself), the Author thereof; therefore it is to be received, because it is the Word of God" (Philadelphia Confession of Faith [1742], *Baptist Confessions, Covenants, and Catechisms,* 57).
7. T. T. Eaton, "Why the Bible and Not Other Standards," in J. M. Frost's *Baptist Why and Why Not,* ed. Timothy and Denise George (Nashville: Broadman and Holman, 1996), 38.
8. Timothy George, "The Priesthood of All Believers and the Quest for Theological Integrity," *Criswell Theological Review* 3 (1989): 292.

9. Ibid., 293.
10. This can be put more formally as follows: For any proposition *P*, if the Bible affirms *P*, then *P*. Notice that, contrary to what some have said, the doctrine of inerrancy can be stated quite simply and does not need to be attended by a detailed list of disclaimers or qualifications.
11. See article I of the *Baptist Faith and Message* (2000).
12. For a helpful history of Baptist attitudes toward the Bible, see L. Russ Bush and Tom J. Nettles, *Baptists and the Bible,* rev. ed. (Nashville: Broadman and Holman, 1999).

20. DISTINCTIVELY AND UNASHAMEDLY BAPTIST

1. Henry Cook, *What Baptists Stand For* (London: Kingsgate Press, 1947), 18.
2. Timothy George, *Baptist Confessions, Covenants, and Catechisms* (Nashville: Broadman & Holman, 1996), 1–5.
3. For example, see 12–14; J. B. Gambrell and others, *Baptist Principles Reset, Consisting of a Series of Articles on Distinctive Baptist Principles,* 3rd ed. (Richmond, Va.: Religious Herald, 1902), 252; and W. R. White, *Baptist Distinctives* (Nashville: Sunday School Board, Southern Baptist Convention, 1946), 1–7.
4. For example, see John A. Broadus, *The Duty of Baptists to Teach Their Distinctive Views* (Philadelphia: American Baptist Publication Society, 1881), 6–11; B. H. Carroll, *Baptists and Their Doctrines; Sermons on Distinctive Baptist Principles,* comp. J. B. Cranfill (Chicago: F. H. Revell Co., 1913), 10–11; and Robert A. Baker, *The Baptist March in History* (Nashville: Convention Press, 1958), 1–11.
5. T. T. Eaton, *The Faith of Baptists* (Louisville: Baptist Book Concern, 1903), 20–41.
6. W. R. White, *Baptist Distinctives* (Nashville: Sunday School Board, Southern Baptist Convention, 1946), 12.
7. *Baptist Principles Reset,* 122.
8. Cook, *What Baptists Stand For,* 167.

21. BLOOD IS THICKER THAN WATER

1. William Cathcart, ed., *The Baptist Encyclopedia* (Philadelphia: Louis H. Everts, 1881; reprint ed., Paris, Ark.: The Baptist Standard Bearer, 1988), 76.

2. R. M. Dudley, "The Distinctive Baptist Way: Our Reasons for the Separate Existence of Baptists," in ed. J. M. Frost (Nashville: Sunday School Board, 1900). This text is reprinted in Timothy and Denise George, ed. *Baptist Why and Why Not* (Nashville: Broadman Press 1900; reprint ed., Nashville: Broadman & Holman, 1996), 31.

22. A BAPTIST BECAUSE OF THE BIBLE

1. E. Y. Mullins, *Baptist Beliefs* (Philadelphia: Judson Press, 1925).
2. John Murray, *Christian Baptism* (Philadelphia: Presbyterian & Reformed, 1970). Further references to this work will be noted in the text of the article.
3. Wayne Grudem, *Systematic Theology* (Leicester, England: Inter-Varsity, and Grand Rapids: Zondervan, 1994), 966–87.

24. SO WHAT'S A NICE SOUTHERN BAPTIST LIKE ME DOING IN A PLACE LIKE THIS?

1. As Dr. Henry said in 1947, "If historic Christianity is again to compete as a vital world ideology, evangelicalism must project a solution for the most pressing world problems. It must offer a formula for a new world mind with spiritual ends, involving evangelical affirmations in political, economical, sociological, and educational realms, local and international" (*The Uneasy Conscience of Modern Fundamentalism,* Eerdmans, p. 68).

26. BAPTIST AFTER ALL: RESURGENT CONSERVATIVES FACE THE FUTURE

1. Larry Chesser, "'Authenticus Baptistus' Growing Extinct, Dilday Tells American Baptists," *Baptists Today,* 13 July 1995, 5.
2. John Roach Straton, "Do True Believers Need to Keep at It?" *Religious Herald,* 19 March 1925, 3.
3. Molly T. Marshall, "A Baptist by Conscience: A Baptist in Hope" in *Why I Am a Baptist: Reflections on Being Baptist in the 21st Century,* ed. Cecil P. Staton, Jr. (Macon, Ga.: Smyth and Helwys, 1999), 93.
4. Edward Erwin, "Reclaiming Baptism's Centrality for Baptists," *Baptists Today,* 4 March 4 1993, 18. See also G. Todd Wilson, "Why Baptists Should Not Rebaptize Christians from Other Denominations" in

Proclaiming the Baptist Vision: Baptism and the Lord's Supper, ed. Walter B. Shurden (Macon, Ga.: Smyth and Helwys, 1999), 41–48.

5. "Most Baptists practice immersion as the mode for baptism, for many compelling reasons," he writes. "To be true to soul competency, however, the timing of our baptism is more important than the mode." Mike Clingenpeel, "Baptists' Hub," *Religious Herald,* 3 August 2000, 8.
6. John A. Broadus, "Only Immersion Is Baptism" in *Baptist Principles Reset,* ed. Jeremiah B. Jeter (Richmond: Religious Herald, 1902), 73.
7. "Taking Baptism Seriously: An Interview with Will Campbell," *Baptist Peacemaker,* Spring-Summer 1994, 12. See also Will Campbell, *Forty Acres and a Goat* (Atlanta: Peachtree Publishers, 1986), 153–54.
8. Ibid., 12.
9. Ibid., 13.
10. Paige Patterson, "What Athens Has to Do with Jerusalem: How to Tighten Greek and Hebrew Requirements and Triple Your M.Div. Enrollment at the Same Time," *Faith and Mission* 17 (Fall 1999): 55.
11. Ibid.
12. W. A. Criswell, *Criswell's Guidebook for Pastors* (Nashville: Broadman Press, 1980), 205.
13. For an excellent treatment of church discipline in Baptist history, see Gregory A. Wills, *Democratic Religion: Freedom, Authority and Church Discipline in the Baptist South, 1895–1900* (New York: Oxford University Press, 1997).
14. Francis Fukuyama, "How to Re-Moralize America," *Wilson Quarterly* 23 (Summer 1999): 44.
15. George W. Truett, *Baptists and Religious Liberty* (Nashville: Sunday School Board of the Southern Baptist Convention, 1920).
16. One moderate leader, for example, suggested that moderate Baptists opposed to the *Baptist Faith and Message* (2000) and other SBC statements on women in ministry might "wait patiently for the government to solve our problem" since "equal opportunity for women is now the law of the land, making discrimination by reason of gender illegal." William E. Hull, "Women and the Southern Baptist Convention," *Christian Ethics Today,* August 2000, 11–12.
17. For an analysis of this, see Russell D. Moore and Gregory A. Thornbury, "The Myths of Mullins in Contemporary Southern Baptist Historiography," *Southern Baptist Journal of Theology* 3 (Winter 1999): 44–57.

18. This is seen, for instance, in the bizarre example of a process philosopher appealing to Baptist "soul competency" to support her claims that God is not Creator but a finite being dependent on the world and evolving right along with it. Nancy R. Howell, "Openness and Process Theism: Respecting the Integrity of the Two Views" in *Searching for an Adequate God: A Dialogue Between Process and Free Will Theists,* ed. John B. Cobb, Jr., and Clark H. Pinnock (Grand Rapids: Eerdmans, 2000), 53. Other moderate leaders have defined "soul competency" to mean that pregnant teenagers should not have to face protesters on the way to the abortion clinic, or that conventions should not refuse to cooperate with churches that "marry" same-sex couples. See, for instance, Grady M. Cothen and James M. Dunn, *Soul Freedom: Baptist Battle Cry* (Macon, Ga.: Smyth and Helwys, 2000), 35–37, 53, 105–106. To say that this is not exactly what E. Y. Mullins and Herschel Hobbs had in mind is an understatement.
19. For an analysis of this coalition, see George H. Nash, *The Conservative Intellectual Movement in America Since 1945* (Wilmington, Del.: Intercollegiate Studies Institute, 1996).
20. For an insightful look at these tensions from a neoconservative perspective, see David Frum, *Dead Right* (New York: Basic Books, 1994).
21. "Interview with James M. Dunn," *Whitsitt Journal* 6 (Spring 2000): 4.